At Home in the
Wilderness

by Morgan Lloyd

illustrated by Burgandy Beam

Scott Foresman
is an imprint of

Glenview, Illinois • Boston, Massachusetts • Mesa, Arizona
Shoreview, Minnesota • Upper Saddle River, New Jersey

Every effort has been made to secure permission and provide appropriate credit for photographic material. The publisher deeply regrets any omission and pledges to correct errors called to its attention in subsequent editions.

Unless otherwise acknowledged, all photographs are the property of Pearson.

Photo locations denoted as follows: Top (T), Center (C), Bottom (B), Left (L), Right (R), Background (Bkgd)

Illustrations by Burgandy Beam

Photograph 16 Corbis

ISBN 13: 978-0-328-39358-9
ISBN 10:   0-328-39358-4

3 4 5 6 7 8 9 10 V0N4 13 12 11 10

"Whoa!" Papa called. The horse and wagon came to a stop.

"This is our homestead," he said. "What do you think?"

Jeremiah and Ruthie looked around. The prairie stretched as far as they could see. It looked like a sea of grass.

"It's a good place for our new home," Mama said.

They had left the east to start a new life. Jeremiah remembered what Papa had said: "Free people need land to live on, and there is free land out west." They had filled a wagon with the things that they would need to make a new home in the wilderness. They had pots and pans, tools, quilts, and a little black stove. Most of the wagon was filled with food: flour, dried fruit, bacon, and seeds for planting. They had even brought four chickens.

That first night was warm and tranquil. Mama made rabbit stew, and they sat around the fire talking. The stars were bright. Back east, you could hardly see the stars, but here, it seemed as though you could see the whole galaxy.

"It will not be easy to farm this land and make it our home," Papa said. "But if we live on it for five years, the land will be ours. We will work hard. And we will always remember how good it is to be free."

At first they slept outside. Late one night, after the Moon had come up, Jeremiah heard a coyote howling in the distance. He was scared, but Papa was right next to him. He pulled the quilt closer. He would be glad when they had a house with walls!

Mama, Papa, Ruthie, and Jeremiah were very busy. It seemed that there was always more work to be done. They dug a well for water. Papa taught Jeremiah how to cut sod for the roof. It was hard work. Jeremiah's hands and back hurt.

Ruthie helped Mama build a coop for the chickens and plant a vegetable garden. They planted potatoes, squash, beans, and watermelons. Later, they plowed the land in order to plant corn.

Slowly, the little plot of land began to feel like home. One afternoon, Jeremiah and Ruthie were out exploring. Jeremiah loved to sit in the tall grass and watch for birds or other wildlife. Suddenly, Ruthie grabbed Jeremiah's hand.

"Jeremiah, look!" she shouted.

Jeremiah looked up and saw a dark, twisting cloud coming towards them. It was a tornado! The two raced home.

"Mama! Papa!" they yelled. "There's a twister coming!"

Jeremiah and Ruthie sat with Mama and Papa inside the little sod house. They could hear the rumbling sound of the wind outside. Minutes passed, and then it was quiet.

They stepped outside to see what had happened. The roof had been badly damaged. Much of the corn lay broken on the ground. Worst of all, the chickens were gone. Ruthie began to cry.

"We are lucky to be safe," Mama said.

Many of the vegetables in the garden were small, so they had not been hurt by the tornado. The family fixed what they could. Weeks went by and the crops grew. Then came a week of rain.

"A little rain will do the crops good," Mama said, trying to smile.

But it was more than a little rain. Soon the roof began to leak. Water dripped in. Clumps of mud began to fall on everything. They even fell on Ruthie.

At last the rain ended. The vegetables in the garden grew ripe from the sun. Soon the corn was ready to harvest. Ruthie and Jeremiah worked hard. They helped pick vegetables from the garden. It was good to have so much food. Jeremiah knew they would need it for the winter.

When winter came, the family stayed inside. Mama and Ruthie worked on a quilt. At night, Papa would play music on his banjo and they would sing.

All winter the wind blew hard and cold. Papa would go hunting. Sometimes he caught a rabbit, but other times there was no meat.

One morning Ruthie did not get up. Mama felt her forehead. "Ruthie has a fever," she said.

Ruthie stayed in bed all day. She did not eat. Jeremiah brought her water and covered her with an extra quilt.

Days passed and Ruthie did not get better. The weather got even worse. It snowed so hard that it got dark outside. Papa brought the horse into the house so it would not freeze to death. By the second day, snow covered the windows and they could not see out. Mama melted snow on the stove for water. They were running out of food.

On the fourth morning, Jeremiah woke up and felt sunlight on his face.

"Ruthie, wake up!" he shouted. "It's stopped snowing!"

Eventually the weather began to get warmer, and Ruthie started to feel well. She ate more and soon she could walk around.

One day Jeremiah and Papa were out walking past the corn fields. Suddenly, a bird shot up in the air in front of them.

"A prairie chicken!" said Papa. The bird landed again not far from them. "See?" Papa pointed down through the grass. Jeremiah saw a nest of grass lined with feathers. The nest was full of eggs.

Papa took off his hat and they filled it with grass. They gently put the eggs in the hat, one by one.

"We can bring them to Ruthie," Jeremiah said, "and she can have chickens again."

As they walked back home, Jeremiah thought about their first year on the homestead. They had lived through many challenges. Their new life was not easy, but Jeremiah knew that together they would make it great.

Life in the Wild

This story is set in Nebraska in the 1870s. Many African Americans joined the thousands of homesteaders who moved west in those years.

The homesteaders faced many challenges. Weather on the plains was harsh. The settlers experienced tornadoes, drought, dust storms, prairie fires, thunderstorms, hail, blizzards, and cold.

They hunted wild animals for food, but animals could also be a threat. Some wild animals damaged crops or hurt livestock. Living alone was perhaps the hardest of all. Neighbors, doctors, and help were far away.

THE ABINGDON SONG BOOK

1

Holy, Holy, Holy

NICAEA. 11. 12. 12. 10.

REGINALD HEBER, 1783-1826

JOHN B. DYKES, 1823-1876

1. Ho-ly, ho-ly, ho - ly! Lord God Al-might - y! Ear - ly in the
2. Ho-ly, ho-ly, ho - ly! all the saints a - dore Thee, Cast - ing down their
3. Ho-ly, ho-ly, ho - ly! though the dark-ness hide Thee, Though the eye of
4. Ho-ly, ho-ly, ho - ly! Lord God Al-might - y! All Thy works shall

morn - ing our song shall rise to Thee; Ho - ly, ho-ly, ho - ly,
gold - en crowns a - round the glass - y sea; Cher-u - bim and ser - a - phim
sin - ful man Thy glo - ry may not see; On - ly Thou art ho - ly;
praise Thy Name, in earth, and sky, and sea; Ho - ly, ho - ly, ho - ly,

mer-ci - ful and might-y! God in Three Per-sons, bless-ed Trin - i - ty.
fall-ing down be-fore Thee, Which wert, and art, and ev - er-more shalt be.
there is none be-side Thee, Per - fect in power, in love, and pu - ri - ty.
mer-ci - ful and might-y! God in Three Per-sons, bless-ed Trin - i - ty! A-MEN.

2 Holy, Holy, Holy, Lord, Thy Disciples

BROMLEY COMMON. 11.12.12.10.

Percy MacKaye, 1875–

Martin Shaw, 1876–

Unison

1. Ho - ly, ho - ly, ho - ly, Lord, Thy dis - ci - ples
2. Ho - ly, ho - ly, ho - ly, still in the morn - ing
3. Ho - ly, ho - ly, ho - ly, Lord, Thy dis - ci - ples

Gath - er in de - vo - tion to sing and dream of Thee:
Mend - ing our fish - er nets, we hail thee by the shore;
Ev - er through the a - ges live a - gain be - cause of Thee:

Ho - ly, ho - ly, ho - ly, beau - ti - ful and gra - cious,
Friend and Guide and Broth - er, by the wells of eve - ning
Ho - ly, ho - ly, ho - ly, all Thy ways we fol - low,

Still in our hearts we dwell in Gal - i - lee.
Deep from Thy voice we drink Thy heal - ing lore.
From Beth - le - hem to dark Geth - sem - a - ne.   A - MEN

Words from The Pilgrim and the Book, a dramatic service of the Bible, by Percy MacKaye, published by Samuel French. Used by permission of the author.
Tune by permission, from Curwen Edition No. 6300, published by J. Curwen & Sons, Ltd., 24 Berners Street, London, W. I.

3   Joyful, Joyful, We Adore Thee

HYMN TO JOY. 8. 7. 8. 7. D.

Henry van Dyke, 1852–1933   Arr. from Ludwig van Beethoven, 1770–1827

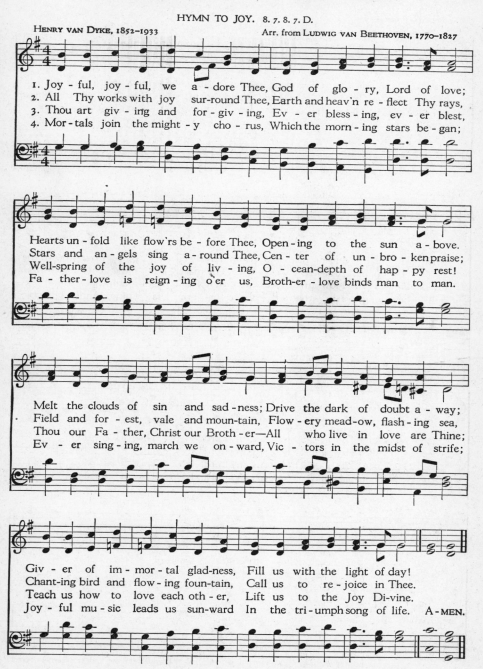

1. Joy - ful, joy - ful, we a - dore Thee, God of glo - ry, Lord of love;
2. All Thy works with joy sur - round Thee, Earth and heav'n re - flect Thy rays,
3. Thou art giv - ing and for - giv - ing, Ev - er bless - ing, ev - er blest,
4. Mor - tals join the might - y cho - rus, Which the morn - ing stars be - gan;

Hearts un - fold like flow'rs be - fore Thee, Open - ing to the sun a - bove.
Stars and an - gels sing a - round Thee, Cen - ter of un - bro - ken praise;
Well-spring of the joy of liv - ing, O - cean-depth of hap - py rest!
Fa - ther - love is reign - ing o'er us, Broth-er - love binds man to man.

Melt the clouds of sin and sad - ness; Drive the dark of doubt a - way;
Field and for - est, vale and moun - tain, Flow - ery mead - ow, flash - ing sea,
Thou our Fa - ther, Christ our Broth - er—All who live in love are Thine;
Ev - er sing - ing, march we on - ward, Vic - tors in the midst of strife;

Giv - er of im - mor - tal glad - ness, Fill us with the light of day!
Chant-ing bird and flow - ing foun-tain, Call us to re - joice in Thee.
Teach us how to love each oth - er, Lift us to the Joy Di - vine.
Joy - ful mu - sic leads us sun-ward In the tri - umph song of life. A - MEN.

4 Jesus, I Thee Adore

SAGINA. 8.8.8.8.

HARRY COLLINS

T. CAMPBELL

1. Je - sus, my Lord, my God, my all, Hear me, blest Sav - iour, when I call; Hear me, and from Thy dwell - ing place Pour down the rich - es of Thy grace. Je - sus, my Lord, I Thee a - dore, O

2. Je - sus, too late I Thee have sought, How can I love Thee as I ought? And how ex - tol Thy match-less fame, The glo - rious beau - ty of Thy Name. Je - sus, my Lord, I Thee a - dore, O

3. Je - sus, what didst Thou find in me, That Thou hast dealt so lov - ing - ly? How great the joy that Thou hast brought, So far ex - ceed - ing hope or thought! Je - sus, my Lord, I Thee a - dore, O

4. Je - sus, of Thee shall be my song, To Thee my heart and soul be - long; All that I have or am is Thine, And Thou, blest Sav - iour, Thou art mine. Je - sus, my Lord, I Thee a - dore, O

make me love Thee more and more. Je - sus, my Lord, I

Je - sus, my Lord,

Jesus, I Thee Adore

Thee a - dore, O make me love Thee more and more.
I Thee a - dore, O make me love Thee

5 We Praise Thee, O God, Our Redeemer

KREMSER. 12. 11. 12. 11.

JULIA BULKLEY CADY, 1882–

Netherlands Folksong from
The Collection by ANDRIANUS VALERIUS

1. We praise Thee, O God, our Re - deem - er, Cre - a - tor,
2. We wor - ship Thee, God, of our fa - thers, we bless Thee;
3. With voic - es u - nit - ed our prais - es we of - fer,

In grate - ful de - vo - tion our trib - ute we bring.
Through life's storm and tem - pest our Guide hast Thou been.
To Thee, great Je - ho - vah, glad an - thems we raise.

We lay it be - fore Thee, we kneel and a - dore Thee,
When per - ils o'er - take us, es - cape Thou wilt make us,
Thy strong arm will guide us, our God is be - side us,

We bless Thy ho - ly name, glad prais - es we sing.
And with Thy help, O Lord, our bat - tles we win.
To Thee, our great Re - deem - er, for ev - er be praise. A - MEN.

6 A Mighty Fortress Is Our God

EIN' FESTE BURG. 8. 7. 8. 7. 6. 6. 6. 6. 7.

MARTIN LUTHER, 1483–1546
Tr. by FREDERICK H. HEDGE, 1805–1890

MARTIN LUTHER, 1483–1546

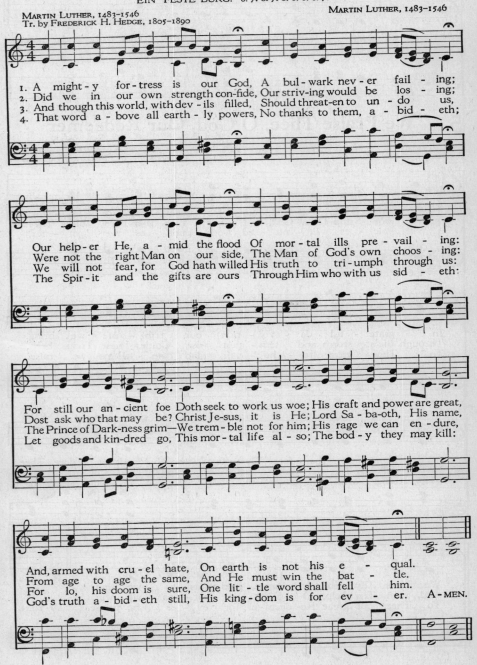

1. A might-y for-tress is our God, A bul-wark nev-er fail-ing;
2. Did we in our own strength con-fide, Our striv-ing would be los-ing;
3. And though this world, with dev-ils filled, Should threat-en to un-do us,
4. That word a-bove all earth-ly powers, No thanks to them, a-bid-eth;

Our help-er He, a-mid the flood Of mor-tal ills pre-vail-ing:
Were not the right Man on our side, The Man of God's own choos-ing:
We will not fear, for God hath willed His truth to tri-umph through us:
The Spir-it and the gifts are ours Through Him who with us sid-eth:

For still our an-cient foe Doth seek to work us woe; His craft and power are great,
Dost ask who that may be? Christ Je-sus, it is He; Lord Sa-ba-oth, His name,
The Prince of Dark-ness grim—We trem-ble not for him; His rage we can en-dure,
Let goods and kin-dred go, This mor-tal life al-so; The bod-y they may kill:

And, armed with cru-el hate, On earth is not his e-qual.
From age to age the same, And He must win the bat-tle.
For lo, his doom is sure, One lit-tle word shall fell him.
God's truth a-bid-eth still, His king-dom is for ev-er. A-MEN.

7   Come, My Soul, Thou Must Be Waking

HAYDN. 8. 4. 7. 8. 4. 7.

FRIEDRICH R. L. VON CANITZ, 1654–1699
Tr. by HENRY J. BUCKOLL, 1803–1871

Arr. from FRANCIS J. HAYDN, 1732–1809

1. Come, my soul, thou must be waking; Now is
2. Glad - ly hail the sun re - turn - ing; Read - y
3. Pray that He may pros - per ev - er Each en -
4. Our God's boun - teous gifts a - buse not, Light re -

break - ing O'er the earth an - oth - er day:
burn - ing Be the in - cense of thy powers;
deav - or, When thine aim is good and true;
fuse not, But His Spir - it's voice o - bey;

Come to Him who made this splen - dor; See thou
For the night is safe - ly end - ed; God hath
But that He may ev - er thwart thee, And con -
Thou with Him shalt dwell, be - hold - ing Light en -

ren - der All thy fee - ble strength can pay.
tend - ed With His care thy help - less hours.
vert thee, When thou e - vil wouldst pur - sue.
fold - ing All things in un - cloud - ed day. A - MEN.

8 Let Us With a Gladsome Mind

INNOCENTS. 7.7.7.7.

John Milton, 1608–1674

The Parish Choir

1. Let us with a glad-some mind Praise the Lord, for He is kind:
2. He with all com-mand-ing might, Filled the new-made world with light;
3. All things liv-ing He doth feed; His full hand sup-plies their need:
4. Let us, then, His praise sing forth, His high ma-jes-ty and worth:

For His mer-cies aye en-dure, Ev-er faith-ful, ev-er sure. A-men.

9 Rejoice, Ye Pure in Heart

MARION. S. M. with Refrain

Edward H. Plumptre, 1821–1891

Arthur H. Messiter, 1831–1916

1. Re - joice, ye pure in heart, Re - joice, give thanks and sing;
2. Bright youth and snow-crowned age, Strong men and maid - ens fair,
3. Yes on thro' life's long path, Still chant - ing as ye go;
4. Still lift your stan - dard high, Still march in firm ar - ray,

Your glo - rious ban - ner wave on high, The cross of Christ your King.
Raise high your free ex - ult - ing song, God's won-drous praise de - clare.
From youth to age, by night and day, In glad-ness and in woe.
As war - riors thro' the dark - ness toil Till dawns the gold - en day.

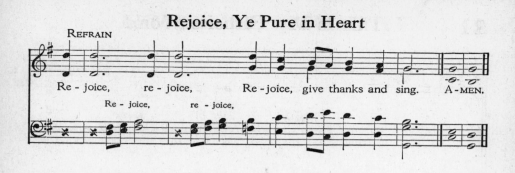

Rejoice, Ye Pure in Heart

REFRAIN

Re - joice, re - joice, Re - joice, give thanks and sing. A - MEN.

Re - joice, re - joice,

10   Come, Thou Almighty King

ITALIAN HYMN. 6. 6. 4. 6. 6. 6. 4.

Anonymous

FELICE DE GIARDINI, 1716–1796

1. Come, Thou al - might - y King, Help us Thy name to sing,
2. Come, Thou in - car - nate Word, Gird on Thy might - y sword;
3. Come, ho - ly Com - fort - er! Thy sa - cred wit - ness bear
4. To Thee, great One in Three, The high - est prais - es be,

Help us to praise: Fa - ther! all - glo - ri - ous, O'er all vic -
Our prayer at - tend: Come, and Thy peo - ple bless, And give Thy
In this glad hour: Thou, who al - might - y art, Now rule in
Hence ev - er - more! His sov - ereign maj - es - ty May we in

to - ri - ous, Come and reign o - ver us, An - cient of Days!
word suc - cess: Spir - it of ho - li - ness! On us de - scend.
ev - ery heart, And ne'er from us de - part, Spir - it of power!
glo - ry see, And to e - ter - ni - ty Love and a - dore. A - MEN.

11 This Is My Father's World

TERRA BEATA. S. M. D.

MALTBIE D. BABCOCK, 1858–1901

FRANKLIN L. SHEPPARD

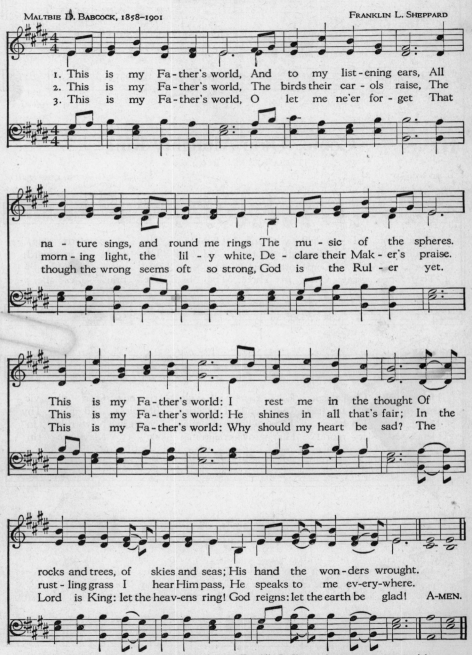

1. This is my Fa-ther's world, And to my list-ening ears, All na-ture sings, and round me rings The mu-sic of the spheres. This is my Fa-ther's world: I rest me in the thought Of rocks and trees, of skies and seas; His hand the won-ders wrought.

2. This is my Fa-ther's world, The birds their car-ols raise, The morn-ing light, the lil-y white, De-clare their Mak-er's praise. This is my Fa-ther's world: He shines in all that's fair; In the rust-ling grass I hear Him pass, He speaks to me ev-ery-where.

3. This is my Fa-ther's world, O let me ne'er for-get That though the wrong seems oft so strong, God is the Rul-er yet. This is my Fa-ther's world: Why should my heart be sad? The Lord is King: let the heav-ens ring! God reigns: let the earth be glad! A-MEN.

12 We Gather Together

KREMSER. Irregular

Anonymous

Netherland Folk Song, 1625
Arr. by EDWARD KREMSER, 1838–1914

1. We gath-er to-geth-er to ask the Lord's bless-ing;
2. Be-side us to guide us, our God with us join-ing,
3. We all do ex-tol Thee, Thou Lead-er tri-um-phant,

He chas-tens and has-tens His will to make known;
Or-dain-ing, main-tain-ing His king-dom di-vine;
And pray that Thou still our De-fend-er wilt be.

The wick-ed op-press-ing now cease from dis-tress-ing,
So from the be-gin-ning the fight we were win-ning:
Let Thy con-gre-ga-tion es-cape trib-u-la-tion:

Sing prais-es to His Name: He for-gets not His own.
Thou, Lord, wast at our side, all glo-ry be Thine!
Thy Name be ev-er praised! O Lord, make us free! A-MEN.

Stanzas one and two in unison; stanza three in harmony

13 We're Marching to Zion

6. 6. 8. 6.

Isaac Watts, 1674–1748   Robert Lowry, 1826–1899

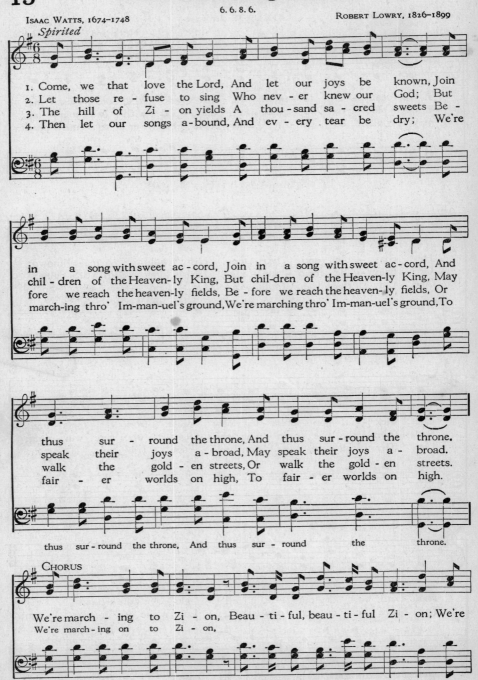

Spirited

1. Come, we that love the Lord, And let our joys be known, Join in a song with sweet ac-cord, Join in a song with sweet ac-cord, And thus sur-round the throne, And thus sur-round the throne.
2. Let those re-fuse to sing Who nev-er knew our God; But chil-dren of the Heaven-ly King, But chil-dren of the Heaven-ly King, May speak their joys a-broad, May speak their joys a-broad.
3. The hill of Zi-on yields A thou-sand sa-cred sweets Be-fore we reach the heaven-ly fields, Be-fore we reach the heaven-ly fields, Or walk the gold-en streets, Or walk the gold-en streets.
4. Then let our songs a-bound, And ev-ery tear be dry; We're march-ing thro' Im-man-uel's ground, We're marching thro' Im-man-uel's ground, To fair-er worlds on high, To fair-er worlds on high.

thus sur-round the throne, And thus sur-round the throne.

Chorus

We're march - ing to Zi - on, Beau - ti - ful, beau - ti - ful Zi - on; We're
We're march - ing on to Zi - on,

We're Marching to Zion

march-ing up-ward to Zi - on, The beau-ti-ful cit-y of God.
Zi - on, Zi - on,

14 O Worship the King

LYONS. 10. 10. 11. 11.

ROBERT GRANT, 1785–1838

Adapted from JOHANN M. HAYDN, 1737–1806

1. O wor-ship the King, all - glo-rious a-bove, O grate-ful-ly sing His
2. The earth, with its store of won-ders un-told, Al - might-y, Thy power hath
3. Thy boun-ti-ful care what tongue can re-cite? It breathes in the air, it
4. Frail chil-dren of dust, and fee-ble as frail, In Thee do we trust, nor

power and His love; Our Shield and De-fend-er, the An-cient of Days,
found-ed of old, Hath stab-lished it fast by a change-less de-cree,
shines in the light, It streams from the hills, it de-scends to the plain,
find Thee to fail; Thy mer-cies how ten-der, how firm to the end,

Pa - vil-ioned in splen-dor, and gird-ed with praise.
And round it hath cast, like a man-tle, the sea.
And sweet-ly dis-tills in the dew and the rain.
Our Mak-er, De-fend-er, Re-deem-er, and Friend. A-MEN.

15 Come, Thou Fount of Every Blessing

NETTLETON. 8. 7. 8. 7. D.

ROBERT ROBINSON, 1735–1790

JOHN WYETH (?), 1770–1858

1. Come, Thou Fount of ev-ery bless-ing, Tune my heart to sing Thy grace;
2. Here I raise mine Eb-en-e-zer; Hith-er by Thy help I'm come;
3. O to grace how great a debt-or Dai-ly I'm con-strained to be!

Streams of mer-cy, nev-er ceas-ing, Call for songs of loud-est praise.
And I hope, by Thy good pleas-ure, Safe-ly to ar-rive at home.
Let Thy good-ness, like a fet-ter, Bind my wan-dering heart to Thee:

Teach me some me-lo-dious son-net Sung by flam-ing tongues a-bove;
Je-sus sought me when a stran-ger, Wan-d'ring from the fold of God;
Prone to wan-der, Lord, I feel it, Prone to leave the God I love;

Praise the mount! I'm fixed up-on it, Mount of Thy re-deem-ing love.
He, to res-cue me from dan-ger, In-ter-posed His pre-cious blood.
Here's my heart, O take and seal it, Seal it for Thy courts a-bove. A-MEN.

16 For the Beauty of the Earth

DIX. 7.7.7.7.7.7.

FOLLIOTT S. PIERPOINT, 1835–1917

Abridged from a chorale by
CONRAD KOCHER, 1786–1872

1. For the beau - ty of the earth, For the glo - ry of the skies,
2. For the beau - ty of each hour Of the day and of the night,
3. For the joy of ear and eye; For the heart and mind's de - light;
4. For the joy of hu - man love, Broth - er, sis - ter, par - ent, child,

For the love which from our birth O - ver and a - round us lies:
Hill and vale, and tree and flower, Sun and moon, and stars of light:
For the mys - tic har - mo - ny Link - ing sense to sound and sight:
Friends on earth, and friends a - bove; For all gen - tle thoughts and mild:

Lord of all, to Thee we raise This our hymn of grate - ful praise. A-MEN.

5 For Thy church, that evermore
　Lifteth holy hands above,
Offering up on every shore
　Her pure sacrifice of love:
Lord of all, to Thee we raise
This our hymn of grateful praise.

6 For Thyself, best Gift Divine!
　To our race so freely given;
For that great, great love of Thine,
　Peace on earth, and joy in heaven:
Lord of all, to Thee we raise
This our hymn of grateful praise.

17 New Every Morning

MELCOMBE. L.M.

JOHN KEBLE, 1792–1866

SAMUEL WEBBE, 1740–1816

1. New ev - ery morn-ing is the love Our wak-'ning and up - ris - ing prove;
2. New mer-cies, each re - turn-ing day, Hov - er a - round us while we pray;
3. Old friends, old scenes, will love-lier be, As more of heav'n in each we see;
4. The triv - ial round, the com-mon task, Will fur - nish all we ought to ask:
5. On - ly, O Lord, in Thy dear love Fit us for per - fect rest a - bove;

Thro' sleep and dark-ness safe-ly brought, Restored to life and power and thought.
New per - ils past, new sins for-given, New tho'ts of God, new hopes of heav'n.
Some soft-'ning gleam of love and pray'r Shall dawn on ev-ery cross and care.
Room to de - ny our-selves, a road To bring us dai - ly near-er God.
And help us this and ev - ery day, To live more near-ly as we pray. A-MEN.

18 Lord of All Being

LOUVAN. L.M.

OLIVER WENDELL HOLMES, 1809–1894

VIRGIL C. TAYLOR, 1817–1891

1. Lord of all be - ing, throned a - far, Thy glo - ry
2. Sun of our life, Thy quick-ening ray Sheds on our
3. Our mid - night is Thy smile with-drawn; Our noon - tide
4. Grant us Thy truth to make us free, And kin - dling

flames from sun and star; Cen - ter and soul of
path the glow of day; Star of our hope, Thy
is Thy gra - cious dawn; Our rain - bow arch, Thy
hearts that burn for Thee; Till all Thy liv - ing

Lord of All Being

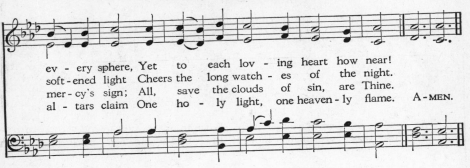

ev - ery sphere, Yet to each lov - ing heart how near!
soft - ened light Cheers the long watch - es of the night.
mer - cy's sign; All, save the clouds of sin, are Thine.
al - tars claim One ho - ly light, one heaven - ly flame. A - MEN.

19 Beauty Around Us

CRUSADERS' HYMN. Irregular

Tr. from the Danish by S. D. RODHOLM

Old German Melody
Arr. by RICHARD S. WILLIS, 1819-1900

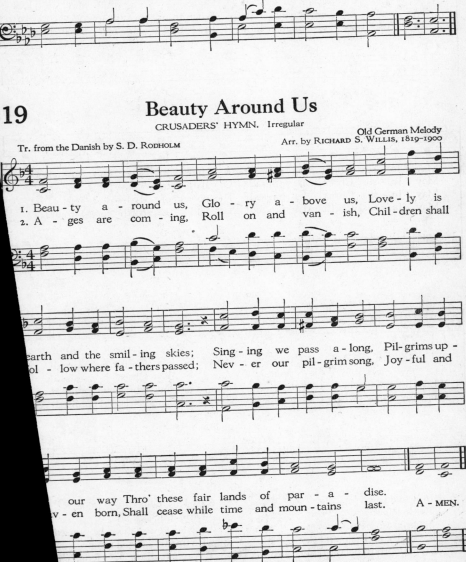

1. Beau - ty a - round us, Glo - ry a - bove us, Love - ly is
2. A - ges are com - ing, Roll on and van - ish, Chil - dren shall

earth and the smil - ing skies; Sing - ing we pass a - long, Pil - grims up -
ol - low where fa - thers passed; Nev - er our pil - grim song, Joy - ful and

our way Thro' these fair lands of par - a - dise.
v - en born, Shall cease while time and moun - tains last. A - MEN.

20 When Morning Gilds the Skies

LAUDES DOMINI. 6. 6. 6. 6. 6. 6.

From the German, c. 1800
Tr. by Edward Caswall, 1814–1878

Joseph Barnby, 1838–1896

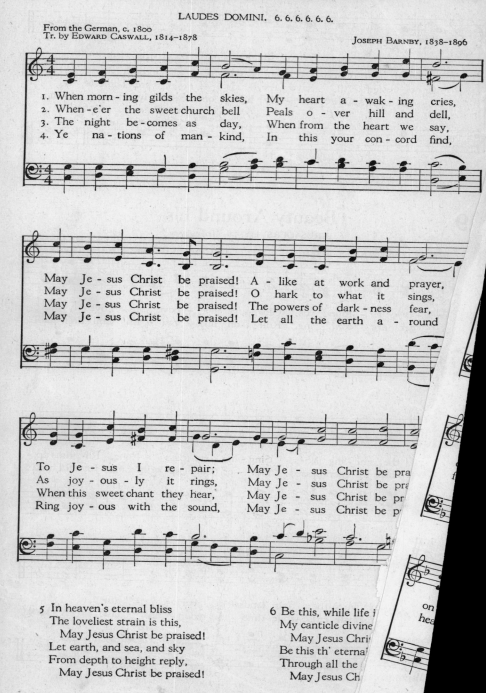

1. When morn - ing gilds the skies, My heart a - wak - ing cries,
2. When - e'er the sweet church bell Peals o - ver hill and dell,
3. The night be - comes as day, When from the heart we say,
4. Ye na - tions of man - kind, In this your con - cord find,

May Je - sus Christ be praised! A - like at work and prayer,
May Je - sus Christ be praised! O hark to what it sings,
May Je - sus Christ be praised! The powers of dark - ness fear,
May Je - sus Christ be praised! Let all the earth a - round

To Je - sus I re - pair; May Je - sus Christ be pra
As joy - ous - ly it rings, May Je - sus Christ be pra
When this sweet chant they hear, May Je - sus Christ be pr
Ring joy - ous with the sound, May Je - sus Christ be p

5 In heaven's eternal bliss
The loveliest strain is this,
 May Jesus Christ be praised!
Let earth, and sea, and sky
From depth to height reply,
 May Jesus Christ be praised!

6 Be this, while life i
My canticle divine
 May Jesus Chri
Be this th' eterna
Through all the
 May Jesus Ch

21 God, That Madest Earth and Heaven

AR HYD Y NOS. 8. 4. 8. 4. 8. 8. 8. 4.

REGINALD HEBER, 1783–1826
FREDERICK L. HOSMER, 1840–1929

Welsh traditional melody
Harmonized by L. O. EMERSON, 1820–1915

1. God, that mad-est earth and heav-en, Dark - ness and light;
2. When the con-stant sun re-turn-ing Un - seals our eyes,

Who the day for toil hast giv-en, For rest the night;
May we, born a-new like morn-ing, To la - bor rise;

May Thine an-gel guards de-fend us, Slum-ber sweet Thy mer - cy send us;
Gird us for the task that calls us, Let not ease and self en-thrall us,

Ho - ly dreams and hopes at-tend us, This live-long night.
Strong thro' Thee what-e'er be-fall us, O God most wise! A - MEN.

22 Day Is Dying in the West

CHATAUQUA (EVENING PRAISE) 7. 7. 7. 7. 4.

MARY A. LATHBURY, 1841–1913   WILLIAM F. SHERWIN, 1826–1888

1. Day is dy-ing in the west, Heaven is touch-ing
2. Lord of life, be-neath the dome Of the u-ni-
3. While the deep-ening shad-ows fall, Heart of Love, en-
4. When for ev-er from our sight Pass the stars, the

earth with rest; Wait and wor-ship while the night
verse, Thy home, Gath-er us, who seek Thy face,
fold-ing all, Through the glo-ry and the grace
day, the night, Lord of an-gels, on our eyes

Sets her eve-ning lamps a-light Through all the sky.
To the fold of Thy em-brace, For Thou art nigh.
Of the stars that veil Thy face, Our hearts as-cend.
Let e-ter-nal morn-ing rise, And shad-ows end!

REFRAIN

Ho-ly, ho-ly, ho-ly, Lord God of Hosts! Heav'n and earth are

full of Thee! Heav'n and earth are praising Thee, O Lord most High! A-MEN.

23 Now, on Land and Sea Descending

VESPER HYMN (Bortniansky). 8. 7. 8. 7. 8. 6. 8. 7.

SAMUEL LONGFELLOW, 1819–1892, alt.

DIMITRI S. BORTNIANSKY, 1752–1825

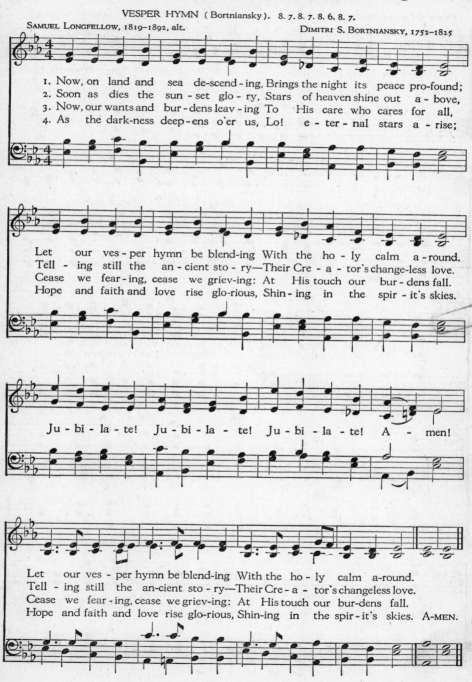

1. Now, on land and sea de-scend-ing, Brings the night its peace pro-found;
2. Soon as dies the sun - set glo - ry, Stars of heaven shine out a - bove,
3. Now, our wants and bur - dens leav - ing To His care who cares for all,
4. As the dark-ness deep-ens o'er us, Lo! e - ter - nal stars a - rise;

Let our ves - per hymn be blend-ing With the ho - ly calm a - round.
Tell - ing still the an - cient sto - ry—Their Cre - a - tor's change-less love.
Cease we fear - ing, cease we griev-ing: At His touch our bur - dens fall.
Hope and faith and love rise glo-rious, Shin - ing in the spir - it's skies.

Ju - bi - la - te! Ju - bi - la - te! Ju - bi - la - te! A - men!

Let our ves - per hymn be blend-ing With the ho - ly calm a-round.
Tell - ing still the an-cient sto - ry—Their Cre - a - tor's changeless love.
Cease we fear - ing, cease we griev-ing: At His touch our bur-dens fall.
Hope and faith and love rise glo-rious, Shin-ing in the spir-it's skies. A-MEN.

24 Praise Him! Praise Him!

Irregular

FANNY J. CROSBY, 1820–1915

CHESTER G. ALLEN

1. Praise Him! Praise Him! Je-sus, our bless-ed Re-deem-er! Sing, O earth, His wonder-ful love pro-claim! Hail Him! Hail Him! High-est arch-an-gels in glo-ry; Strength and hon-or give to His ho-ly Name! Like a shep-herd, Je-sus will guard His chil-dren, In His arms He car-ries them all day long: Praise Him! Praise Him!

2. Praise Him! Praise Him! Je-sus, our bless-ed Re-deem-er! For our sins He suf-fered, and bled, and died; He our Rock, our hope of e-ter-nal sal-va-tion, Hail Him! Hail Him! Je-sus the Cru-ci-fied. Sound His prais-es! Je-sus who bore our sor-rows, Love un-bound-ed, won-der-ful, deep, and strong:

3. Praise Him! Praise Him! Je-sus, our bless-ed Re-deem-er! Heav'nly por-tals loud with ho-san-nas ring! Je-sus, Sav-iour, reign-eth for ev-er and ev-er; Crown Him! Crown Him! Proph-et, and Priest, and King! Christ is com-ing! O-ver the world vic-to-rious, Power and glo-ry un-to the Lord be-long:

REFRAIN

Praise Him! Praise Him!

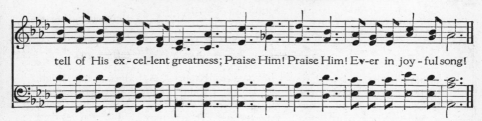

tell of His ex-cel-lent greatness; Praise Him! Praise Him! Ev-er in joy-ful song!

25   Sun of My Soul

HURSLEY. L.M.

John Keble, 1792–1866   Adapted from Katholisches Gesangbuch, c. 1774

1. Sun of my soul, Thou Sav - iour dear, It is not
2. When the soft dews of kind - ly sleep My wea - ried
3. A - bide with me from morn till eve, For with - out
4. If some poor wan - dering child of Thine Have spurned, to -

night if Thou be near: O may no earth - born
eye - lids gent - ly steep, Be my last thought, how
Thee I can - not live; A - bide with me when
day, the voice di - vine, Now, Lord, the gra - cious

cloud a - rise To hide Thee from Thy ser - vant's eyes.
sweet to rest For ev - er on my Sav - iour's breast.
night is nigh, For with - out Thee I dare not die.
work be - gin; Let him no more lie down in sin.   A - men.

5 Watch by the sick; enrich the poor
With blessings from Thy boundless store;
Be every mourner's sleep to-night,
Like infants' slumbers, pure and light.

6 Come near and bless us when we wake,
Ere through the world our way we take;
Till, in the ocean of Thy love,
We lose ourselves in heaven above.

26 Now the Day Is Over

LYNDHURST. 6. 5. 6. 5. D.

SABINE BARING-GOULD, 1834–1914

Anonymous, in CHURCH PRAISE, 1883

1. Now the day is o - ver, Night is draw - ing nigh,
2. Je - sus, give the wea - ry Calm and sweet re - pose;
3. Com - fort ev - ery suf - ferer Watch - ing late in pain;
4. When the morn - ing wak - ens, Then may I a - rise

Shad - ows of the eve - ning Steal a - cross the sky.
With Thy ten - derest bless - ing May mine eye - lids close.
Those who plan some e - vil From their sin re - strain.
Pure, and fresh, and sin - less In Thy ho - ly eyes.

Now the dark - ness gath - ers, Stars be - gin to peep;
Grant to lit - tle chil - dren Vis - ions bright of Thee;
Through the long night watch - es May Thine an - gels spread
Glo - ry to the Fa - ther, Glo - ry to the Son,

Birds and beasts and flow - ers Soon will be a - sleep.
Guard the sail - ors, toss - ing On the deep blue sea.
Their white wings a - bove me, Watch - ing round my bed.
And to Thee, blest Spir - it, Whilst all a - ges run. A - MEN.

27 Come, Ye Thankful People, Come

ST. GEORGE'S, WINDSOR. 7.7.7.7. D.

Henry Alford, 1810–1871
Anna L. Barbauld, 1743–1825
Alt. by Hugh Hartshorne

George J. Elvey, 1816–1893

1. Come, ye thank-ful peo-ple, come, Raise the song of har-vest home;
2. All the bless-ings of the field, All the stores the gar-dens yield;
3. These to thee, our God, we owe, Source whence all our bless-ings flow;

All is safe-ly gath-ered in, Ere the win-ter storms be-gin;
All the fruits in full sup-ply, Rip-ened 'neath the sum-mer sky;
And for these our souls shall raise Grate-ful vows and sol-emn praise.

God, our Mak-er, doth pro-vide For our wants to be sup-plied;
All that spring with boun-teous hand Scat-ters o'er the smil-ing land;
Come, then, thank-ful peo-ple, come, Raise the song of har-vest home;

Come to God's own tem-ple, come, Raise the song of har-vest home.
All that lib-eral au-tumn pours From her rich o'er-flow-ing stores:
Come to God's own tem-ple, come, Raise the song of har-vest home. A-MEN.

28 Hark! The Herald Angels Sing

MENDELSSOHN. 7. 7. 7. 7. D. with Refrain

CHARLES WESLEY, 1707–1788
Alt. by GEORGE WHITEFIELD, 1714–1770

FELIX MENDELSSOHN-BARTHOLDY, 1809–1847
Adapted by WILLIAM H. CUMMINGS, 1831–1915

1. Hark! the her - ald an - gels sing, "Glo - ry to the new - born King;
2. Christ, by high - est heaven a - dored, Christ, the ev - er - last - ing Lord:
3. Hail the heav'n-born Prince of Peace! Hail the Sun of right-eous-ness!

Peace on earth, and mer - cy mild; God and sin - ners rec - on - ciled."
Long de - sired, be - hold Him come, Find - ing here His hum - ble home.
Light and life to all He brings, Risen with heal - ing in His wings.

Joy - ful, all ye na - tions, rise, Join the tri - umph of the skies;
Veiled in flesh the God - head see, Hail th' in - car - nate De - i - ty!
Mild He lays His glo - ry by, Born that man no more may die,

With an - gel - ic hosts pro-claim, "Christ is born in Beth - le - hem!"
Pleased as man with men to dwell, Je - sus our Im - man - u - el.
Born to raise the sons of earth, Born to give them sec - ond birth.

Hark! the her - ald an - gels sing, "Glo - ry to the new-born King." A - MEN.

29 Joy to the World!

ANTIOCH. C. M.

From Psalm XCVIII
Isaac Watts, 1674-1748

Arr. from George F. Handel, 1685-1759

1. Joy to the world! the Lord is come: Let earth re-
2. Joy to the world! the Sav-iour reigns: Let men their
3. No more let sins and sor-rows grow, Nor thorns in-
4. He rules the world with truth and grace, And makes the

ceive her King; Let ev-ery heart pre-pare Him room,
songs em-ploy; While fields and floods, rocks, hills and plains,
fest the ground; He comes to make His bless-ings flow
na-tions prove The glo-ries of His right-eous-ness,

And heaven and na-ture sing, And heaven and na-ture
Re-peat the sound-ing joy, Re-peat the sound-ing
Far as the curse is found, Far as the curse is
And won-ders of His love, And won-ders of His

And heaven and na-ture sing,
Re-peat the sound-ing joy,
Far as the curse is found,
And won-ders of His love,

And
Re-
Far
And

sing, And heaven, and heaven and na-ture sing.
joy, Re-peat, re-peat the sound-ing joy.
found, Far as, far as the curse is found.
love, And won-ders, won-ders of His love. A-men.

heaven and na-ture sing,
peat the sound-ing joy,
as the curse is found,
won-ders of His love,

30 O Come, All Ye Faithful

ADESTE FIDELES (PORTUGUESE HYMN). Irregular, with Refrain

Anonymous. Latin, 18th century
Tr. by FREDERICK OAKELEY, 1802–1880, and others

Source unknown, 18th century melody

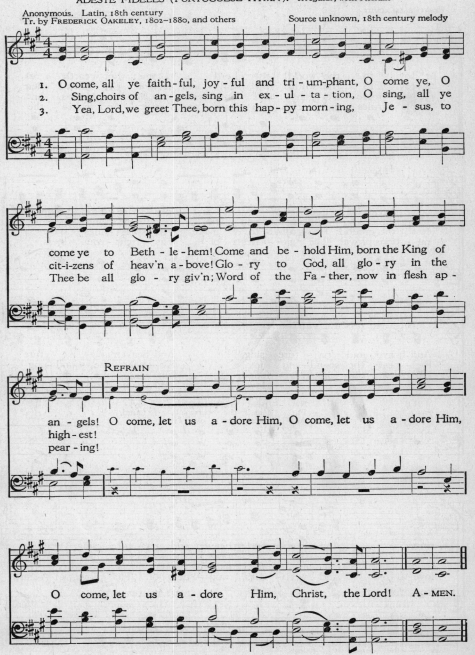

1. O come, all ye faith-ful, joy-ful and tri-um-phant, O come ye, O
2. Sing, choirs of an-gels, sing in ex-ul-ta-tion, O sing, all ye
3. Yea, Lord, we greet Thee, born this hap-py morn-ing, Je-sus, to

come ye to Beth-le-hem! Come and be-hold Him, born the King of
cit-i-zens of heav'n a-bove! Glo-ry to God, all glo-ry in the
Thee be all glo-ry giv'n; Word of the Fa-ther, now in flesh ap-

REFRAIN

an-gels! O come, let us a-dore Him, O come, let us a-dore Him,
high-est!
pear-ing!

O come, let us a-dore Him, Christ, the Lord! A-MEN.

31 O Little Town of Bethlehem

ST. LOUIS. 8. 6. 8. 6. 7. 6. 8. 6.

PHILLIPS BROOKS, 1835–1893

LEWIS H. REDNER, 1831–1908

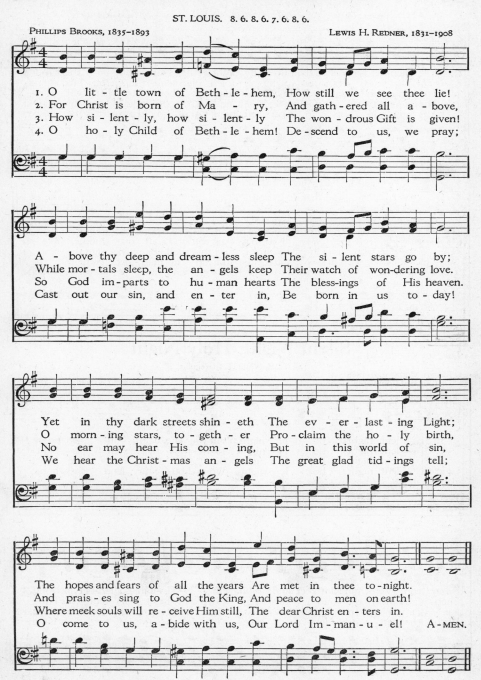

1. O lit - tle town of Beth - le - hem, How still we see thee lie!
2. For Christ is born of Ma - ry, And gath - ered all a - bove,
3. How si - lent - ly, how si - lent - ly The won - drous Gift is given!
4. O ho - ly Child of Beth - le - hem! De - scend to us, we pray;

A - bove thy deep and dream - less sleep The si - lent stars go by;
While mor - tals sleep, the an - gels keep Their watch of won-dering love.
So God im - parts to hu - man hearts The bless - ings of His heaven.
Cast out our sin, and en - ter in, Be born in us to - day!

Yet in thy dark streets shin - eth The ev - er - last - ing Light;
O morn - ing stars, to - geth - er Pro - claim the ho - ly birth,
No ear may hear His com - ing, But in this world of sin,
We hear the Christ - mas an - gels The great glad tid - ings tell;

The hopes and fears of all the years Are met in thee to - night.
And prais - es sing to God the King, And peace to men on earth!
Where meek souls will re - ceive Him still, The dear Christ en - ters in.
O come to us, a - bide with us, Our Lord Im - man - u - el! A - MEN.

32　While Shepherds Watched Their Flocks

ST. ANNE.　C. M.

NAHUM TATE, 1652–1715

WILLIAM CROFT, 1678–1727

1. While shep-herds watched their flocks by night, All seat-ed on the ground,
2. "Fear not!" said he; for might-y dread Had seized their trou-bled mind,
3. "To you, in Da-vid's town, this day Is born of Da-vid's line,
4. "The Heav'n-ly Babe you there shall find To hu-man view dis-played,
5. "All glo-ry be to God on high, And to the earth be peace:

The an-gel of the Lord came down, And glo-ry shone a-round.
"Glad tid-ings of great joy I bring, To you and all man-kind."
The Sav-iour, who is Christ the Lord; And this shall be the sign."
All mean-ly wrapped in swath-ing bands, And in a man-ger laid."
Good will hence-forth from heav'n to men, Be-gin and nev-er cease." A-MEN.

33　Silent Night, Holy Night

STILLE NACHT.　Irregular

JOSEPH MOHR, 1792–1848
Tr. compiled from various sources

FRANZ GRUBER, 1787–1863

1. Si-lent night, ho-ly night, All is calm, all is bright;
2. Si-lent night, ho-ly night, Dark-ness flies, all is light;
3. Si-lent night, ho-ly night, Son of God, love's pure light;
4. Si-lent night, ho-ly night, Won-drous Star, lend thy light;

Round yon Vir-gin Moth-er and Child! Ho-ly In-fant, so ten-der and mild,
Shep-herds hear the an-gels sing, "Al-le-lu-ia! hail the King!
Ra-diant beams from Thy ho-ly face, With the dawn of re-deem-ing grace,
With the an-gels let us sing, Al-le-lu-ia! to our King;

Silent Night, Holy Night

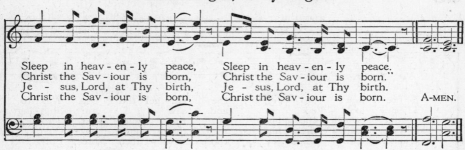

Sleep in heav - en - ly peace, Sleep in heav - en - ly peace."
Christ the Sav - iour is born, Christ the Sav - iour is born."
Je - sus, Lord, at Thy birth, Je - sus, Lord, at Thy birth.
Christ the Sav - iour is born, Christ the Sav - iour is born. A-MEN.

34 There's a Song in the Air

CHRISTMAS SONG. 6.6.6.6.12.12.

JOSIAH G. HOLLAND, 1819–1881   KARL P. HARRINGTON, 1861–

1. There's a song in the air! There's a star in the sky! There's a moth-er's deep
2. There's a tu-mult of joy O'er the won-der-ful birth, For the Vir-gin's sweet
3. In the light of that star Lie the a-ges im-pearled; And that song from a-
4. We re-joice in the light, And we ech-o the song That comes down thro' the

prayer And a ba-by's low cry! And the star rains its fire while the
boy Is the Lord of the earth. Ay! the star rains its fire while the
far Has swept o - ver the world. Ev-ery hearth is a-flame, and the
night From the heav-en-ly throng. Ay! we shout to the love-ly e-

beau-ti-ful sing, For the man-ger of Beth-le-hem cra-dles a King!
beau-ti-ful sing, For the man-ger of Beth-le-hem cra-dles a King!
beau-ti-ful sing In the homes of the na-tions that Je - sus is King!
van-gel they bring, And we greet in His cra-dle our Sav-iour and King! A-MEN.

Words used by permission of Charles Scribner's Sons
Music copyright by Karl P. Harrington. Renewal, 1933

The First Noel

THE FIRST NOEL. Irregular with Refrain

Old English carol

Traditional melody, from
W. SANDYS' CHRISTMAS CAROLS, 1833

1. The first No - el, the an - gel did say, Was to cer - tain poor shep-herds in fields as they lay; In fields where they lay keep - ing their sheep, On a cold win - ter's night that was so deep. No - el, No - el, No -

2. They look - ed up and saw a star Shin - ing in the east, be - yond them far, And to the earth it gave great light, And so it con - tin-ued both day and night.

3. And by the light of that same star Three wise - men came from coun - try far; To seek for a king was their in - tent, And to fol - low the star wher - ev - er it went.

4. This star drew nigh to the north - west, O'er Beth - le - hem it took its rest, And there it did both stop and stay, Right o - ver the place where Je - sus lay.

5. Then en - tered in those wise - men three, Full rev - er - ent - ly up - on the knee, And of - fered there, in His pres - ence, Their gold and myrrh and frank - in - cense.

REFRAIN

The First Noel

el, No - el, Born is the King of Is - ra - el.

36 Away in a Manger

MÜLLER. 11. 11. 11. 11.

Anonymous

CARL MÜLLER (?), ?

1. A - way in a man - ger, no crib for a bed, The lit - tle Lord
2. The cat - tle are low - ing, the Ba - by a - wakes, But lit - tle Lord
3. Be near me, Lord Je - sus, I ask Thee to stay Close by me for

Je - sus laid down His sweet head. The stars in the sky looked
Je - sus, no cry - ing He makes. I love Thee, Lord Je - sus, look
ev - er, and love me, I pray. Bless all the dear chil - dren in

down where He lay, The lit - tle Lord Je - sus, a - sleep on the hay,
down from the sky, And stay by my cra - dle till morn - ing is nigh.
Thy ten - der care, And fit us for heav - en to live with Thee there.

37   We Three Kings of Orient Are

KINGS OF ORIENT. 8. 8. 8. 6. with Refrain

JOHN H. HOPKINS, 1820–1891   JOHN H. HOPKINS, 1820–1891

1. We three kings of O - ri - ent are; Bear-ing gifts we trav-erse a - far
2. Born a King on Beth - le-hem's plain, Gold I bring to crown Him a - gain,
3. Frank-in-cense to of - fer have I; In - cense owns a De - i - ty nigh;
4. Myrrh is mine: its bit - ter per - fume Breathes a life of gath - er - ing gloom:
5. Glo-rious now be - hold Him a - rise, King and God and Sac - ri - fice;

Field and foun - tain, moor and moun-tain, Fol - low-ing yon - der star.
King for ev - er, ceas - ing nev - er O - ver us all to reign.
Prayer and prais - ing all men rais - ing, Wor-ship Him, God on high.
Sor - rowing, sigh-ing, bleed-ing, dy - ing, Sealed in the stone-cold tomb.
Al - le - lu - ia, Al - le - lu - ia! Sounds thro' the earth and skies.

REFRAIN

O star of won - der, star of night, Star with roy - al beau - ty bright,

West-ward lead-ing, still pro-ceed-ing, Guide us to Thy per - fect light. A - MEN.

38 Hosanna, Loud Hosanna

ELLACOMBE. 7. 6. 7. 6. D.

JEANNETTE THRELFALL, 1821–1880

GESANGBUCH DER HERZOGL.
WIRTEMBURGISCHEN KATHOLISCHEN HOFKAPELLE, 1784

1. Ho - san - na, loud ho - san - na The lit - tle chil - dren sang;
2. From Ol - i - vet they fol - lowed 'Mid an ex - ult - ant crowd,
3. "Ho - san - na in the high - est!" That an - cient song we sing,

Through pil - lared court and tem - ple The love - ly an - them rang;
The vic - tor palm-branch wav - ing, And chant - ing clear and loud;
For Christ is our Re - deem - er, The Lord of heaven our King.

To Je - sus, who had blessed them Close fold - ed to His breast,
The Lord of men and an - gels Rode on in low - ly state,
O may we ev - er praise Him With heart and life and voice,

The chil - dren sang their prais - es, The sim - plest and the best.
Nor scorned that lit - tle chil - dren Should on His bid - ding wait.
And in His bliss - ful pres - ence E - ter - nal - ly re - joice! A - MEN.

39 Beneath the Cross of Jesus

ST. CHRISTOPHER. 7. 6. 8. 6. 8. 6. 8. 6.

Elizabeth C. Clephane, 1830-1869

Frederick C. Maker, 1844-1927

1. Be - neath the cross of Je - sus I fain would take my stand,
2. Up - on that cross of Je - sus Mine eye at times can see
3. I take, O cross, thy shad - ow For my a - bid - ing place;

The shad - ow of a might - y rock With - in a wea - ry land;
The ver - y dy - ing form of One Who suf - fered there for me;
I ask no oth - er sun - shine than The sun - shine of His face;

A home with - in the wil - der - ness, A rest up - on the way,
And from my strick - en heart with tears Two won - ders I con - fess:
Con - tent to let the world go by, To know no gain nor loss,

From the burn - ing of the noon - tide heat, And the bur - den of the day.
The won - ders of re - deem - ing love And my own worth - less - ness.
My sin - ful self my on - ly shame, My glo - ry all the cross. A - MEN.

40 At the Cross

8. 6. 8. 6. with Chorus

Isaac Watts, 1674–1748

R. E. Hudson

1. A - las! and did my Sav - iour bleed? And did my Sov - 'reign die?
2. Was it for crimes that I had done, He groaned up - on the tree?
3. Well might the sun in dark - ness hide, And shut his glo - ries in,
4. But drops of grief can ne'er re - pay The debt of love I owe:

Would He de - vote that sa - cred head For such a worm as I?
A - maz - ing pit - y! grace un - known! And love be - yond de - gree!
When Christ, the might - y Mak - er, died For man the crea-ture's sin.
Here, Lord, I give my - self a - way,—'Tis all that I can do.

Chorus

At the cross, at the cross where I first saw the light, And the
bur - den of my heart rolled a - way,
rolled a - way,
It was there by
faith I re - ceived my sight, And now I am hap - py all the day.

41 Above the Hills of Time

LONDONDERRY. 11. 10. 11. 10. D.

Thomas Tiplady, 1882–

Irish traditional melody

1. A - bove the hills of time the cross is gleam-ing, Fair as the
2. The cross, O Christ, Thy won-drous love re - veal - ing, A - wakes our

sun when night has turned to day; And from it love's pure light is rich - ly
hearts as with the light of morn, And par-don o'er our sin - ful spir - its

stream-ing, To cleanse the heart and ban - ish sin a - way.
steal - ing Tells us that we, in Thee, have been re - born.

To this dear cross the eyes of men are turn - ing To - day as
Like ech - oes to sweet tem - ple bells re - ply - ing, Our hearts, O

Above the Hills of Time

in the a-ges lost to sight; And so for Thee, O Christ, men's hearts are
Lord, make an-swer to Thy love; And we will love Thee with a love un-

yearn-ing As ship-wrecked sea-men yearn for morn-ing light.
dy-ing, Till we are gath-ered to Thy home a-bove. A-MEN.

Words used by permission of Thomas Tiplady

42   Jesus, Keep Me Near the Cross

NEAR THE CROSS. 7.6.7.6. with Refrain

FANNY J. CROSBY, 1823–1915   WILLIAM H. DOANE, 1832–1915

1. Je - sus, keep me near the cross; There a pre-cious foun-tain, Free to all—a
2. Near the cross, a trem-bling soul, Love and mer - cy found me; There the bright and
3. Near the cross! O Lamb of God, Bring its scenes be - fore me; Help me walk from
4. Near the cross I'll watch and wait, Hop-ing, trust-ing ev - er, Till I reach the

REFRAIN

heal-ing stream—Flows from Cal-va-ry's moun-tain. In the cross, in the cross, Be my glo-ry
morn - ing Star Shed its beams a-round me.
day to day With its shad-ow o'er me.
gold - en strand Just be-yond the riv - er.

ev - er, Till my rap-tured soul shall find Rest be-yond the riv - er. A-MEN.

43 In the Cross of Christ I Glory

RATHBUN. 8. 7. 8. 7.

JOHN BOWRING, 1792–1872

ITHAMAR CONKEY, 1815–1867

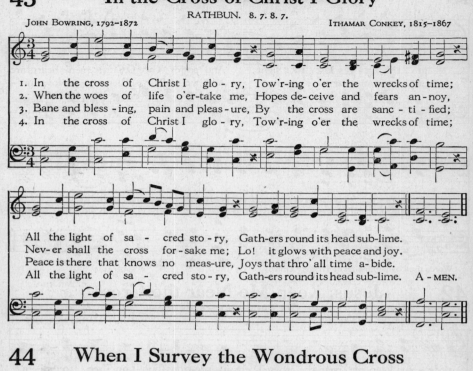

1. In the cross of Christ I glo-ry, Tow'r-ing o'er the wrecks of time;
2. When the woes of life o'er-take me, Hopes de-ceive and fears an-noy,
3. Bane and bless-ing, pain and pleas-ure, By the cross are sanc-ti-fied;
4. In the cross of Christ I glo-ry, Tow'r-ing o'er the wrecks of time;

All the light of sa-cred sto-ry, Gath-ers round its head sub-lime.
Nev-er shall the cross for-sake me; Lo! it glows with peace and joy.
Peace is there that knows no meas-ure, Joys that thro' all time a-bide.
All the light of sa-cred sto-ry, Gath-ers round its head sub-lime. A-MEN.

44 When I Survey the Wondrous Cross

HAMBURG. L. M.

ISAAC WATTS, 1674–1748

Arr. by LOWELL MASON, 1792–1872

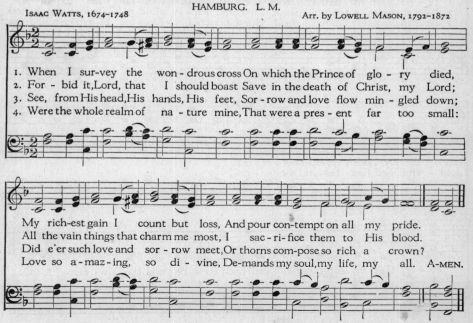

1. When I sur-vey the won-drous cross On which the Prince of glo-ry died,
2. For-bid it, Lord, that I should boast Save in the death of Christ, my Lord;
3. See, from His head, His hands, His feet, Sor-row and love flow min-gled down;
4. Were the whole realm of na-ture mine, That were a pres-ent far too small:

My rich-est gain I count but loss, And pour con-tempt on all my pride.
All the vain things that charm me most, I sac-ri-fice them to His blood.
Did e'er such love and sor-row meet, Or thorns com-pose so rich a crown?
Love so a-maz-ing, so di-vine, De-mands my soul, my life, my all. A-MEN.

45 I Am Coming to the Cross

COMING TO THE CROSS. 7. 7. 7. 7. with Refrain

WILLIAM McDONALD, 1820–1901   WILLIAM G. FISCHER, 1835–1912

1. I am com-ing to the cross; I am poor, and weak, and blind;
2. Long my heart has sighed for Thee; Long has e-vil reigned with-in;
3. Here I give my all to Thee—Friends, and time, and earth-ly store;
4. Je-sus comes! He fills my soul! Per-fect-ed in Him I am;

I am count-ing all but dross; I shall full sal-va-tion find.
Je-sus sweet-ly speaks to me, "I will cleanse you from all sin."
Soul and bod-y Thine to be, Whol-ly Thine for ev-er-more.
I am ev-ery whit made whole—Glo-ry, glo-ry to the Lamb!

REFRAIN

I am trust-ing, Lord, in Thee, Blest Lamb of Cal-va-ry;

Hum-bly at Thy cross I bow, Save me, Je-sus, save me now. A-MEN.

46 The Old Rugged Cross

GEO. BENNARD   Irregular   GEO. BENNARD

1. On a hill far a-way stood an old rug-ged cross, The em-blem of
2. On that old rug-ged cross, so de-spised by the world, Has a won-drous at-
3. In the old rug-ged cross, stain'd with blood so di-vine, A won-drous
4. To the old rug-ged cross I will ev-er be true, Its shame and re-

suf-f'ring and shame, And I love that old cross where the dear-est and best
trac-tion for me; For the dear Lamb of God left His glo-ry a-bove,
beau-ty I see, For 'twas on that old cross Je-sus suf-fered and died,
proach glad-ly bear, Then He'll call me some day to my home far a-way,

CHORUS

For a world of lost sin-ners was slain. So I'll cher-ish the old rug-ged
To bear it to dark Cal-va-ry.
To par-don and sanc-ti-fy me.
Where His glo-ry for ev-er I'll share. cross, the

cross, Till my tro-phies at last I lay down; I will cling to the
old rug-ged cross,

old rug-ged cross, And ex-change it some day for a crown.
cross, the old rug-ged cross,

47 Low in the Grave He Lay

6. 5. 6. 4. with Refrain

ROBERT LOWRY, 1826–1899

ROBERT LOWRY, 1826–1899

1. Low in the grave He lay— Je - sus my Sav - iour! Wait - ing the
2. Vain - ly they watch His bed— Je - sus my Sav - iour! Vain - ly they
3. Death can - not keep his prey— Je - sus my Sav - iour! He tore the

REFRAIN. *Faster*

com - ing day—Je - sus my Lord! Up from the grave He a - rose,
seal the dead—Je - sus my Lord!
bars a - way—Je - sus my Lord! He a - rose,

With a might - y tri - umph o'er His foes; He a - rose a
He a - rose!

Vic - tor from the dark do - main, And He lives for - ev - er with His saints to reign.

He a - rose! He a - rose! Hal - le - lu - jah! Christ a - rose!
He a - rose! He a - rose!

48 Christ the Lord Is Risen Today

EASTER HYMN. 7. 7. 7. 7. with Alleluias

CHARLES WESLEY, 1707-1788, and others

From LYRA DAVIDICA, 1708

1. Christ the Lord is risen to-day, Al - - - le - lu - ia!
2. Lives a-gain our glo-rious King, Al - - - le - lu - ia!
3. Love's re-deem-ing work is done, Al - - - le - lu - ia!
4. Soar we now where Christ has led, Al - - - le - lu - ia!

Sons of men and an-gels say, Al - - - le - lu - ia!
Where, O death, is now thy sting? Al - - - le - lu - ia!
Fought the fight, the bat-tle won, Al - - - le - lu - ia!
Fol-lowing our ex-alt-ed Head, Al - - - le - lu - ia!

Raise your joys and tri-umphs high, Al - - le - lu - ia!
Once He died, our souls to save, Al - - le - lu - ia!
Death in vain for-bids Him rise, Al - - le - lu - ia!
Made like Him, like Him we rise, Al - - le - lu - ia!

Sing, ye heavens, and earth re - ply, Al - le - lu - ia!
Where's thy vic-tory, boast-ing grave? Al - le - lu - ia!
Christ hath o-pened par - a - dise, Al - le - lu - ia!
Ours the cross, the grave, the skies, Al - le - lu - ia! A-MEN.

49 Sing With All the Sons of Glory

HYMN TO JOY. 8. 7. 8. 7. D.

WILLIAM J. IRONS, 1812–1883

Arr. from LUDWIG VAN BEETHOVEN, 1770–1827

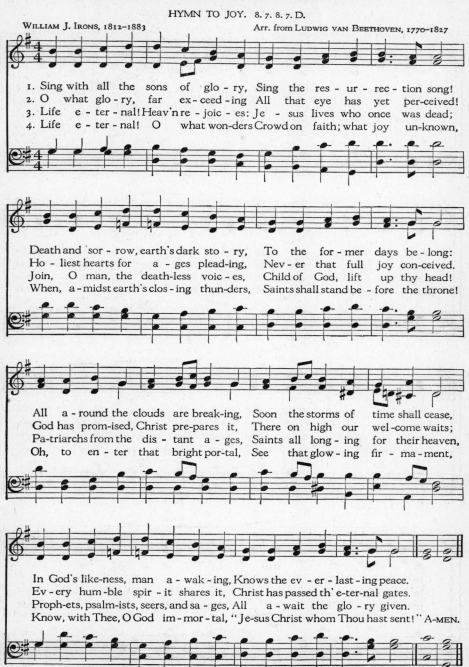

1. Sing with all the sons of glo - ry, Sing the res - ur - rec - tion song!
2. O what glo - ry, far ex - ceed - ing All that eye has yet per-ceived!
3. Life e - ter - nal! Heav'n re - joic - es: Je - sus lives who once was dead;
4. Life e - ter - nal! O what won-ders Crowd on faith; what joy un-known,

Death and sor - row, earth's dark sto - ry, To the for - mer days be - long:
Ho - liest hearts for a - ges plead-ing, Nev - er that full joy con-ceived.
Join, O man, the death-less voic - es, Child of God, lift up thy head!
When, a-midst earth's clos-ing thun-ders, Saints shall stand be - fore the throne!

All a - round the clouds are break-ing, Soon the storms of time shall cease,
God has prom-ised, Christ pre-pares it, There on high our wel-come waits;
Pa-triarchs from the dis - tant a - ges, Saints all long - ing for their heaven,
Oh, to en - ter that bright por-tal, See that glow - ing fir - ma-ment,

In God's like-ness, man a - wak-ing, Knows the ev - er - last-ing peace.
Ev - ery hum-ble spir - it shares it, Christ has passed th' e-ter-nal gates.
Proph-ets, psalm-ists, seers, and sa - ges, All a - wait the glo - ry given.
Know, with Thee, O God im - mor - tal, "Je-sus Christ whom Thou hast sent!" A-MEN.

50 Ask Ye What Great Thing I Know

HENDON. 7. 7. 7. 7. 7.

JOHANN C. SCHWEDLER, 1672–1730
Tr. by BENJAMIN H. KENNEDY, 1804–1889

H. A. CÉSAR MALAN, 1787–1864

1. Ask ye what great thing I know
2. Who de - feats my fier - cest foes?
3. Who is life in life to me?
4. This is that great thing I know;

That de - lights and stirs me so? What the high re -
Who con - soles my sad - dest woes? Who re - vives my
Who the death of death will be? Who will place me
This de - lights and stirs me so: Faith in Him who

ward I win? Whose the Name I glo - ry in?
faint - ing heart, Heal - ing all its hid - den smart?
on His right, With the count - less hosts of light?
died to save, Him who tri - umphed o'er the grave,

Je - sus Christ, the Cru - ci - fied.
Je - sus Christ, the Cru - ci - fied.
Je - sus Christ, the Cru - ci - fied.
Je - sus Christ, the Cru - ci - fied. A - MEN.

51 "Welcome, Happy Morning!"

FORTUNATUS. 11. 11. 11. 11. with Refrain

VENANTIUS FORTUNATUS, c. 530–609
Tr. by JOHN ELLERTON, 1826–1893

ARTHUR S. SULLIVAN, 1842–1900

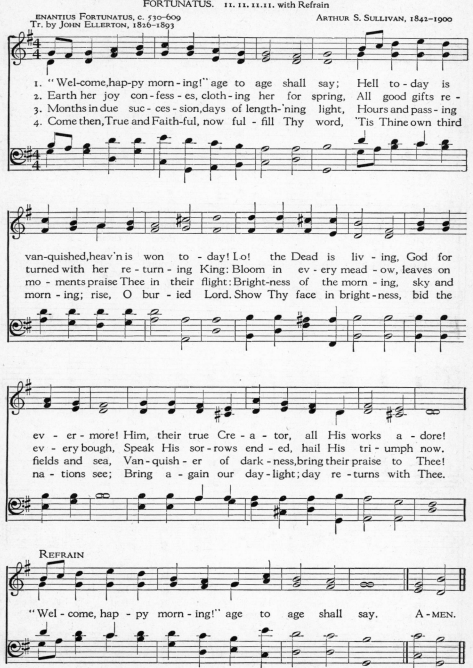

1. "Wel-come, hap-py morn-ing!" age to age shall say; Hell to-day is van-quished, heav'n is won to-day! Lo! the Dead is liv-ing, God for ev-er-more! Him, their true Cre-a-tor, all His works a-dore!

2. Earth her joy con-fess-es, cloth-ing her for spring, All good gifts re-turned with her re-turn-ing King: Bloom in ev-ery mead-ow, leaves on ev-ery bough, Speak His sor-rows end-ed, hail His tri-umph now.

3. Months in due suc-ces-sion, days of length-'ning light, Hours and pass-ing mo-ments praise Thee in their flight: Bright-ness of the morn-ing, sky and fields and sea, Van-quish-er of dark-ness, bring their praise to Thee!

4. Come then, True and Faith-ful, now ful-fill Thy word, 'Tis Thine own third morn-ing; rise, O bur-ied Lord. Show Thy face in bright-ness, bid the na-tions see; Bring a-gain our day-light; day re-turns with Thee.

REFRAIN

"Wel-come, hap-py morn-ing!" age to age shall say. A-MEN.

52 The Strife Is O'er, the Battle Done

VICTORY. 8. 8. 8. 4. with Alleluias

Authorship uncertain
Tr. by FRANCIS POTT, 1832–1909

GIOVANNI P. DA PALESTRINA, 1525–1594

Al - le - lu - ia! Al - le - lu - ia! Al - le - lu - ia!

Org.

1. The strife is o'er, the bat - tle done;
2. The pow'rs of death have done their worst,
3. The three sad days have quick - ly sped;
4. Lord, by the stripes which wound - ed Thee,

The vic - to - ry of life is won; The song of
But Christ their le - gions hath dis - persed; Let shouts of
He ris - es glo - rious from the dead: All glo - ry
From death's dread sting Thy ser - vants free, That we may

D.S.

tri - umph has be - gun. Al - le - lu - ia!
ho - ly joy out - burst. Al - le - lu - ia!
to our ris - en Head! Al - le - lu - ia!
live and sing to Thee. Al - le - lu - ia! A - MEN.

53 All Hail the Power of Jesus' Name

CORONATION. C. M.

(*First Tune*)

EDWARD PERRONET, 1726–1792
Alt. by JOHN RIPPON, 1751–1836

OLIVER HOLDEN, 1765–1844

1. All hail the power of Je-sus' name! Let an-gels pros-trate fall;
2. Ye cho-sen seed of Is-rael's race, Ye ran-somed from the fall,
3. Sin-ners, whose love can ne'er for-get The worm-wood and the gall,

Bring forth the roy-al di-a-dem, And crown Him Lord of all;
Hail Him who saves you by His grace, And crown Him Lord of all;
Go, spread your tro-phies at His feet, And crown Him Lord of all;

Bring forth the roy-al di-a-dem, And crown Him Lord of all.
Hail Him who saves you by His grace, And crown Him Lord of all.
Go, spread your tro-phies at His feet, And crown Him Lord of all. A-MEN.

4 Let every kindred, every tribe,
  On this terrestrial ball,
To Him all majesty ascribe,
  And crown Him Lord of all.

5 O that with yonder sacred throng
  We at His feet may fall!
We'll join the everlasting song,
  And crown Him Lord of all.

54 All Hail the Power of Jesus' Name

DIADEM, C. M.
(Second Tune)

Edward Perronet, 1726-1792
Alt. by John Rippon, 1751-1836

James Ellor, 1819-1899

1. All hail the power of Je - sus' name! Let an - gels pros-trate
2. Ye cho - sen seed of Is - rael's race, Ye ran-somed from the
3. Sin - ners, whose love can ne'er for - get The worm-wood and the
4. Let ev - ery kin - dred, ev - ery tribe, On this ter - res - trial
5. O that with yon - der sa - cred throng We at His feet may

fall, Let an - gels pros - trate fall; Bring forth the roy - al
fall, Ye ran - somed from the fall; Hail Him who saves you
gall, The worm - wood and the gall, Go, spread your tro - phies
ball, On this ter - res - trial ball, To Him all maj - es -
fall, We at His feet may fall! We'll join the ev - er -

di - a - dem, And crown . . . . Him,
by His grace, And crown . . . . Him,
at His feet, And crown . . . . Him,
ty as - cribe, And crown . . . . Him,
last - ing song, And crown . . . . Him,

crown Him, crown Him, crown Him, crown Him,

crown . . . .

crown Him, crown Him, crown Him, And crown Him Lord of all. A - MEN.

Him,

55 Fairest Lord Jesus

CRUSADER'S HYMN. 5.6.8.5.5.8.

From the German, 17th century

From SCHLESISCHE VOLKSLIEDER, 1842
Arr. by RICHARD S. WILLIS, 1819–1900

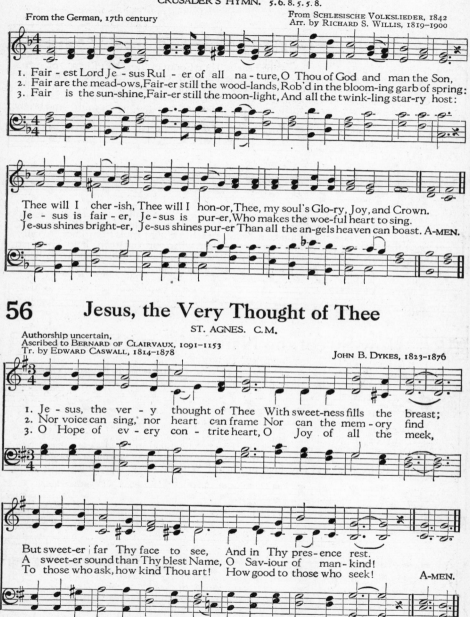

1. Fair - est Lord Je - sus Rul - er of all na - ture, O Thou of God and man the Son,
2. Fair are the mead-ows, Fair-er still the wood-lands, Rob'd in the bloom-ing garb of spring:
3. Fair is the sun-shine, Fair-er still the moon-light, And all the twink-ling star-ry host:

Thee will I cher-ish, Thee will I hon-or, Thee, my soul's Glo-ry, Joy, and Crown.
Je - sus is fair - er, Je-sus is pur-er, Who makes the woe-ful heart to sing.
Je-sus shines bright-er, Je-sus shines pur-er Than all the an-gels heaven can boast. A-MEN.

56 Jesus, the Very Thought of Thee

ST. AGNES. C.M.

Authorship uncertain,
Ascribed to BERNARD of CLAIRVAUX, 1091–1153
Tr. by EDWARD CASWALL, 1814–1878

JOHN B. DYKES, 1823–1876

1. Je - sus, the ver - y thought of Thee With sweet-ness fills the breast;
2. Nor voice can sing, nor heart can frame Nor can the mem - ory find
3. O Hope of ev - ery con - trite heart, O Joy of all the meek,

But sweet-er far Thy face to see, And in Thy pres-ence rest.
A sweet-er sound than Thy blest Name, O Sav-iour of man-kind!
To those who ask, how kind Thou art! How good to those who seek!

A-MEN.

4 But what to those who find? Ah, this
  Nor tongue nor pen can show:
The love of Jesus, what it is
  None but His loved ones know.

5 Jesus, our only joy be Thou,
  As Thou our prize wilt be;
Jesus, be Thou our glory now,
  And through eternity.

57 Jesus, Thou Joy of Loving Hearts

GERMANY. L. M.

BERNARD OF CLAIRVAUX, 1091-1153

Arr. from LUDWIG VAN BEETHOVEN, 1770-1827

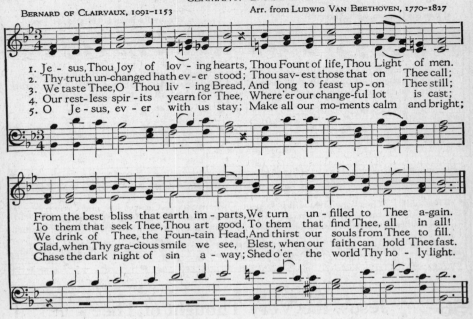

1. Je - sus, Thou Joy of lov - ing hearts, Thou Fount of life, Thou Light of men.
2. Thy truth un-changed hath ev - er stood; Thou sav - est those that on Thee call;
3. We taste Thee, O Thou liv - ing Bread, And long to feast up - on Thee still;
4. Our rest - less spir - its yearn for Thee, Where'er our change-ful lot is cast;
5. O Je - sus, ev - er with us stay; Make all our mo-ments calm and bright;

From the best bliss that earth im - parts, We turn un - filled to Thee a-gain.
To them that seek Thee, Thou art good, To them that find Thee, all in all!
We drink of Thee, the Foun-tain Head, And thirst our souls from Thee to fill.
Glad, when Thy gra-cious smile we see, Blest, when our faith can hold Thee fast.
Chase the dark night of sin a - way; Shed o'er the world Thy ho - ly light.

58 How Sweet the Name of Jesus Sounds

ST. PETER'S, OXFORD. C.M.

JOHN NEWTON, 1725-1807

ALEXANDER R. REINAGLE, 1799-1877

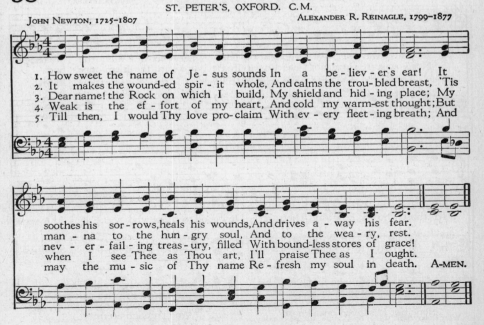

1. How sweet the name of Je - sus sounds In a be - liev - er's ear! It
2. It makes the wound-ed spir - it whole, And calms the trou-bled breast, 'Tis
3. Dear name! the Rock on which I build, My shield and hid - ing place; My
4. Weak is the ef - fort of my heart, And cold my warm-est thought; But
5. Till then, I would Thy love pro - claim With ev - ery fleet - ing breath; And

soothes his sor - rows, heals his wounds, And drives a - way his fear.
man - na to the hun - gry soul, And to the wea - ry, rest.
nev - er - fail - ing treas - ury, filled With bound-less stores of grace!
when I see Thee as Thou art, I'll praise Thee as I ought.
may the mu - sic of Thy name Re - fresh my soul in death. A-MEN.

59   O Master Workman of the Race

ST. MICHEL'S. C. M. D.

Jay T. Stocking, 1870–1936

From W. Gawler's Hymns and Psalms, 1789

1. O Mas - ter Work-man of the race, Thou Man of Gal - i - lee,
2. O Car - pen - ter of Naz - a - reth, Build - er of life di - vine,
3. O Thou who dost the vi - sion send And giv - est each his task,

Who with the eyes of ear - ly youth E - ter - nal things did see:
Who shap - est man to God's own law, Thy - self the fair de - sign:
And with the task suf - fi - cient strength: Show us Thy will, we ask;

We thank Thee for Thy boy - hood faith That shone Thy whole life through;
Build us a tower of Christ-like height, That we the land may view,
Give us a con-science bold and good; Give us a pur - pose true,

"Did ye not know it is my work My Fa - ther's work to do?"
And see, like Thee, our no-blest work Our Fa - ther's work to do.
That it may be our high - est joy, Our Fa - ther's work to do. A-MEN.

60 Jesus! The Name High Over All

AZMON. C.M.

CHARLES WESLEY, 1707–1788

CARL G. GLÄSER, 1784–1829
Arr. by LOWELL MASON, 1792–1872

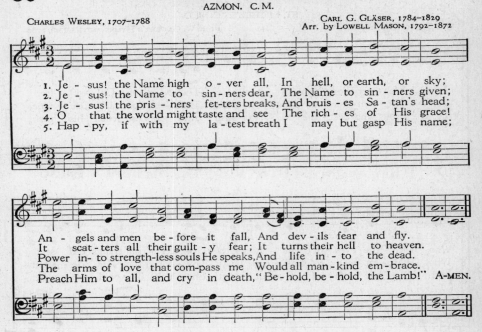

1. Je - sus! the Name high o - ver all, In hell, or earth, or sky;
2. Je - sus! the Name to sin - ners dear, The Name to sin - ners given;
3. Je - sus! the pris - 'ners' fet-ters breaks, And bruis - es Sa - tan's head;
4. O that the world might taste and see The rich - es of His grace!
5. Hap - py, if with my la - test breath I may but gasp His name;

An - gels and men be - fore it fall, And dev - ils fear and fly.
It scat - ters all their guilt - y fear; It turns their hell to heaven.
Power in - to strength-less souls He speaks, And life in - to the dead.
The arms of love that com-pass me Would all man - kind em - brace.
Preach Him to all, and cry in death, "Be - hold, be - hold, the Lamb!" A-MEN.

61 O Son of Man, Thou Madest Known

BROOKFIELD. L.M.

MILTON S. LITTLEFIELD, 1864–1934

THOMAS B. SOUTHGATE, 1814–1868

1. O Son of Man, Thou mad - est known, Through qui - et
2. O Work - man true, may we ful - fill in dai - ly
3. Thou Mas - ter Work - man, grant us grace The chal - lenge
4. And thus we pray in deed and word, Thy king - dom

work in shop and home; The sa - cred - ness of com - mon
life Thy Fa - ther's will: In du - ty's call, Thy call we
of our tasks to face; By loy - al scorn of sec - ond
come on earth, O Lord; In work that gives ef - fect to

O Son of Man, Thou Madest Known

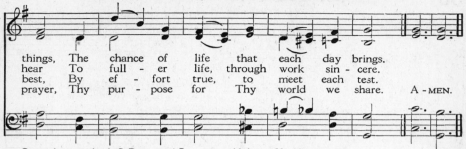

things, The chance of life that each day brings.
hear, To full - er life, through work sin - cere.
best, By ef - fort true, to meet each test.
prayer, Thy pur - pose for Thy world we share. A - MEN.

62 I Know Not How That Bethlehem's Babe

VERITAS. C. M.

HARRY WEBB FARRINGTON, 1880-1931

JOHN N. BURNHAM

Andante religioso

1. I know not how that Beth - l'hem's Babe Could in the
2. I know not how that Cal - v'ry's cross A world from
3. I know not how that Jo - seph's tomb Could solve death's

God - head be: I on - ly know the
sin could free: I on - ly know its
mys - ter - y: I on - ly know a

Man - ger Child Has brought God's life to me.
match-less love Has brought God's love to me.
liv - ing Christ, Our im - mor - tal - i - ty. A - MEN.

63 Far, Far Away Is Bethlehem

ALL SAINTS, NEW. C. M. D.

WALTER RUSSELL BOWIE, 1882–

HENRY S. CUTLER, 1824–1902

1. Far, far a-way is Beth-le-hem, And years are long and dim
2. Be-yond the sea is Gal-i-lee, And ways which Je-sus trod;
3. O Life that seems so long a-go, And yet is ev-er new,

Since Ma-ry held the ho-ly Child And an-gels sang to Him;
And hid-den there are those high hills Where He com-muned with God;
The fel-low-ship of love with Thee, Thro' all the years is true.

But still to hearts where love and faith Make room for Christ in them;
Yet on the plains of com-mon life Thro' all the world of men,
O Mas-ter o-ver death and time, Re-veal Thy-self we pray;

He comes a-gain, the Child from God, To find His Beth-le-hem.
The voice that once said "Fol-low Me" Speaks to our hearts a-gain.
And as be-fore a-mongst Thine own, So dwell with us to-day. A-MEN.

64 Jesus, Thou Divine Companion

LOVE DIVINE. 8.7.8.7.D.

Henry van Dyke, 1852–1933

George F. Le Jeune, 1842–1904

1. Je - sus, Thou di - vine Com - pan - ion, By Thy low - ly hu - man birth
2. They who tread the path of la - bor Fol - low where Thy feet have trod;
3. Ev - ery task, how - ev - er sim - ple, Sets the soul that does it free;

Thou hast come to join the work - ers, Bur - den bear - ers of the earth.
They who work with - out com - plain - ing Do the ho - ly will of God.
Ev - ery deed of love and kind - ness Done to man is done to Thee.

Thou, the Car - pen - ter of Naza - reth, Toil - ing for Thy dai - ly food,
Thou, the Peace that pass - eth knowl - edge, Dwell - est in the dai - ly strife;
Je - sus, Thou di - vine Com - pan - ion, Help us all to work our best;

By Thy pa - tience and Thy cour - age, Thou hast taught us toil is good.
Thou, the Bread of heaven, art bro - ken In the sac - ra - ment of life.
Bless us in our dai - ly la - bor, Lead us to our Sab - bath rest. A-MEN.

65 Take the Name of Jesus With You

PRECIOUS NAME. 8. 7. 8. 7. with Refrain

LYDIA BAXTER, 1809-1874

WILLIAM H. DOANE, 1832-1915

1. Take the Name of Je - sus with you, Child of [sor - row and of woe;
2. Take the Name of Je - sus ev - er, As a shield from ev - ery snare;
3. O the pre - cious Name of Je - sus! How it thrills our souls with joy,
4. At the Name of Je - sus bow - ing, Fall - ing pros - trate at His feet,

It will joy and com-fort give you — Take it, then, wher-e'er you go.
If temp - ta - tions round you gath - er, Breathe that ho - ly Name in prayer.
When His lov - ing arms re - ceive us, And His songs our tongues em-ploy!
King of kings in heaven we'll crown Him, When our jour-ney is com-plete.

REFRAIN

Pre-cious Name, O how sweet! Hope of earth and joy of heaven;

Pre-cious Name, O how sweet!

Pre-cious Name, O how sweet! Hope of earth and joy of heaven. A-MEN.

Pre-cious Name, O how sweet, how sweet!

66 Crown Him With Many Crowns

DIADEMATA. S. M. D.

MATTHEW BRIDGES, 1800-1894 and
GODFREY THRING, 1823-1903

GEORGE J. ELVEY, 1816-1893

1. Crown Him with man - y crowns, The Lamb up - on His throne;
2. Crown Him the Lord of life, Who tri - umphed o'er the grave,
3. Crown Him the Lord of peace, Whose power a scep - ter sways
4. Crown Him the Lord of love; Be - hold His hands and side,

Hark! how the heaven-ly an - them drowns All mu - sic but its own!
And rose vic - to - rious in the strife For those He came to save;
From pole to pole, that wars may cease, And all be prayer and praise:
Those wounds, yet vis - i - ble a - bove, In beau-ty glo - ri - fied:

A - wake, my soul, and sing Of Him who died for thee,
His glo - ries now we sing Who died, and rose on high,
His reign shall know no end, And round His pierc - ed feet
All hail, Re - deem - er, hail! For Thou hast died for me:

And hail Him as thy match-less King Through all e - ter - ni - ty.
Who died — e - ter - nal life to bring, And lives, that death may die.
Fair flowers of par - a - dise ex - tend Their fra-grance ev - er sweet.
Thy praise and glo - ry shall not fail Through-out e - ter - ni - ty. A - MEN.

3

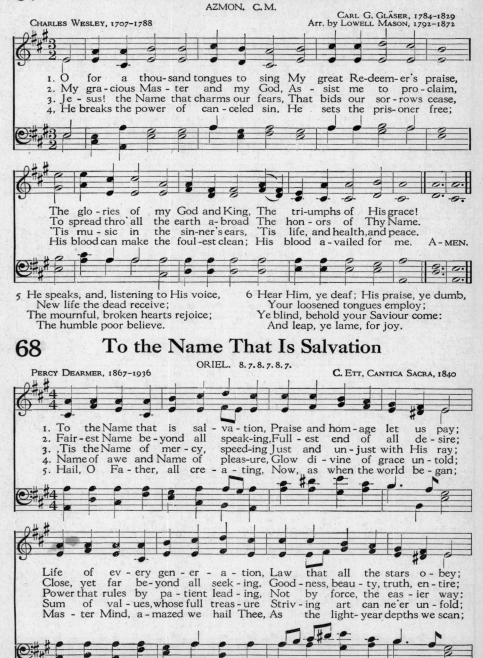

67 O For a Thousand Tongues

AZMON. C. M.

CHARLES WESLEY, 1707-1788

CARL G. GLÄSER, 1784-1829
Arr. by LOWELL MASON, 1792-1872

1. O for a thou-sand tongues to sing My great Re-deem-er's praise,
2. My gra-cious Mas-ter and my God, As-sist me to pro-claim,
3. Je-sus! the Name that charms our fears, That bids our sor-rows cease,
4. He breaks the power of can-celed sin, He sets the pris-oner free;

The glo-ries of my God and King, The tri-umphs of His grace!
To spread thro' all the earth a-broad The hon-ors of Thy Name.
'Tis mu-sic in the sin-ner's ears, 'Tis life, and health, and peace.
His blood can make the foul-est clean; His blood a-vailed for me. A-MEN.

5 He speaks, and, listening to His voice,
New life the dead receive;
The mournful, broken hearts rejoice;
The humble poor believe.

6 Hear Him, ye deaf; His praise, ye dumb,
Your loosened tongues employ;
Ye blind, behold your Saviour come:
And leap, ye lame, for joy.

68 To the Name That Is Salvation

ORIEL. 8.7.8.7.8.7.

PERCY DEARMER, 1867-1936

C. ETT, CANTICA SACRA, 1840

1. To the Name that is sal-va-tion, Praise and hom-age let us pay;
2. Fair-est Name be-yond all speak-ing, Full-est end of all de-sire;
3. 'Tis the Name of mer-cy, speed-ing Just and un-just with His ray;
4. Name of awe and Name of pleas-ure, Glow di-vine of grace un-told;
5. Hail, O Fa-ther, all cre-a-ting, Now, as when the world be-gan;

Life of ev-ery gen-er-a-tion, Law that all the stars o-bey;
Close, yet far be-yond all seek-ing, Good-ness, beau-ty, truth, en-tire;
Power that rules by pa-tient lead-ing, Not by force, the eas-ier way:
Sum of val-ues, whose full treas-ure Striv-ing art can ne'er un-fold;
Mas-ter Mind, a-mazed we hail Thee, As the light-year depths we scan;

To the Name That Is Salvation

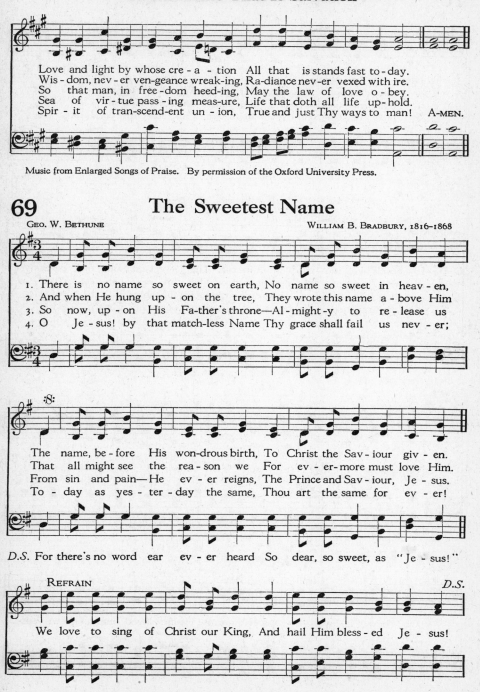

Love and light by whose cre - a - tion All that is stands fast to - day.
Wis - dom, nev - er ven-geance wreak-ing, Ra-diance nev - er vexed with ire.
So that man, in free - dom heed-ing, May the law of love o - bey.
Sea of vir - tue pass - ing meas-ure, Life that doth all life up - hold.
Spir - it of tran-scend-ent un - ion, True and just Thy ways to man! A-MEN.

Music from Enlarged Songs of Praise. By permission of the Oxford University Press.

69 The Sweetest Name

GEO. W. BETHUNE

WILLIAM B. BRADBURY, 1816-1868

1. There is no name so sweet on earth, No name so sweet in heav - en,
2. And when He hung up - on the tree, They wrote this name a - bove Him
3. So now, up - on His Fa - ther's throne—Al - might-y to re - lease us
4. O Je - sus! by that match-less Name Thy grace shall fail us nev - er;

The name, be - fore His won-drous birth, To Christ the Sav - iour giv - en.
That all might see the rea - son we For ev - er-more must love Him.
From sin and pain—He ev - er reigns, The Prince and Sav-iour, Je - sus.
To - day as yes - ter - day the same, Thou art the same for ev - er!

D.S. For there's no word ear ev - er heard So dear, so sweet, as "Je - sus!"

REFRAIN

D.S.

We love to sing of Christ our King, And hail Him bless - ed Je - sus!

70 There Is a Name I Love to Hear

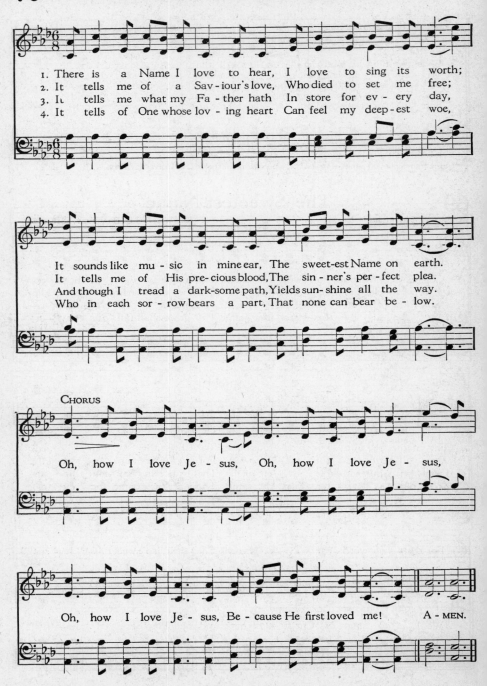

1. There is a Name I love to hear, I love to sing its worth;
2. It tells me of a Saviour's love, Who died to set me free;
3. It tells me what my Father hath In store for every day,
4. It tells of One whose loving heart Can feel my deepest woe,

It sounds like music in mine ear, The sweetest Name on earth.
It tells me of His precious blood, The sinner's perfect plea.
And though I tread a darksome path, Yields sunshine all the way.
Who in each sorrow bears a part, That none can bear below.

CHORUS

Oh, how I love Jesus, Oh, how I love Jesus,

Oh, how I love Jesus, Because He first loved me! A-MEN.

71 Thou Hidden Source of Calm Repose

ST. PETERSBURG. 8. 8. 8. 8. 8. 8.

CHARLES WESLEY, 1707-1788

DIMITRI S. BORTNIANSKY, 1752-1825

1. Thou hid - den Source of calm re - pose, Thou all - suf
2. Thy might - y Name sal - va - tion is, And keeps my
3. Je - sus, my All - in - All Thou art: My rest in
4. In want my plen - ti - ful sup - ply, In weak - ness

fi - cient Love di - vine, My help and ref - uge from my foes,
hap - py soul a - bove: Com - fort it brings, and pow'r, and peace,
toil, my ease in pain, The heal - ing of my bro - ken heart,
my al - might - y pow'r, In bonds my per - fect lib - er - ty,

Se - cure I am while Thou art mine; And lo! from sin, and
And joy, and ev - er - last - ing love: To me, with Thy great
In war my peace, in loss my gain, My smile be - neath the
My light in Sa - tan's dark - est hour, In grief my joy un -

grief, and shame, I hide me, Je - sus, in Thy name.
Name, are given Par - don, and ho - li - ness and heaven.
ty - rant's frown: In shame my glo - ry and my crown,
speak - a - ble, My life in death: my All - in - All. A - MEN.

72 Come, Holy Spirit, Heavenly Dove

AZMON. C. M.

Isaac Watts, 1674–1748

Carl G. Gläser, 1784–1829
Arr. by Lowell Mason, 1792–1872

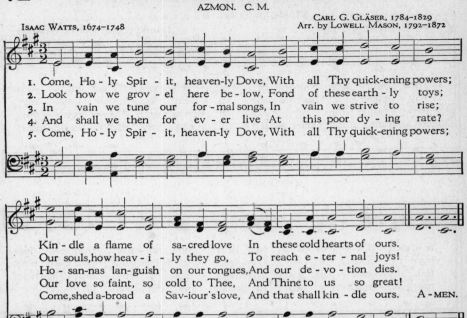

1. Come, Ho - ly Spir - it, heaven-ly Dove, With all Thy quick-ening powers;
2. Look how we grov - el here be - low, Fond of these earth - ly toys;
3. In vain we tune our for - mal songs, In vain we strive to rise;
4. And shall we then for ev - er live At this poor dy - ing rate?
5. Come, Ho - ly Spir - it, heaven-ly Dove, With all Thy quick-ening powers;

Kin - dle a flame of sa-cred love In these cold hearts of ours.
Our souls, how heav - i - ly they go, To reach e - ter - nal joys!
Ho - san-nas lan - guish on our tongues, And our de - vo - tion dies.
Our love so faint, so cold to Thee, And Thine to us so great!
Come, shed a-broad a Sav-iour's love, And that shall kin - dle ours. A - MEN.

73 Gracious Spirit, Dwell With Me

REDHEAD. 7. 7. 7. 7. 7. 7.

Thomas Toke Lynch, 1818–1871

Richard Redhead, 1820–1901

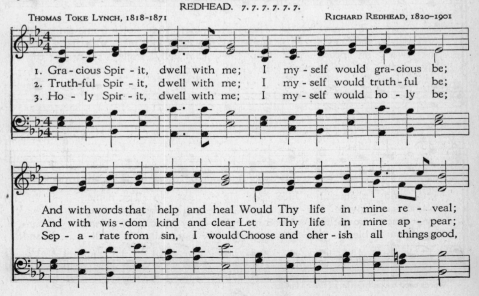

1. Gra - cious Spir - it, dwell with me; I my - self would gra - cious be;
2. Truth-ful Spir - it, dwell with me; I my - self would truth - ful be;
3. Ho - ly Spir - it, dwell with me; I my - self would ho - ly be;

And with words that help and heal Would Thy life in mine re - veal;
And with wis - dom kind and clear Let Thy life in mine ap - pear;
Sep - a - rate from sin, I would Choose and cher - ish all things good,

75 Spirit of God, Descend Upon My Heart

MORECAMBE. 10. 10. 10. 10.

GEORGE CROLY, 1780-1860

FREDERICK C. ATKINSON, 1841-1897

1. Spir - it of God, de-scend up - on my heart; Wean it from earth; thro'
2. I ask no dream, no proph-et ec - sta - sies, No sud-den rend - ing
3. Hast Thou not bid me love Thee, God and King? All, all Thine own— soul,
4. Teach me to feel that Thou art al-ways nigh; Teach me the strug-gles

all its puls - es move; Stoop to my weak - ness, might - y as Thou art,
of the veil of clay, No an - gel vis - it - ant, no o-pening skies;
heart, and strength, and mind. I see Thy cross— there teach my heart to cling:
of the soul to bear, To check the ris - ing doubt, the reb - el sigh;

And make me love Thee as I ought to love.
But take the dim - ness of my soul a - way.
O let me seek Thee, and O let me find!
Teach me the pa - tience of un - an - swered prayer. A - MEN.

5 Teach me to love Thee as Thine angels love,
One holy passion filling all my frame;
The kindling of the heaven-descended Dove,
My heart an altar, and Thy love the flame.

76 Breathe on Me, Breath of God

6.6.8.6.

EDWIN HATCH, 1835-1889

LOWELL MASON, 1792-1872

1. Breathe on me, Breath of God, Fill me with life a - new,
2. Breathe on me, Breath of God, Un - til my heart is pure,
3. Breathe on me, Breath of God, Till I am whol - ly Thine.
4. Breathe on me, Breath of God, So shall I nev - er die,

That I may love what Thou dost love, And do what Thou wouldst do.
Un - til with Thee I will one will, To do or to en - dure.
Till all this earth - ly part of me Glows with Thy fire di - vine.
But live with Thee the per - fect life Of Thine e - ter - ni - ty. A - MEN.

77 Our Blest Redeemer, Ere He Breathed

8.6.8.4.

HARRIET AUBER, 1773-1862

JOHN B. DYKES, 1823-1876

1. Our blest Re - deem - er, ere He breathed His ten - der last fare - well,
2. He came in tongues of liv - ing flame, To teach, con - vince, sub - due;
3. He comes, sweet in - fluence to im - part, A gra - cious, will - ing Guest,
4. And His that gen - tle voice we hear, Soft as the breath of even,
5. Spir - it of pur - i - ty and grace, Our weak - ness, pity - ing see;

A Guide, a Com - fort - er be - queathed, With us to dwell.
All - pow'r - ful as the wind He came, As view - less, too.
While He can find one hum - ble heart Where - in to rest.
That checks each fault, that calms each fear, And speaks of heaven.
O make our hearts Thy dwell - ing place, And wor - thier Thee. A - MEN.

78 O Spirit of the Living God

ST. LEONARD. C. M. D.

HENRY H. TWEEDY, 1868–

HENRY HILES, 1826–1904

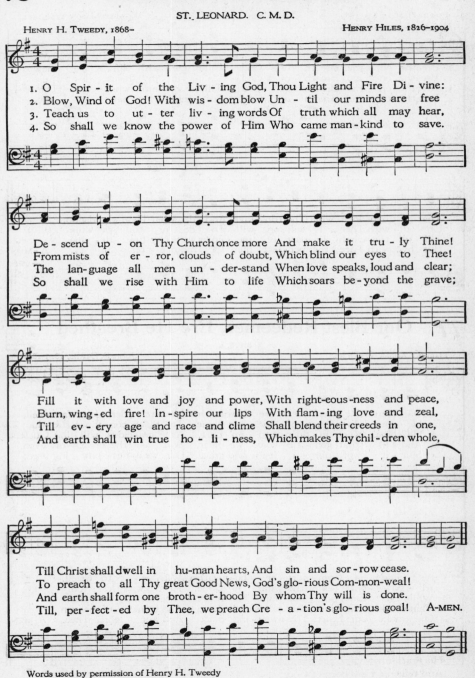

1. O Spir-it of the Liv-ing God, Thou Light and Fire Di- vine:
2. Blow, Wind of God! With wis-dom blow Un - til our minds are free
3. Teach us to ut - ter liv-ing words Of truth which all may hear,
4. So shall we know the power of Him Who came man-kind to save.

De - scend up - on Thy Church once more And make it tru-ly Thine!
From mists of er - ror, clouds of doubt, Which blind our eyes to Thee!
The lan-guage all men un - der-stand When love speaks, loud and clear;
So shall we rise with Him to life Which soars be-yond the grave;

Fill it with love and joy and power, With right-eous-ness and peace,
Burn, wing-ed fire! In-spire our lips With flam-ing love and zeal,
Till ev - ery age and race and clime Shall blend their creeds in one,
And earth shall win true ho - li - ness, Which makes Thy chil-dren whole,

Till Christ shall dwell in hu-man hearts, And sin and sor-row cease.
To preach to all Thy great Good News, God's glo- rious Com-mon-weal!
And earth shall form one broth-er-hood By whom Thy will is done.
Till, per-fect-ed by Thee, we preach Cre - a-tion's glo- rious goal! A-MEN.

Words used by permission of Henry H. Tweedy

79 Arise, My Soul, Arise

LENOX. 6. 6. 6. 6. 8. 8.

CHARLES WESLEY, 1707–1788

LEWIS EDSON, 1748–1820

1. A - rise, my soul, a - rise; Shake off thy guilt - y fears:
2. He ev - er lives a - bove, For me to in - ter - cede;
3. Five bleed - ing wounds He bears, Re - ceived on Cal - va - ry;

The bleed - ing Sac - ri - fice In my be - half ap - pears:
His all - re - deem - ing love, His pre - cious blood, to plead;
They pour ef - fect - ual prayers, They strong - ly plead for me:

Be - fore the throne my Sure - ty stands, Be - fore the throne my
His blood a - toned for all our race, His blood a - toned for
"For - give him, O for - give," they cry, "For - give him, O for -

Sure - ty stands, My name is writ - ten on His hands.
all our race, And sprin - kles now the throne of grace.
give," they cry, "Nor let that ran - somed sin - ner die!" A-MEN.

4 The Father hears Him pray,
His dear Anointed One;
He cannot turn away
The presence of His Son;
His Spirit answers to the blood,
And tells me I am born of God.

5 My God is reconciled;
His pardoning voice I hear;
He owns me for His child,
I can no longer fear:
With confidence I now draw nigh,
And, "Father, Abba, Father," cry.

80 And Can It Be That I Should Gain

FILLMORE. 8. 8. 8. 8. 8. 8.

CHARLES WESLEY, 1707-1788

JEREMIAH INGALLS, 1764-1828

1. And can it be that I should gain An in-terest in the Sav-iour's blood? Died He for me, who caused His pain? For me, who Him to death pur-sued? A-maz-ing love! How can it be That Thou, my Lord, shouldst die for me?

2. 'Tis mys-tery all! Th' im-mor-tal dies! Who can ex-plore His strange de-sign? In vain the first-born ser-aph tries To sound the depths of love di-vine; 'Tis mer-cy all! Let an-gel minds in-quire no more.

3. He left His Fa-ther's throne a-bove, So free, so in-fi-nite His grace! Emp-tied Him-self of all but love, And bled for Ad-am's help-less race; 'Tis mer-cy all! Im-mense and free, For, O my God, it found out me!

4. Long my im-pris-oned spir-it lay, Fast bound in sin and na-ture's night; Thine eye dif-fused a quick-ening ray, I woke, the dun-geon flamed with light: My chains fell off, my heart was free, I rose, went forth, and fol-lowed Thee.

5. No con-dem-na-tion now I dread, Je-sus, with all in Him, is mine; A-live in Him, my liv-ing Head, And clothed in right-eous-ness di-vine, Bold I ap-proach th' e-ter-nal throne, And claim the crown, thro' Christ, my own. A-MEN.

81 There Is a Fountain Filled With Blood

CLEANSING FOUNTAIN. C. M. D.

WILLIAM COWPER, 1731–1800

Early American melody
Arr. from LOWELL MASON, 1792–1872

1. There is a foun-tain filled with blood Drawn from Im-man-uel's veins;
2. The dy-ing thief re-joiced to see That foun-tain in his day;
3. Dear dy-ing Lamb, Thy pre-cious blood Shall nev-er lose its power,
4. E'er since, by faith, I saw the stream Thy flow-ing wounds sup-ply,
5. Then in a no-bler, sweet-er song, I'll sing Thy power to save,

And sin-ners, plunged be-neath that flood, Lose all their guilt-y stains,
And there may I, though vile as he, Wash all my sins a-way,
Till all the ran-somed Church of God Be saved, to sin no more,
Re-deem-ing love has been my theme, And shall be till I die,
When this poor lisp-ing, stam-mering tongue Lies si-lent in the grave,

Lose all their guilt-y stains, Lose all their guilt-y stains; And
Wash all my sins a-way, Wash all my sins a-way; And
Be saved, to sin no more, Be saved, to sin no more; Till
And shall be till I die, And shall be till I die; Re-
Lies si-lent in the grave, Lies si-lent in the grave; When

sin-ners, plunged be-neath that flood, Lose all their guilt-y stains.
there may I, though vile as he, Wash all my sins a-way.
all the ran-somed Church of God Be saved, to sin no more.
deem-ing love has been my theme, And shall be till I die.
this poor lisp-ing, stam-mering tongue Lies si-lent in the grave. A-MEN.

82 My Hope Is Built on Nothing Less

THE SOLID ROCK. L. M. with Refrain

EDWARD MOTE, 1797–1874

WILLIAM B. BRADBURY, 1816–1868

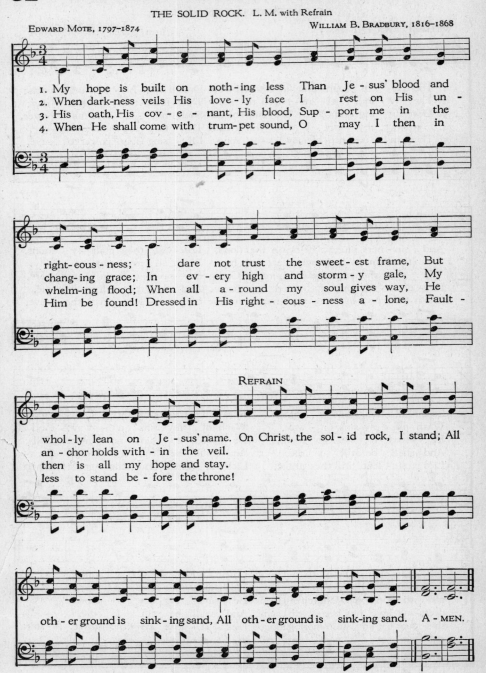

1. My hope is built on noth-ing less Than Je-sus' blood and right-eous-ness; I dare not trust the sweet-est frame, But whol-ly lean on Je-sus' name.
2. When dark-ness veils His love-ly face I rest on His un-chang-ing grace; In ev-ery high and storm-y gale, My an-chor holds with-in the veil.
3. His oath, His cov-e-nant, His blood, Sup-port me in the whelm-ing flood; When all a-round my soul gives way, He then is all my hope and stay.
4. When He shall come with trum-pet sound, O may I then in Him be found! Dressed in His right-eous-ness a-lone, Fault-less to stand be-fore the throne!

REFRAIN

On Christ, the sol-id rock, I stand; All oth-er ground is sink-ing sand, All oth-er ground is sink-ing sand. A-MEN.

83 I Have a Saviour, He's Pleading in Glory

I AM PRAYING FOR YOU. 11. 11. 12. 11. with Refrain

SAMUEL O'M. CLOUGH ?

IRA D. SANKEY, 1840-1908

1. I have a Sav-iour, He's plead-ing in glo-ry, A dear, lov-ing
2. I have a Fa-ther; to me He has giv-en A hope for e-
3. When Je-sus finds you, tell oth-ers the sto-ry, That your lov-ing

Sav-iour, tho' earth-friends be few; And now He is watch-ing in
ter-ni-ty, bless-ed and true; And soon He will call me to
Sav-iour is their Sav-iour, too; Then pray that the Fa-ther will

ten-der-ness o'er me, But oh, that my Sav-iour were your Sav-iour, too!
meet Him in glo-ry, But oh, that He'd let me bring you with me, too!
bring them to glo-ry, And pray'r will be an-swered; 'twas an-swered for you!

REFRAIN

For you I am pray-ing, For you I am pray-ing, For

you I am pray-ing, I'm pray-ing for you. A-MEN.

84 I Love to Tell the Story

HANKEY. 7. 6. 7. 6. D. with Refrain

KATHERINE HANKEY, 1834–1911
Refrain added

WILLIAM G. FISCHER, 1835–1912

1. I love to tell the story Of un-seen things a-bove, Of Je - sus and His glo - ry, Of Je - sus and His love. I love to tell the story, Be - cause I know 'tis true; It sat - is - fies my long-ings As noth - ing else can do.

2. I love to tell the story; More won-der-ful it seems Than all the gold-en fan - cies Of all our gold-en dreams. I love to tell the story, It did so much for me; And that is just the rea - son I tell it now to thee.

3. I love to tell the story; 'Tis pleas-ant to re-peat What seems, each time I tell it, More won-der-ful-ly sweet. I love to tell the story, For some have nev - er heard The mes-sage of sal - va tion From God's own ho-ly Word.

4. I love to tell the story, For those who know it best Seem hun - ger-ing and thirst-ing To hear it like the rest. And when, in scenes of glo - ry, I sing the new, new song, 'Twill be the old, old sto - ry That I have loved so long.

REFRAIN

I love to tell the sto - ry, 'Twill be my theme in glo-ry, To tell the old, old sto - ry Of Je - sus and His love. A - MEN.

85 Ye Must Be Born Again

W. T. Sleeper   11.11.11.5   George C. Stebbins, 1846–

1. A ru-ler once came to Je-sus by night, To
2. Ye chil-dren of men, at-tend to the word So
3. O ye who would en-ter that glo-ri-ous rest, And
4. A dear one in heav-en thy heart yearns to see, At the

ask Him the way of sal-va-tion and light; The
sol-emn-ly ut-tered by Je-sus, the Lord, And
sing with the ran-somed the song of the blest; The
beau-ti-ful gate may be watch-ing for thee; Then

Mas-ter made an-swer in words true and plain, "Ye must be born a-gain."
let not the mes-sage to you be in vain, "Ye must be born a-gain."
life ev-er-last-ing if ye would ob-tain, "Ye must be born a-gain."
list to the note of this sol-emn re-frain, "Ye must be born a-gain."

a-gain,"

CHORUS

"Ye must be born a-gain," "Ye must be born a-gain,"

a-gain,"   a-gain,"

I ver-i-ly, ver-i-ly, say un-to thee, "Ye must be born a-gain."

a-gain,"

86 Brightly Beams Our Father's Mercy

LOWER LIGHTS.   8. 7. 8. 7. with Refrain

PHILIP P. BLISS, 1838–1876

PHILIP P. BLISS, 1838–1876

1. Bright-ly beams our Fa-ther's mer - cy From His light - house ev - er - more;
2. Dark the night of sin has set-tled, Loud the an - gry bil - lows roar:
3. Trim your fee - ble lamp, my broth-er! Some poor sea - man, tem-pest-tossed,

But to us He gives the keep-ing Of the lights a - long the shore.
Ea - ger eyes are watch-ing, long-ing, For the lights a - long the shore.
Try - ing now to make the har - bor, In the dark-ness may be lost.

REFRAIN

Let the low - er lights be burn-ing! Send a gleam a - cross the wave!

Some poor faint-ing, strug-gling sea-man You may res-cue, you may save.   A - MEN.

Lord Jesus, Thou Art Standing

ST. HILDA. 7. 6. 7. 6. D.

WILLIAM W. HOW, 1823-1897

JUSTIN H. KNECHT, 1752-1817
EDWARD HUSBAND, 1843-1908

1. Lord Je - sus, Thou art stand-ing Out - side the fast-closed door,
2. Lord Je - sus, Thou art knock-ing: And lo, that hand is scarred,
3. Lord Je - sus, Thou art plead-ing In ac - cents meek and low,

In low - ly pa-tience wait-ing To pass the thresh-old o'er:
And thorns Thy brow en - cir - cle, And tears Thy face have marred.
"I died for you, my chil-dren, And will ye treat me so?"

Shame on us, Chris - tian breth-ren, His Name and sign who bear;
O love that pass-eth know-ledge, So pa - tient-ly to wait!
O Lord, with shame and sor - row We o - pen now the door;

O shame, thrice shame up - on us, To keep Him stand-ing there!
O sin that hath no e - qual, So fast to bar the gate!
Dear Sav - iour, en - ter, en - ter, And leave us nev - er - more. A-MEN.

Saviour, Thy Dying Love

SOMETHING FOR JESUS. 6. 4. 6. 4. 6. 6. 6. 4.

SYLVANUS D. PHELPS, 1816–1895

ROBERT LOWRY, 1826–1899

1. Sav - iour, Thy dy - ing love   Thou gav - est   me,   Nor should I
2. At   the blest mer - cy seat,   Plead - ing for   me,   My   fee - ble
3. Give me   a faith - ful heart,   Like - ness to   Thee,   That each de -
4. All that   I   am and have,   Thy gifts so   free,   In   joy, in

aught with-hold, Dear Lord, from Thee; In   love my soul would bow, My heart ful
faith looks up,   Je - sus,   to Thee; Help me the cross to bear, Thy won-drous
part - ing day   Hence-forth may see   Some work of love be-gun, Some deed of
grief, through life,   Dear Lord, for   Thee! And when Thy face I see,   My ran-somed

fill   its vow, Some   of - f'ring bring Thee now,   Some-thing for Thee.
love de-clare, Some   song to raise, or prayer,   Some-thing for Thee.
kind-ness done, Some   wan-derer sought and won,   Some-thing for Thee.
soul shall be, Through all e - ter - ni - ty,   Some-thing for Thee.   A-MEN.

Copyright property of Mary Runyan Lowry.   Used by permission.

Revive Us Again

WM. PATON MACKAY

J. J. HUSBAND

1. We praise Thee, O God!   for the Son of Thy love,   For   Je - sus who
2. We praise Thee, O God!   for Thy Spir - it of light,   Who has shown us   our
3. All   glo - ry and praise   to the Lamb that was slain,   Who has borne all   our
4. All   glo - ry and praise   to the God of   all grace,   Who has bought us, and
5. Re - vive us   a - gain;   fill each heart with Thy love;   May each soul be re -

Revive Us Again

REFRAIN

died and is now gone a-bove. Hal-le-lu-jah! Thine the glo-ry; Hal-le-
Sav-iour and scat-tered our night.
sins, and has cleansed ev-ery stain.
sought us, and guid-ed our ways.
kin-dled with fire from a-bove.

lu-jah! A-men! Hal-le-lu-jah! Thine the glo-ry; Re-vive us a-gain.

90 All to Christ I Owe

Elvina M. Hall

John T. Grape

1. I hear the Sav-iour say, "Thy strength in-deed is small; Child of
2. Lord, now in-deed I find Thy power, and thine a-lone Can
3. When from my dy-ing bed My ran-somed soul shall rise, Then
4. And when be-fore the throne I stand in Him com-plete, I'll

CHORUS

weak-ness, watch and pray, Find in me thine all in all." Je-sus paid it all,
change the lep-er's spots, And melt the heart of stone.
"Je-sus paid it all" Shall rend the vault-ed skies.
lay my tro-phies down, All down at Je-sus' feet.

All to him I owe; Sin had left a crim-son stain: He wash'd it white as snow.

91 What a Friend We Have in Jesus

CONVERSE. 8. 7. 8. 7. D.

JOSEPH SCRIVEN, 1820–1886   CHARLES C. CONVERSE, 1832–1918

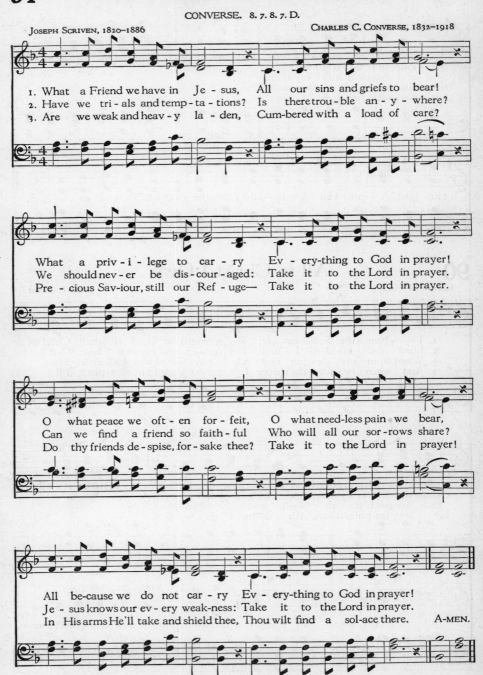

1. What a Friend we have in Je - sus, All our sins and griefs to bear!
2. Have we tri - als and temp - ta - tions? Is there trou - ble an - y - where?
3. Are we weak and heav - y la - den, Cum-bered with a load of care?

What a priv - i - lege to car - ry Ev - ery-thing to God in prayer!
We should nev - er be dis - cour - aged: Take it to the Lord in prayer.
Pre - cious Sav-iour, still our Ref - uge— Take it to the Lord in prayer.

O what peace we oft - en for - feit, O what need-less pain we bear,
Can we find a friend so faith - ful Who will all our sor - rows share?
Do thy friends de - spise, for - sake thee? Take it to the Lord in prayer!

All be-cause we do not car - ry Ev - ery-thing to God in prayer!
Je - sus knows our ev - ery weak-ness: Take it to the Lord in prayer.
In His arms He'll take and shield thee, Thou wilt find a sol-ace there.

A-MEN.

Holy Spirit, Faithful Guide

HOLY SPIRIT, FAITHFUL GUIDE. 7. 7. 7. 7. D.

MARCUS M. WELLS, 1815–1895   MARCUS M. WELLS, 1815–1895

1. Ho - ly Spir - it, faith - ful Guide, Ev - er near the Chris-tian's side;
2. Ev - er pres - ent, tru - est Friend, Ev - er near Thine aid to lend,
3. When our days of toil shall cease, Wait-ing still for sweet re - lease,

Gen - tly lead us by the hand, Pil - grims in a des - ert land;
Leave us not to doubt and fear, Grop - ing on in dark - ness drear;
Noth - ing left but heav'n and prayer, Won-dering if our names were there;

Wea - ry souls for - e'er re - joice, While they hear that sweet-est voice,
When the storms are rag - ing sore, Hearts grow faint, and hopes give o'er,
Wad - ing deep the dis - mal flood, Plead - ing naught but Je - sus' blood,

Whis-p'ring soft - ly, "Wan-d'rer, come! Fol - low me, I'll guide thee home."
Whis - per soft - ly, "Wan-d'rer, come! Fol - low me, I'll guide thee home."
Whis - per soft - ly, "Wan-d'rer, come! Fol - low me, I'll guide thee home." A-MEN.

93 There Were Ninety and Nine

THE NINETY AND NINE. Irregular

Elizabeth C. Clephane, 1830–1869

Ira D. Sankey, 1840–1908

1. There were nine-ty 'and nine that safe-ly lay In the shel-ter of the fold, But one was out on the hills a-way, Far off from the gates of gold— A-way on the moun-tains wild and bare, A-way from the ten-der

2. "Lord, Thou hast here Thy nine-ty and nine; Are they not e-nough for Thee?" But the Shep-herd made an-swer: "This of mine Has wan-dered a-way from me; And al-though the road be rough and steep I go to the des-ert to

3. But none of the ran-somed ev-er knew How deep were the wa-ters crossed; Nor how dark was the night that the Lord passed thro' Ere He found His sheep that was lost. Out in the des-ert He heard its cry— So sick and so help-less and

4. "Lord, whence are those blood-drops all the way That mark out the moun-tain's track?"—"They were shed for one who had gone a-stray Ere the Shep-herd could bring him back."— "Lord, whence are Thy hands so rent and torn?"—"They are pierc'd to-night by

5. But all thro' the moun-tains, thun-der-riv-en, And up from the rock-y steep, There a-rose a glad cry to the gate of heaven, "Re-joice! I have found my sheep!' And the an-gels ech-oed a-round the throne, "Re-joice, for the Lord brings

There Were Ninety and Nine

Shep-herd's care, A - way from the ten - der Shep-herd's care.
find my sheep, I go to the des-ert to find my sheep."
read-y to die, So sick and so help-less and read-y to die.
man-y a thorn, They are pierc'd to - night by man-y a thorn."
back His own, Re-joice, for the Lord brings back His own!" A-MEN.

---

94 ## I Need Thee Every Hour

I NEED THEE EVERY HOUR. 6. 4. 6. 4. with Refrain

ANNIE S. HAWKS, 1835–1918 · · · ROBERT LOWRY, 1826–1899

1. I need Thee ev-ery hour, Most gra - cious Lord; No ten-der voice like Thine
2. I need Thee ev-ery hour; Stay Thou near by; Temp-ta-tions lose their power
3. I need Thee ev-ery hour, In joy or pain; Come quick-ly and a - bide,
4. I need Thee ev-ery hour; Teach me Thy will; And Thy rich prom-is - es

REFRAIN

Can peace af - ford. I need Thee, O I need Thee. Ev-ery hour I
When Thou art nigh.
Or life is vain.
In me ful - fill.

need Thee; O bless me now, my Sav-iour, I come to Thee! A-MEN.

95 I Was a Wandering Sheep

6.6.8.6.D.

HORATIUS BONAR, 1808–1889

JOHN ZUNDEL, 1815–1882

1. I was a wan-dering sheep, I did not love the fold;
2. The Shep-herd sought His sheep, The Fa-ther sought His child,
3. Je-sus my Shep-herd is, 'Twas He that loved my soul,
4. I was a wan-dering sheep, I would not be con-trolled;

I did not love my Shep-herd's voice, I would not be con-trolled.
They fol-lowed me o'er vale and hill, O'er des-erts waste and wild:
'Twas He that washed me in His blood, 'Twas He that made me whole;
But now I love the Shep-herd's voice, I love, I love the fold;

I was a way-ward child, I did not love my home;
They found me nigh to death, Fam-ished and faint, and lone;
'Twas He that sought the lost, That found the wan-dering sheep,
I was a way-ward child, I once pre-ferred to roam;

I did not love my Fa-ther's voice; I loved a-far to roam.
They bound me with the bands of love; They saved the wan-dering one.
'Twas He that brought me to the fold, 'Tis He that still doth keep.
But now I love my Fa-ther's voice, I love, I love His home.

96 In Tenderness He Sought Me

7. 6. 7. 6. 8. 8.

W. Spencer Walton

Adoniram J. Gordon, 1836–1895

1. In ten-der-ness He sought me, Wea-ry and sick with sin,
2. He wash'd the bleed-ing sin-wounds, And poured in oil and wine;
3. He point-ed to the nail-prints, For me His blood was shed,
4. I'm sit-ting in His pres-ence, The sun-shine of His face,
5. So while the hours are pass-ing, All now is per-fect rest,

And on His shoul-ders brought me, Back to His fold a-gain.
He whis-pered to as-sure me, "I've found thee, thou art Mine;"
A mock-ing crown so thorn-y, Was placed up-on His head:
While with a-dor-ing won-der His bless-ings I re-trace.
I'm wait-ing for the morn-ing, The bright-est and the best,

While an-gels in His pres-ence sang Un-til the courts of Heav-en rang.
I nev-er heard a sweet-er voice, It made my ach-ing heart re-joice!
I won-dered what He saw in me, To suf-fer such deep ag-o-ny.
It seems as if e-ter-nal days Are far too short to sound His praise.
When He will call us to His side, To be with Him, His spot-less bride.

Chorus

Oh, the love that sought me! Oh, the blood that bought me, Oh, the grace that

brought me to the fold, Won-drous grace that brought me to the fold!

97 Launch Out

11.8.11.9.

A. B. SIMPSON

R. KELSO CARTER

1. The mer - cy of God is an o - cean di - vine, A
2. But man - y, a - las! on - ly stand on the shore, And
3. And oth - ers just ven - ture a - way from the land, And
4. Oh, let us launch out on this o - cean so broad, Where the

bound - less and fath - om - less flood; Launch out in the deep, cut a -
gaze on the o - cean so wide; They nev - er have ven - tured its
lin - ger so near to the shore, That the surf and the slime that beat
floods of sal - va - tion o'er - flow; Oh, let us be lost in the

way the shore - line, And be lost in the full - ness of God.
depths to ex - plore, Or to launch on the fath - om - less tide.
o - ver the strand, Dash o'er them in floods ev - er - more.
mer - cy of God, Till the depths of His full - ness we know.

CHORUS

Launch out in - to the deep, Oh, let the shore-line go;
Oh, launch out in the deep,

Launch out, launch out in the o - cean di - vine, Out where the full tides flow.

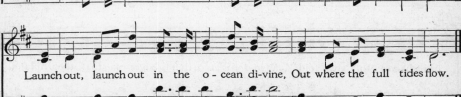

98 He Leadeth Me: O Blessed Thought!

HE LEADETH ME. L. M. with Refrain

Joseph H. Gilmore, 1834–1918

William B. Bradbury, 1816–1868

1. He lead-eth me: O bless-ed thought! O words with heavenly com-fort fraught!
2. Sometimes 'mid scenes of deep-est gloom, Sometimes where E-den's bow-ers bloom,
3. Lord, I would place my hand in Thine, Nor ev-er mur-mur nor re-pine;
4. And when my task on earth is done, When, by Thy grace, the vic-tory's won,

What-e'er I do, wher-e'er I be, Still 'tis God's hand that lead-eth me.
By wa-ters still, o'er trou-bled sea, Still 'tis His hand that lead-eth me.
Con-tent, what-ev-er lot I see, Since 'tis my God that lead-eth me.
E'en death's cold wave I will not flee, Since God thro' Jor-dan lead-eth me.

Refrain

He lead-eth me, He lead-eth me, By His own hand He lead-eth me:

His faith-ful fol-lower I would be, For by His hand He lead-eth me. A-men.

99 Amazing Grace! How Sweet the Sound

AMAZING GRACE. C. M.

JOHN NEWTON, 1725–1807

Early American Melody

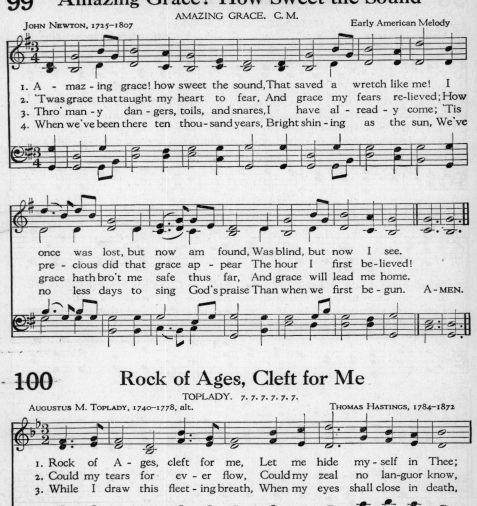

1. A - maz - ing grace! how sweet the sound, That saved a wretch like me! I
2. 'Twas grace that taught my heart to fear, And grace my fears re-lieved; How
3. Thro' man - y dan - gers, toils, and snares, I have al - read - y come; 'Tis
4. When we've been there ten thou - sand years, Bright shin - ing as the sun, We've

once was lost, but now am found, Was blind, but now I see.
pre - cious did that grace ap - pear The hour I first be - lieved!
grace hath bro't me safe thus far, And grace will lead me home.
no less days to sing God's praise Than when we first be - gun. A-MEN.

100 Rock of Ages, Cleft for Me

TOPLADY. 7. 7. 7. 7. 7. 7.

AUGUSTUS M. TOPLADY, 1740–1778, alt.

THOMAS HASTINGS, 1784–1872

1. Rock of A - ges, cleft for me, Let me hide my - self in Thee;
2. Could my tears for ev - er flow, Could my zeal no lan - guor know,
3. While I draw this fleet - ing breath, When my eyes shall close in death,

Let the wa - ter and the blood, From Thy wound - ed side which flowed,
These for sin could not a - tone; Thou must save, and Thou a - lone:
When I rise to worlds un - known, And be - hold Thee on Thy throne:

Rock of Ages, Cleft for Me

Be of sin the dou-ble cure, Save from wrath and make me pure.
In my hand no price I bring; Sim-ply to Thy cross I cling.
Rock of A-ges, cleft for me, Let me hide my-self in Thee. A-MEN.

101 I Sought the Lord

PEACE. 10. 10. 10. 6.

Anonymous, c. 1904

GEORGE W. CHADWICK, 1854–1931

1. I sought the Lord, and af-ter-ward I knew He moved my
2. Thou didst reach forth Thy hand and mine en-fold; I walked and
3. I find, I walk, I love, but, oh, the whole Of love is

soul to seek Him, seek-ing me; It was not I that
sank not on the storm-vexed sea; 'Twas not so much that
but my an-swer, Lord, to Thee! For Thou wert long be-

found, O Sav-iour true, No, I was found of Thee.
I on Thee took hold As Thou, dear Lord, on me.
fore-hand with my soul; Al-ways Thou lov-edst me. A-MEN.

102 My Faith It Is an Oaken Staff

MUSWELL HILL. 8. 6. 8. 6. 8. 8. 8. 6.

THOMAS T. LYNCH, 1818-1871

Traditional Melody
Arr. by CAREY BONNER

1. My faith it is an oak-en staff, The trav-eler's well-loved aid; My faith it is a weap-on stout, The sol-dier's trust-ed blade. I'll trav-el on and still be stirred By si-lent thought or so-cial word, By all my per-ils

2. I have a Guide, and in His steps When trav-elers lone have trod, Wheth-er be-neath was flint-y rock Or yield-ing grass-y sod, They cared not, but with force un-spent, Un-moved by pain they on-ward went, Un-stayed by pleas-ures

3. My faith it is an oak-en staff, O let me on it lean; My faith it is a trust-y sword, May false-hood find it keen, Thy spir-it, Lord, to me im-part, O make me what Thou ev-er art, Of pa-tient and cour-

My Faith It Is an Oaken Staff

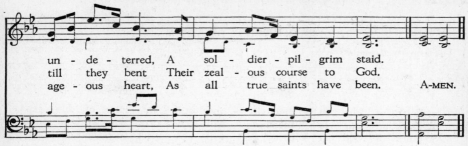

un - de - terred, A sol - dier - pil - grim staid.
till they bent Their zeal - ous course to God.
age - ous heart, As all true saints have been. A-MEN.

103   My Faith Looks Up to Thee

OLIVET. 6. 6. 4. 6. 6. 6. 4.

RAY PALMER, 1808-1887   LOWELL MASON, 1792-1872

1. My faith looks up to Thee, Thou Lamb of Cal - va - ry,
2. May Thy rich grace im - part Strength to my faint - ing heart,
3. When life's dark maze I tread, And griefs a - round me spread,
4. When ends life's tran - sient dream, When death's cold, sul - len stream

Sav - iour di - vine! Now hear me while I pray, Take all my
My zeal in - spire; As Thou hast died for me, O may my
Be Thou my guide; Bid dark - ness turn to day, Wipe sor - row's
Shall o'er me roll; Blest Sav - iour, then, in love, Fear and dis -

guilt a - way, O let me from this day Be whol - ly Thine!
love to Thee Pure, warm, and change-less be, A liv - ing fire!
tears a - way, Nor let me ev - er stray From Thee a - side.
trust re-move; O bear me safe a - bove, A ran-somed soul! A-MEN.

104 Faith of Our Fathers! Living Still

ST. CATHERINE. 8. 8. 8. 8. 8. 8.

FREDERICK W. FABER, 1814–1863

HENRI F. HEMY, 1818–1888
Adapted by JAMES G. WALTON, 1821–1905

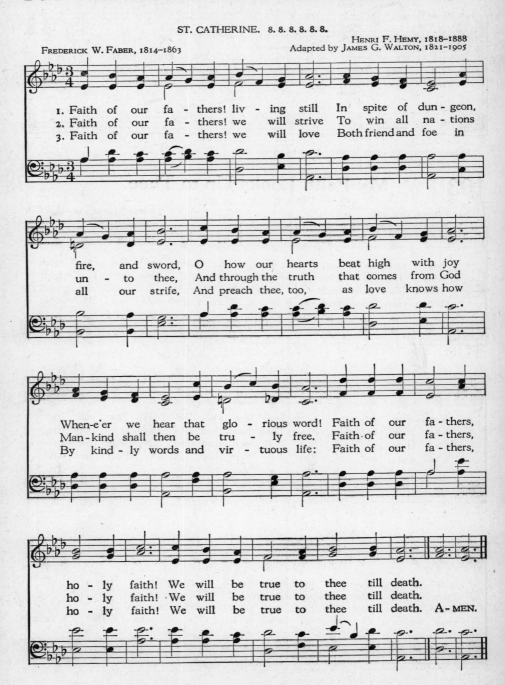

1. Faith of our fa - thers! liv - ing still In spite of dun - geon,
   fire, and sword, O how our hearts beat high with joy When-e'er we hear that glo - rious word! Faith of our fa - thers, ho - ly faith! We will be true to thee till death.

2. Faith of our fa - thers! we will strive To win all na - tions un - to thee, And through the truth that comes from God Man-kind shall then be tru - ly free. Faith of our fa - thers, ho - ly faith! We will be true to thee till death.

3. Faith of our fa - thers! we will love Both friend and foe in all our strife, And preach thee, too, as love knows how By kind - ly words and vir - tuous life: Faith of our fa - thers, ho - ly faith! We will be true to thee till death. A - MEN.

105 Father, I Stretch My Hands to Thee

8. 6. 8. 6.

CHARLES WESLEY, 1707–1788

Unknown
Fine

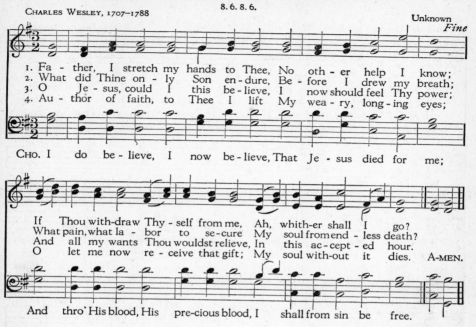

1. Fa - ther, I stretch my hands to Thee, No oth - er help I know;
2. What did Thine on - ly Son en - dure, Be - fore I drew my breath;
3. O Je - sus, could I this be - lieve, I now should feel Thy power;
4. Au - thor of faith, to Thee I lift My wea - ry, long - ing eyes;

CHO. I do be - lieve, I now be - lieve, That Je - sus died for me;

If Thou with-draw Thy - self from me, Ah, whith-er shall I go?
What pain, what la - bor to se - cure My soul from end - less death?
And all my wants Thou wouldst relieve, In this ac - cept - ed hour.
O let me now re - ceive that gift; My soul with-out it dies. A-MEN.

And thro' His blood, His pre-cious blood, I shall from sin be free.

106 I Am Trusting Thee, Lord Jesus

BULLINGER. 8. 5. 8. 3.

FRANCES R. HAVERGAL, 1836–1879

ETHELBERT W. BULLINGER, 1837–1913

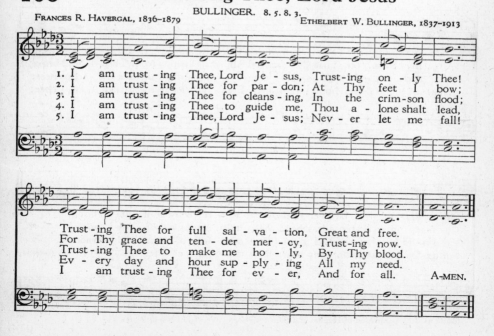

1. I am trust - ing Thee, Lord Je - sus, Trust - ing on - ly Thee!
2. I am trust - ing Thee for par - don; At Thy feet I bow;
3. I am trust - ing Thee for cleans - ing, In the crim - son flood;
4. I am trust - ing Thee to guide me, Thou a - lone shalt lead,
5. I am trust - ing Thee, Lord Je - sus; Nev - er let me fall!

Trust - ing Thee for full sal - va - tion, Great and free.
For Thy grace and ten - der mer - cy, Trust - ing now.
Trust - ing Thee to make me ho - ly, By Thy blood.
Ev - ery day and hour sup - ply - ing All my need.
I am trust - ing Thee for ev - er, And for all. A-MEN.

107 Jesus, Lover of My Soul

ABERYSTWYTH. 7.7.7.7.D.

(First Tune)

CHARLES WESLEY, 1707–1788

JOSEPH PARRY, 1841–1903

1. Je - sus, Lov - er of my soul, Let me to Thy bos - om fly,
2. Oth - er ref - uge have I none; Hangs my help - less soul on Thee;
3. Thou, O Christ, art all I want; More than all in Thee I find:
4. Plen - teous grace with Thee is found, Grace to cov - er all my sin;

While the near - er wa - ters roll, While the tem - pest still is high:
Leave, ah! leave me not a - lone, Still sup - port and com - fort me:
Raise the fall - en, cheer the faint, Heal the sick, and lead the blind.
Let the heal - ing streams a - bound; Make and keep me pure with - in.

Hide me, O my Sav - iour, hide, Till the storm of life is past;
All my trust on Thee is stayed, All my help from Thee I bring;
Just and ho - ly is Thy Name, I am all un - right - eous - ness;
Thou of life the Foun - tain art, Free - ly let me take of Thee:

Safe in - to the ha - ven guide; O re - ceive my soul at last!
Cov - er my de - fense - less head With the shad - ow of Thy wing.
False and full of sin I am, Thou art full of truth and grace.
Spring Thou up with - in my heart, Rise to all e - ter - ni - ty. A - MEN.

Music used by permission of Hughes and Son, Publishers, Wrexham, North Wales.

107 Jesus, Lover of My Soul

MARTYN. 7. 7. 7. 7. D.

(Second Tune)

CHARLES WESLEY, 1707–1788

SIMEON B. MARSH, 1798–1875

1. Je - sus, Lov - er of my soul, Let me to Thy bos - om fly,
2. Oth - er ref - uge have I none; Hangs my help - less soul on Thee;
3. Thou, O Christ, art all I want; More than all in Thee I find:
4. Plen-teous grace with Thee is found, Grace to cov - er all my sin;

While the near - er wa - ters roll, While the tem - pest still is high:
Leave, ah! leave me not a - lone, Still sup - port and com - fort me:
Raise the fall - en, cheer the faint, Heal the sick, and lead the blind.
Let the heal - ing streams a - bound; Make and keep me pure with - in.

Hide me, O my Sav - iour, hide, Till the storm of life is past;
All my trust on Thee is stayed, All my help from Thee I bring;
Just and ho - ly is Thy Name, I am all un - right - eous - ness;
Thou of life the Foun - tain art, Free - ly let me take of Thee:

Safe in - to the ha - ven guide; O re - ceive my soul at last!
Cov - er my de-fense - less head With the shad - ow of Thy wing.
False and full of sin I am, Thou art full of truth and grace.
Spring Thou up with - in my heart, Rise to all e - ter - ni - ty. A - MEN.

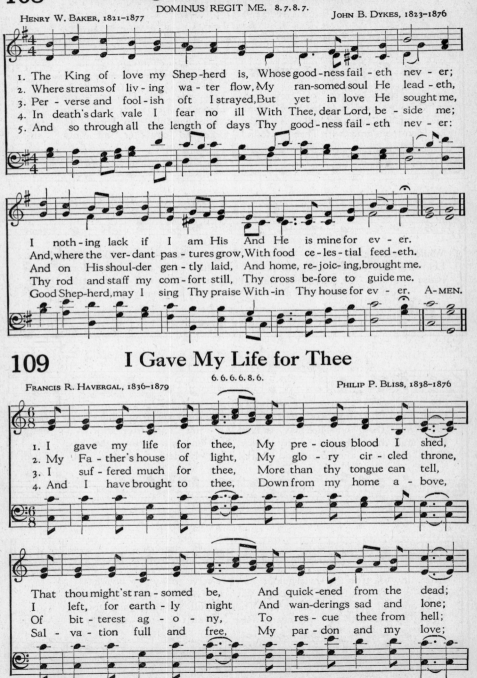

108 The King of Love My Shepherd Is

DOMINUS REGIT ME. 8.7.8.7.

HENRY W. BAKER, 1821–1877

JOHN B. DYKES, 1823–1876

1. The King of love my Shep-herd is, Whose good-ness fail-eth nev-er;
2. Where streams of liv-ing wa-ter flow, My ran-somed soul He lead-eth,
3. Per-verse and fool-ish oft I strayed, But yet in love He sought me,
4. In death's dark vale I fear no ill With Thee, dear Lord, be-side me;
5. And so through all the length of days Thy good-ness fail-eth nev-er:

I noth-ing lack if I am His And He is mine for ev-er.
And, where the ver-dant pas-tures grow, With food ce-les-tial feed-eth.
And on His shoul-der gen-tly laid, And home, re-joic-ing, brought me.
Thy rod and staff my com-fort still, Thy cross be-fore to guide me.
Good Shep-herd, may I sing Thy praise With-in Thy house for ev-er. A-MEN.

109 I Gave My Life for Thee

6.6.6.6.8.6.

FRANCIS R. HAVERGAL, 1836–1879

PHILIP P. BLISS, 1838–1876

1. I gave my life for thee, My pre-cious blood I shed,
2. My Fa-ther's house of light, My glo-ry cir-cled throne,
3. I suf-fered much for thee, More than thy tongue can tell,
4. And I have brought to thee, Down from my home a-bove,

That thou might'st ran-somed be, And quick-ened from the dead;
I left, for earth-ly night And wan-derings sad and lone;
Of bit-terest ag-o-ny, To res-cue thee from hell;
Sal-va-tion full and free, My par-don and my love;

I Gave My Life for Thee

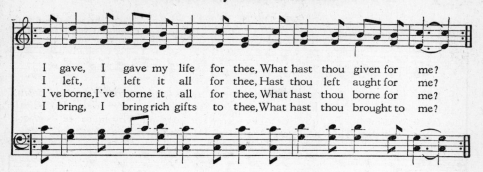

I gave, I gave my life for thee, What hast thou given for me?
I left, I left it all for thee, Hast thou left aught for me?
I've borne, I've borne it all for thee, What hast thou borne for me?
I bring, I bring rich gifts to thee, What hast thou brought to me?

110 More Love to Thee, O Christ

MORE LOVE TO THEE. 6. 4. 6. 4. 6. 6. 4.

ELIZABETH P. PRENTISS, 1818–1878

WILLIAM H. DOANE, 1832–1916

1. More love to Thee, O Christ, More love to Thee! Hear Thou the prayer I make On bend-ed knee; This is my ear-nest plea, More love, O Christ, to Thee, More love to Thee, More love to Thee!

2. Once earth-ly joy I craved, Sought peace and rest; Now Thee a-lone I seek, Give what is best: This all my prayer shall be, More love, O Christ, to Thee, More love to Thee, More love to Thee!

3. Then shall my lat-est breath Whis-per Thy praise; This be the part-ing cry My heart shall raise; This still its prayer shall be, More love, O Christ, to Thee, More love to Thee, More love to Thee! A-MEN.

111 Love Divine, All Loves Excelling

LOVE DIVINE. 8. 7. 8. 7. D.

CHARLES WESLEY, 1707-1788

JOHN ZUNDEL, 1815-1882

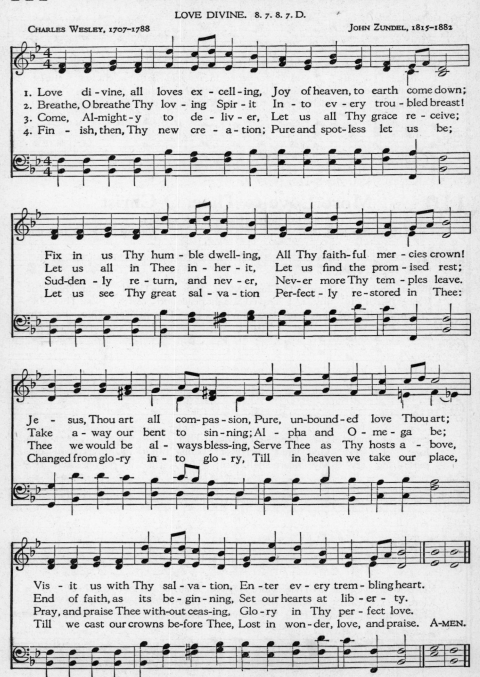

1. Love di-vine, all loves ex-cell-ing, Joy of heaven, to earth come down;
2. Breathe, O breathe Thy lov-ing Spir-it In-to ev-ery trou-bled breast!
3. Come, Al-might-y to de-liv-er, Let us all Thy grace re-ceive;
4. Fin-ish, then, Thy new cre-a-tion; Pure and spot-less let us be;

Fix in us Thy hum-ble dwell-ing, All Thy faith-ful mer-cies crown!
Let us all in Thee in-her-it, Let us find the prom-ised rest;
Sud-den-ly re-turn, and nev-er, Nev-er more Thy tem-ples leave.
Let us see Thy great sal-va-tion Per-fect-ly re-stored in Thee:

Je-sus, Thou art all com-pas-sion, Pure, un-bound-ed love Thou art;
Take a-way our bent to sin-ning; Al-pha and O-me-ga be;
Thee we would be al-ways bless-ing, Serve Thee as Thy hosts a-bove,
Changed from glo-ry in-to glo-ry, Till in heaven we take our place,

Vis-it us with Thy sal-va-tion, En-ter ev-ery trem-bling heart.
End of faith, as its be-gin-ning, Set our hearts at lib-er-ty.
Pray, and praise Thee with-out ceas-ing, Glo-ry in Thy per-fect love.
Till we cast our crowns be-fore Thee, Lost in won-der, love, and praise. A-MEN.

112 Make Me a Captive, Lord

LEOMINSTER. S. M. D.

GEORGE MATHESON, 1842–1906

GEORGE W. MARTIN, 1828–1881
Arr. by ARTHUR S. SULLIVAN, 1842–1900

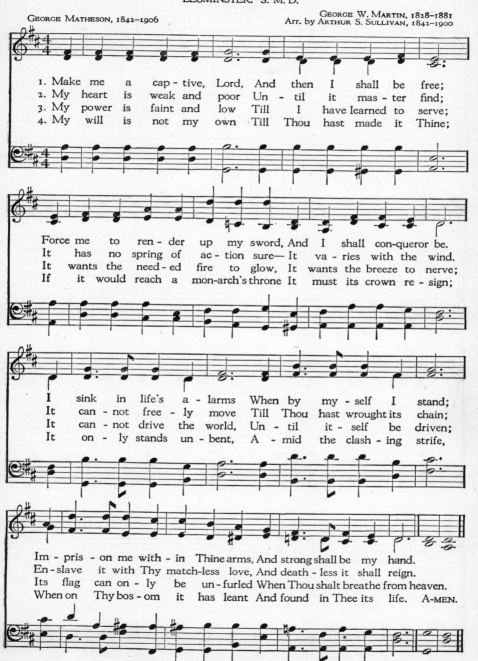

1. Make me a cap-tive, Lord, And then I shall be free;
   Force me to ren-der up my sword, And I shall con-queror be.
   I sink in life's a-larms When by my-self I stand;
   Im-pris-on me with-in Thine arms, And strong shall be my hand.

2. My heart is weak and poor Un-til it mas-ter find;
   It has no spring of ac-tion sure— It va-ries with the wind.
   It can-not free-ly move Till Thou hast wrought its chain;
   En-slave it with Thy match-less love, And death-less it shall reign.

3. My power is faint and low Till I have learned to serve;
   It wants the need-ed fire to glow, It wants the breeze to nerve;
   It can-not drive the world, Un-til it-self be driven;
   Its flag can on-ly be un-furled When Thou shalt breathe from heaven.

4. My will is not my own Till Thou hast made it Thine;
   If it would reach a mon-arch's throne It must its crown re-sign;
   It on-ly stands un-bent, A-mid the clash-ing strife,
   When on Thy bos-om it has leant And found in Thee its life. A-MEN.

113 We Would Be Building

FINLANDIA. 10. 10. 10. 10. 10. 10

PURD E. DEITZ

JEAN SIBELIUS, 1865–
Arr. for THE HYMNAL, 1933

May be sung in unison

1. We would be build-ing; tem-ples still un-done O'er crum-bling walls their cross-es scarce-ly lift; Wait-ing till love can raise the bro-ken stone, And hearts cre-a-tive bridge the hu-man rift; We would be build-ing, Mas-ter, let Thy plan

2. Teach us to build; up-on the sol-id rock We set the dream that hard-ens in-to deed, Ribbed with the steel that time and change doth mock, Th' un-fail-ing pur-pose of our no-blest creed; Teach us to build; O Mas-ter, lend us sight

3. O keep us build-ing, Mas-ter; may our hands Ne'er fal-ter when the dream is in our hearts, When to our ears there come di-vine com-mands And all the pride of sin-ful will de-parts; We build with Thee, O grant en-dur-ing worth

We Would Be Building

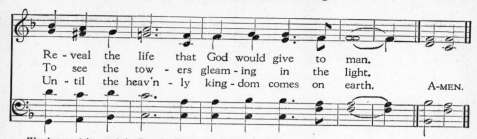

Re - veal the life that God would give to man.
To see the tow - ers gleam - ing in the light.
Un - til the heav'n - ly king - dom comes on earth. A-MEN.

114 Nearer, My God, to Thee

BETHANY. 6. 4. 6. 4. 6. 6. 4.

SARAH F. ADAMS, 1805-1848
Arr. by LOWELL MASON, 1792-1872

1. Near - er, my God, to Thee, Near - er to Thee! E'en though it
2. Though like the wan - der - er, The sun gone down, Dark - ness be
3. There let the way ap - pear, Steps un - to Heav'n: All that Thou
4. Then, with my wak - ing tho'ts Bright with Thy praise, Out of my
5. Or if on joy - ful wing, Cleav - ing the sky, Sun, moon, and

be a - cross That rais - eth me; Still all my song shall be,
o - ver me, My rest a stone; Yet in my dreams I'd be
send - est me, In mer - cy given: An - gels to beck - on me,
sto - ny griefs Beth - el I'll raise; So by my woes to be
stars for - got, Up - ward I'll fly, Still all my song shall be,

Near - er, my God, to Thee, Near - er, my God, to Thee, Near - er to Thee! A-MEN.

115 God of Grace and God of Glory

REGENT SQUARE. 8.7.8.7.8.7.

HARRY EMERSON FOSDICK, 1878–   HENRY SMART, 1813–1879

1. God of grace and God of glo-ry, On Thy peo-ple
2. Lo! the hosts of e-vil round us Scorn thy Christ, as-
3. Cure Thy chil-dren's war-ring mad-ness, Bend our pride to
4. Set our feet on loft-y plac-es; Gird our lives, that
5. Save us from weak res-ig-na-tion To the e-vils

pour Thy power; Crown Thine an-cient Church's sto-ry;
sail His ways! From the fears that long have bound us
Thy con-trol; Shame our wan-ton, self-ish glad-ness,
they may be Ar-mored with all Christ-like grac-es
we de-plore; Let the search for Thy sal-va-tion

Bring her bud to glo-rious flower. Grant us wis-dom,
Free our hearts to faith and praise: Grant us wis-dom,
Rich in things and poor in soul. Grant us wis-dom,
In the fight to set men free. Grant us wis-dom,
Be our glo-ry ev-er-more. Grant us wis-dom,

Grant us cour-age, For the fac-ing of this hour.
Grant us cour-age, For the liv-ing of these days.
Grant us cour-age, Lest we miss Thy king-dom's goal.
Grant us cour-age, That we fail not man nor Thee!
Grant us cour-age, Serv-ing Thee whom we a-dore. A-MEN.

Printed with permission of author and publisher.

116 O Master, Let Me Walk With Thee

SAXBY. L. M.

WASHINGTON GLADDEN, 1836–1918

TIMOTHY R. MATTHEWS, 1826–1910

1. O Mas-ter, let me walk with Thee In low-ly paths of ser-vice free;
2. Help me the slow of heart to move By some clear win-ning word of love;
3. Teach me Thy pa-tience; still with Thee In clos-er, dear-er com-pa-ny,
4. In hope that sends a shin-ing ray Far down the fu-ture's broadening way;

Tell me Thy se-cret; help me bear The strain of toil, the fret of care.
Teach me the way-ward feet to stay, And guide them in the home-ward way.
In work that keeps faith sweet and strong, In trust that triumphs o-ver wrong;
In peace that on-ly Thou canst give, With Thee, O Mas-ter, let me live. A-MEN.

117 O For a Heart of Calm Repose

SPOHR. C. M.

Anonymous

Adapted from LOUIS SPOHR, 1784–1859

1. O for a heart of calm re-pose A-mid the world's loud roar,
2. Come, Ho-ly Spir-it! still my heart With gen-tle-ness di-vine;
3. A-bove these scenes of storm and strife There spreads a re-gion fair;
4. Come, Ho-ly Spir-it! breathe that peace, That vic-tory make me win;

A life that like a riv-er flows A-long a peace-ful shore!
In-dwell-ing peace Thou canst im-part; O make that bless-ing mine!
Give me to live that high-er life, And breathe that heaven-ly air.
Then shall my soul her con-flict cease, And find a heaven with-in. A-MEN.

118 We Would See Jesus

CONSOLATION. 11. 10. 11. 10.

ANNA B. WARNER

Arr. from FELIX MENDELSSOHN-BARTHOLDY, 1809-1847

1. We would see Je - sus— for the shad - ows length - en
2. We would see Je - sus— the great Rock Foun - da - tion,
3. We would see Je - sus— oth - er lights are pal - ing,
4. We would see Je - sus— this is all we're need - ing,

A - cross this lit - tle land - scape of our life;
Where - on our feet were set with sov - ereign grace;
Which for long years we have re - joiced to see:
Strength, joy, and will - ing - ness come with the sight;

We would see Je - sus, our weak faith to strength - en
Not life, nor death, with all their ag - i - ta - tion,
The bless - ings of our pil - grim - age are fail - ing,
We would see Je - sus, dy - ing, ris - en, plead - ing,

For the last wea - ri - ness—the fi - nal strife.
Can thence re - move us, if we see His face.
We should not mourn them, for we go to Thee.
Then wel - come day, and fare - well mor - tal night! A - MEN.

119 I Would Be True

PEEK. 11. 10. 11. 10.

Howard Arnold Walter, 1883-1918

Joseph Yates Peek

1. I would be true, for there are those who trust me;
2. I would be friend of all— the foe, the friend-less;

I would be pure, for there are those who care;
I would be giv - ing, and for - get the gift,

I would be strong, for there is much to suf - fer;
I would be hum - ble, for I know my weak - ness;

I would be brave, for there is much to dare,
I would look up, and laugh, and love, and lift,

I would be brave, for there is much to dare.
I would look up, and laugh, and love, and lift. A - MEN.

120 Blessed Assurance, Jesus Is Mine!

ASSURANCE. 9. 10. 9. 9. with Refrain

FANNY J. CROSBY, 1820-1915

Mrs. JOSEPH F. KNAPP, 1839-1908

1. Bless-ed as-sur-ance, Je-sus is mine! O what a fore-taste of glo-ry di-
2. Per-fect sub-mis-sion, per-fect de-light, Vi-sions of rap-ture now burst on my
3. Per-fect sub-mis-sion, all is at rest, I in my Sav-iour am hap-py and

vine! Heir of sal-va-tion, pur-chase of God, Born of His
sight; An-gels de-scend-ing, bring from a-bove, Ech-oes of
blest, Watch-ing and wait-ing, look-ing a-bove, Filled with His

REFRAIN

Spir-it, washed in His blood. This is my sto-ry, this is my
mer-cy, whis-pers of love.
good-ness, lost in His love.

song, Prais-ing my Sav-iour all the day long; This is my

sto-ry, this is my song, Praising my Sav-iour all the day long. A-MEN.

121 Be Still, My Soul

FINLANDIA. 10. 10. 10. 10. 10. 10.

KATHARINA VON SCHLEGEL, 1697–?
Tr. by JANE L. BORTHWICK, 1813–1897

JEAN SIBELIUS, 1865–
Arr. for THE HYMNAL, 1933

1. Be still, my soul: the Lord is on thy side; Bear pa-tient-ly the
2. Be still, my soul: thy God doth un-der-take To guide the fu-ture
3. Be still, my soul: the hour is has-tening on When we shall be for

cross of grief or pain; Leave to thy God to or-der and pro-vide;
as He has the past. Thy hope, thy con-fi-dence let noth-ing shake;
ev-er with the Lord, When dis-ap-point-ment, grief, and fear are gone,

In ev-ery change He faith-ful will re-main. Be still, my soul: thy
All now mys-te-rious shall be bright at last. Be still, my soul: the
Sor-row for-got, love's pur-est joys re-stored. Be still, my soul: when

best, thy heavenly Friend Thro' thorn-y ways leads to a joy-ful end.
waves and winds still know His voice who ruled them while He dwelt be-low.
change and tears are past, All safe and bless-ed we shall meet at last. A-MEN.

122 How Firm a Foundation

ADESTE FIDELES (PORTUGUESE HYMN). 11. 11. 11. 11.

"K" in Rippon's Selection, 1787   From John F. Wade's Cantus Diversi, 1751

1. How firm a foun-da-tion, ye saints of the Lord, Is laid for your
2. "Fear not, I am with thee; O be not dis-mayed, For I am thy
3. "When thro' the deep wa-ters I call thee to go, The riv-ers of

faith in His ex-cel-lent Word! What more can He say than to
God, and will still give thee aid; I'll strength-en thee, help thee, and
woe shall not thee o-ver-flow; For I will be with thee thy

you He hath said, To you who for ref-uge to Je-sus have fled?
cause thee to stand, Up-held by my right-eous, om-nip-o-tent hand,
trou-bles to bless, And sanc-ti-fy to thee thy deep-est dis-tress,

To you who for ref-uge to Je-sus have fled?
Up-held by my right-eous, om-nip-o-tent hand.
And sanc-ti-fy to thee thy deep-est dis-tress. A-MEN.

4 "When through fiery trials thy pathway shall lie,
  My grace, all-sufficient, shall be thy supply,
  The flame shall not hurt thee; I only design
  Thy dross to consume, and thy gold to refine.

5 "The soul that on Jesus still leans for repose,
  I will not, I will not desert to his foes;
  That soul, though all hell should endeavor to shake,
  I'll never, no, never, no, never forsake!"

The Lord's My Shepherd

123

C. M.

Robt. H. Wilson

1. The Lord's my Shep-herd, I'll not want, He makes me down to lie
2. My soul He doth re-store a-gain, And me to walk doth make
3. Yea, tho' I walk thro' death's dark vale, Yet will I fear no ill,
4. A ta-ble Thou hast fur-nished me In pres-ence of my foes;
5. Good-ness and mer-cy all my life Shall sure-ly fol-low me,

In pas-tures green; He lead-eth me The qui-et wa-ters by.
With-in the paths of right-eous-ness, Even for His own name's sake.
For Thou art with me, and Thy rod And staff me com-fort still.
My head Thou dost with oil a-noint, And my cup o-ver-flows.
And in God's house for ev-er-more My dwell-ing place shall be.

Chorus

He lead-eth me, He lead-eth me,

rit. *a tempo*

In the green pas-tures and by the still wa-ters He lead-eth me. A-men.

124 All the Way My Saviour Leads Me

8.7.8.7.D.

Fanny J. Crosby, 1820–1915

R. Lowry, 1826–1899

1. All the way my Sav-iour leads me; What have I to ask be-side?
2. All the way my Sav-iour leads me; Cheers each wind-ing path I tread;
3. All the way my Sav-iour leads me; Oh, the full-ness of His love!

Can I doubt His ten-der mer-cy, Who thro' life has been my Guide?
Gives me grace for ev-ery tri-al, Feeds me with the liv-ing bread;
Per-fect rest to me is prom-ised In my Fa-ther's house a-bove;

Heaven-ly peace, di-vin-est com-fort, Here by faith in Him to dwell!
Though my wea-ry steps may fal-ter, And my soul a-thirst may be,
When my spir-it, clothed im-mor-tal, Wings its flight to realms of day,

For I know what-e'er be-fall me, Je-sus do-eth all things
Gush-ing from the Rock be-fore me, Lo! a spring of joy I
This my song through end-less a-ges—"Je-sus led me all the

All the Way My Saviour Leads Me

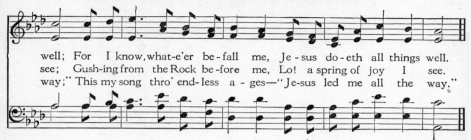

well; For I know, what-e'er be-fall me, Je-sus do-eth all things well.
see; Gush-ing from the Rock be-fore me, Lo! a spring of joy I see.
way;" This my song thro' end-less a-ges—"Je-sus led me all the way."

125 That Cause Can Neither Be Lost Nor Stayed

DANISH FOLK TUNE. 9. 9. 10. 10.

Tr. by J. A. Aaberg

Christian Ostergaard

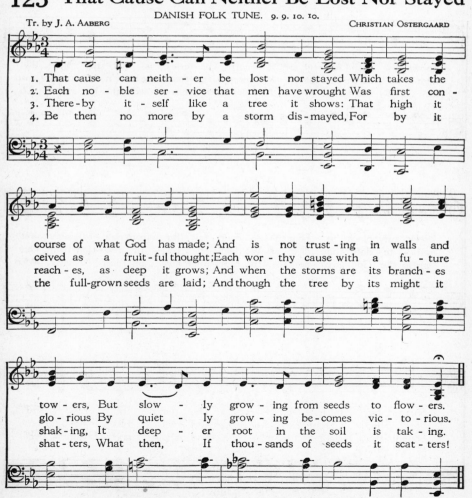

1. That cause can neith-er be lost nor stayed Which takes the
2. Each no-ble ser-vice that men have wrought Was first con-
3. There-by it-self like a tree it shows: That high it
4. Be then no more by a storm dis-mayed, For by it

course of what God has made; And is not trust-ing in walls and
ceived as a fruit-ful thought; Each wor-thy cause with a fu-ture
reach-es, as deep it grows; And when the storms are its branch-es
the full-grown seeds are laid; And though the tree by its might it

tow-ers, But slow-ly grow-ing from seeds to flow-ers.
glo-rious By quiet-ly grow-ing be-comes vic-to-rious.
shak-ing, It deep-er root in the soil is tak-ing.
shat-ters, What then, If thou-sands of seeds it scat-ters!

126 How Happy Every Child of Grace
C. M. D.

CHARLES WESLEY, 1707-1788

D. B. THOMPSON?

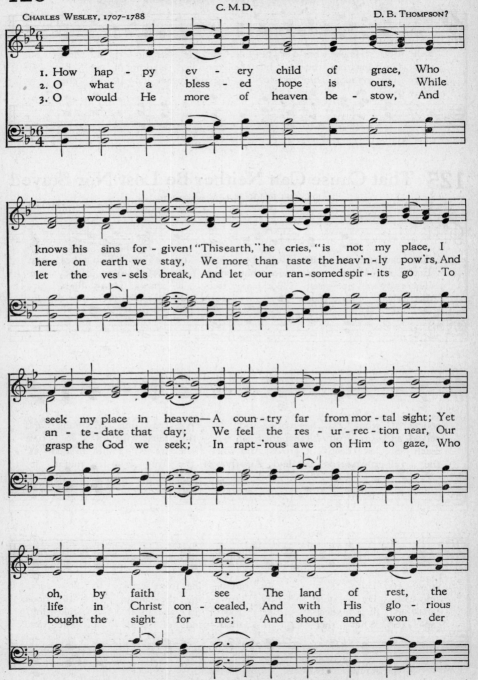

1. How hap - py ev - ery child of grace, Who knows his sins for - given! "This earth," he cries, "is not my place, I seek my place in heaven—A coun - try far from mor - tal sight; Yet oh, by faith I see The land of rest, the

2. O what a bless - ed hope is ours, While here on earth we stay, We more than taste the heav'n - ly pow'rs, And an - te - date that day; We feel the res - ur - rec - tion near, Our life in Christ con - cealed, And with His glo - rious

3. O would He more of heaven be - stow, And let the ves - sels break, And let our ran - somed spir - its go To grasp the God we seek; In rapt - 'rous awe on Him to gaze, Who bought the sight for me; And shout and won - der

How Happy Every Child of Grace

saints' de - light, The heaven pre-pared for me."
pres - ence here Our earth - en ves - sels filled.
at His grace Thro' all e - ter - ni - ty. A-MEN.

127   Guide of My Spirit

LANGRAN. 10. 10. 10. 10.

ALLEN EASTMAN CROSS, 1864-

JAMES LANGRAN, 1835-1909

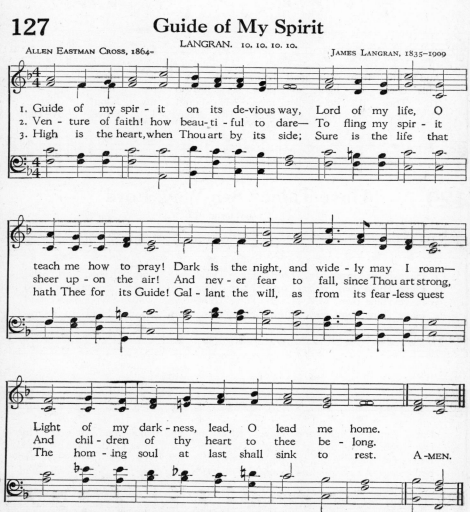

1. Guide of my spir - it on its de-vious way, Lord of my life, O
2. Ven - ture of faith! how beau-ti - ful to dare— To fling my spir - it
3. High is the heart, when Thou art by its side; Sure is the life that

teach me how to pray! Dark is the night, and wide - ly may I roam—
sheer up - on the air! And nev - er fear to fall, since Thou art strong,
hath Thee for its Guide! Gal - lant the will, as from its fear -less quest

Light of my dark - ness, lead, O lead me home.
And chil - dren of thy heart to thee be - long.
The hom - ing soul at last shall sink to rest. A -MEN.

128 I Am Thine Own, O Christ

6. 6. 6. 4.

H. Bradley

A. A. Wright

1. I am Thine own, O Christ; Hence-forth en-tire-ly Thine;
2. No earth-ly joy can lure My qui-et soul from Thee;
3. My joy-ful song of praise In sweet con-tent I sing:
4. O peace— O ho-ly rest, O balm-y breath of love;

And life from this glad hour, New life is mine.
This deep de-light, so pure, Is heaven to me.
To Thee the note I raise, My King! my King!
O heart, di-vin-est, best— Thy depth I prove. A-men.

129 Have Thine Own Way, Lord

5. 4. 5. 4. 5. 4.

Adelaide A. Pollard

George Stebbins, 1846-

1. Have Thine own way, Lord! Have Thine own way! Thou art the
2. Have Thine own way, Lord! Have Thine own way! Search me and
3. Have Thine own way, Lord! Have Thine own way! Wound-ed and
4. Have Thine own way, Lord! Have Thine own way! Hold o'er my

Pot-ter; I am the clay. Mold me and make me Aft-er Thy
try me, Mas-ter, to-day! Whit-er than snow, Lord, Wash me just
wea-ry, Help me, I pray! Pow-er— all pow-er— Sure-ly is
be-ing Ab-so-lute sway! Fill with Thy Spir-it Till all shall

Have Thine Own Way, Lord

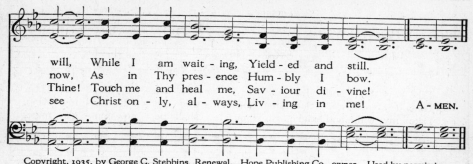

will, While I am wait-ing, Yield-ed and still.
now, As in Thy pres-ence Hum-bly I bow.
Thine! Touch me and heal me, Sav-iour di-vine!
see Christ on-ly, al-ways, Liv-ing in me! A-MEN.

130 O Love That Wilt Not Let Me Go

ST. MARGARET. 8. 8. 8. 8. 6.

GEORGE MATHESON, 1842–1906 ALBERT L. PEACE, 1844–1912

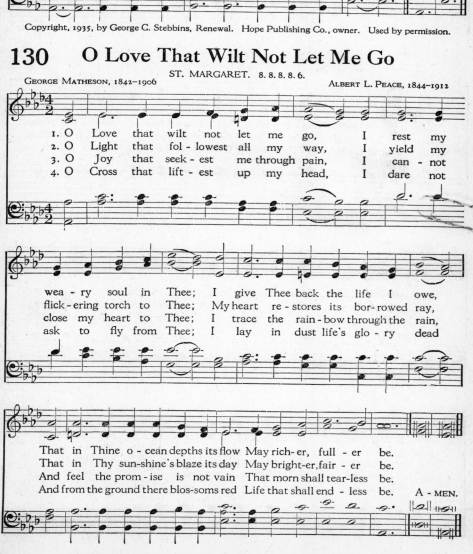

1. O Love that wilt not let me go, I rest my
2. O Light that fol-lowest all my way, I yield my
3. O Joy that seek-est me through pain, I can-not
4. O Cross that lift-est up my head, I dare not

wea-ry soul in Thee; I give Thee back the life I owe,
flick-ering torch to Thee; My heart re-stores its bor-rowed ray,
close my heart to Thee; I trace the rain-bow through the rain,
ask to fly from Thee; I lay in dust life's glo-ry dead

That in Thine o-cean depths its flow May rich-er, full-er be.
That in Thy sun-shine's blaze its day May bright-er, fair-er be.
And feel the prom-ise is not vain That morn shall tear-less be.
And from the ground there blos-soms red Life that shall end-less be. A-MEN.

131 Take My Life, and Let It Be

MESSIAH. 7. 7. 7. 7. D.

Frances R. Havergal, 1836–1879

Louis J. F. Herold, 1791–1833
Arr. by George Kingsley, 1811–1884

1. Take my life, and let it be Con - se - cra - ted, Lord, to Thee.
2. Take my voice, and let me sing, Al - ways, on - ly, for my King.
3. Take my will, and make it Thine; It shall be no lon - ger mine.

Take my mo - ments and my days; Let them flow in cease - less praise.
Take my lips, and let them be Filled with mes - sag - es from Thee.
Take my heart, it is Thine own; It shall be Thy roy - al throne.

Take my hands, and let them move At the im - pulse of Thy love.
Take my sil - ver and my gold; Not a mite would I with - hold.
Take my love; my Lord, I pour At Thy feet its treas - ure - store.

Take my feet, and let them be Swift and beau - ti - ful for Thee.
Take my in - tel - lect, and use Ev - ery pow'r as Thou shalt choose.
Take my - self, and I will be Ev - er, on - ly, all for Thee. A - men.

Lord Jesus, I Have Promised

ANGEL'S STORY. 7. 6. 7. 6. D.

John E. Bode, 1816–1874

Arthur H. Mann, 1850–1929

1. Lord Je - sus, I have prom - ised To serve Thee to the end;
2. O let me feel Thee near me! The world is ev - er near;
3. O let me hear Thee speak - ing, In ac - cents clear and still,
4. Lord Je - sus, Thou hast prom - ised To all who fol - low Thee

Be Thou for ev - er near me, My Mas - ter and my Friend:
I see the sights that daz - zle, The tempt - ing sounds I hear;
A - bove the storms of pas - sion, The mur - murs of self - will;
That where Thou art in glo - ry There shall Thy ser - vant be;

I shall not fear the bat - tle If Thou art by my side,
My foes are ev - er near me, A - round me and with - in;
O speak to re - as - sure me, To has - ten or con - trol;
And, Je - sus, I have prom - ised To serve Thee to the end;

Nor wan - der from the path - way If Thou wilt be my guide.
But, Je - sus, draw Thou near - er, And shield my soul from sin.
O speak, and make me lis - ten, Thou Guard - ian of my soul.
O give me grace to fol - low, My Mas - ter and my Friend. A - men.

133 Thy Will, Not Mine, O Lord

NYACK. 6. 6. 8. 6.

CHAS. C. WASHBURN

CHAS. C. WASHBURN

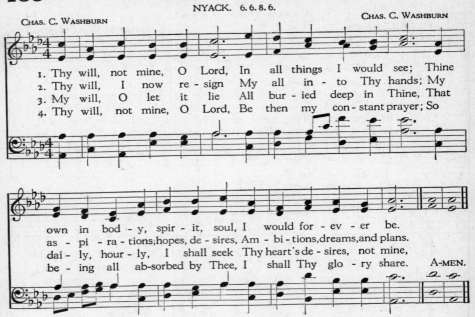

1. Thy will, not mine, O Lord, In all things I would see; Thine
2. Thy will, I now re-sign My all in-to Thy hands; My
3. My will, O let it lie All bur-ied deep in Thine, That
4. Thy will, not mine, O Lord, Be then my con-stant prayer; So

own in bod-y, spir-it, soul, I would for-ev-er be.
as-pi-ra-tions,hopes, de-sires, Am-bi-tions,dreams,and plans.
dai-ly, hour-ly, I shall seek Thy heart's de-sires, not mine,
be-ing all ab-sorbed by Thee, I shall Thy glo-ry share. A-MEN.

134 The Body, Lord, Is Ours to Keep

DOLUT. 8. 8. 8. 8. 8. 5.

ELEANOR B. STOCK

SEBASTIAN W. MEYER

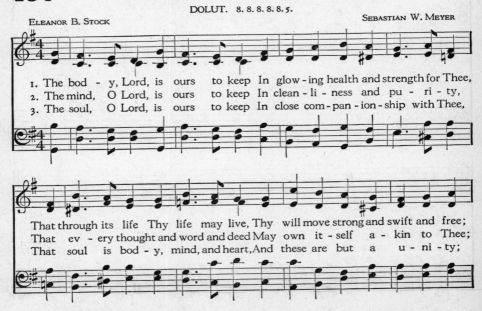

1. The bod-y, Lord, is ours to keep In glow-ing health and strength for Thee,
2. The mind, O Lord, is ours to keep In clean-li-ness and pu-ri-ty,
3. The soul, O Lord, is ours to keep In close com-pan-ion-ship with Thee,

That through its life Thy life may live, Thy will move strong and swift and free;
That ev-ery thought and word and deed May own it-self a-kin to Thee;
That soul is bod-y, mind, and heart, And these are but a u-ni-ty;

The Body, Lord, Is Ours to Keep

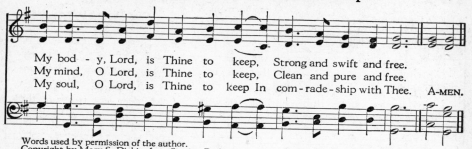

My bod - y, Lord, is Thine to keep, Strong and swift and free.
My mind, O Lord, is Thine to keep, Clean and pure and free.
My soul, O Lord, is Thine to keep In com - rade - ship with Thee. A-MEN.

135   Jesus, Master, Whose I Am

ST. PETERSBURG. 8. 8. 8. 8. 8. 8.

FRANCES R. HAVERGAL, 1836–1879   D. BORTNIANSKI, 1752–1825

1. Je - sus, Mas - ter, whose I am, Pur-chased, Thine a - lone to be,
2. Oth - er lords have long held sway; Now, Thy name a - lone to bear,
3. Je - sus, Mas - ter, Whom I serve, Though so fee - bly and so ill,
4. Je - sus, Mas - ter, wilt Thou use One who owes Thee more than all?

By Thy blood, O spot - less Lamb, Shed so will - ing - ly for me,
Thy dear voice a - lone o - bey, Is my dai - ly, hour - ly prayer:
Strength-en hand and heart and nerve All Thy bid - ding to ful - fill;
As Thou wilt! I would not choose: On - ly let me hear Thy call.

Let my heart be all Thine own, Let me live to Thee a - lone.
Whom have I in heaven but Thee? Noth-ing else my joy can be.
O - pen Thou mine eyes to see All the work Thou hast for me.
Je - sus, let me al - ways be, In Thy ser - vice, glad and free. A-MEN.

136 Living for Jesus

10. 10. 10. 10.

T. O. CHISHOLM
Not fast

CARL HAROLD LOWDEN, 1883–

1. Liv-ing for Je-sus a life that is true, Striv-ing to please Him in
2. Liv-ing for Je-sus who died in my place, Bear-ing on Cal-v'ry my
3. Liv-ing for Je-sus wher-ev-er I am, Do-ing each du-ty in
4. Liv-ing for Je-sus thro' earth's lit-tle while, My dear-est treas-ure the

all that I do, Yield-ing al-le-giance, glad-heart-ed and free,
sin and dis-grace, Such love con-strains me to an-swer His call,
His ho-ly Name, Will-ing to suf-fer af-flic-tion and loss,
light of His smile, Seek-ing the lost ones He died to re-deem,

*CHORUS. Unison. Slower

This is the path-way of bless-ing for me. O Je-sus, Lord and
Fol-low His lead-ing and give Him my all.
Deem-ing each tri-al a part of my cross.
Bring-ing the wea-ry to find rest in Him.

Sav-iour, I give my-self to Thee, For Thou, in Thine a-tone-ment, Didst

give Thy-self for me; I own no oth-er Mas-ter, My heart shall be Thy

*Melody in lower notes. A two-part effect may be had by having the men sing the melody, the women tak-ing the middle notes.

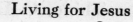

Living for Jesus

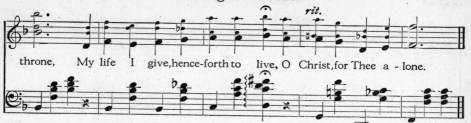

throne, My life I give, hence-forth to live, O Christ, for Thee a-lone.

137 Dear Lord and Father of Mankind

REST (ELTON). 8. 6. 8. 8. 6.

JOHN G. WHITTIER, 1807–1892

FREDERICK C. MAKER, 1844–1927

1. Dear Lord and Fa-ther of man-kind, For-give our fev-'rish ways!
2. In sim-ple trust like theirs who heard, Be-side the Syr-ian sea
3. O Sab-bath rest by Gal-i-lee! O calm of hills a-bove,
4. Drop Thy still dews of qui-et-ness, Till all our striv-ings cease;
5. Breathe thro' the heats of our de-sire Thy cool-ness and Thy balm;

Re-clothe us in our right-ful mind; In pur-er lives Thy
The gra-cious call-ing of the Lord, Let us, like them, with-
Where Je-sus knelt to share with thee The si-lence of e-
Take from our souls the strain and stress, And let our or-dered
Let sense be dumb, let flesh re-tire; Speak thro' the earth-quake,

ser-vice find, In deep-er rev-'rence, praise.
out a word, Rise up and fol-low Thee.
ter-ni-ty, In-ter-pret-ed by love!
lives con-fess The beau-ty of Thy peace.
wind, and fire, O still small voice of calm! A-MEN.

138   I Am Thine, O Lord

I AM THINE. 10. 7. 10. 7. with Refrain

FANNY J. CROSBY, 1820–1915   WILLIAM H. DOANE, 1832–1915

1. I am Thine, O Lord, I have heard Thy voice, And it told Thy love to
2. Con - se - crate me now to Thy serv - ice, Lord, By the pow'r of grace di -
3. O the pure de - light of a sin - gle hour That be - fore Thy throne I
4. There are depths of love that I can - not know Till I cross the nar - row

me; But I long to rise in the arms of faith, And be
vine; Let my soul look up with a stead - fast hope, And my
spend, When I kneel in prayer, and with Thee, my God, I com -
sea; There are heights of joy that I may not reach Till I

REFRAIN

clos - er drawn to Thee. Draw me near - er, near - er, bless - ed Lord,
will be lost in Thine.
mune as friend with friend!
rest in peace with Thee.   near - er, near - er,

To the cross where Thou hast died; Draw me near - er, near - er,

near - er, bless - ed Lord, To Thy pre - cious, bleed - ing side.   A-MEN.

139 · Live Out Thy Life Within Me

ST. HILDA. 7.6.7.6.D.

FRANCES R. HAVERGAL, 1836–1879

H. HUSBAND

1. Live out Thy life with-in me, O Je - sus, King of kings!
2. The tem - ple has been yield-ed, And pu - ri - fied of sin;
3. Its mem - bers ev - ery mo-ment Held sub - ject to Thy call;
4. But rest-ful, calm, and pli - ant, From bend and bi - as free,

Be Thou Thy-self the an - swer To all my ques - tion - ings.
Let Thy She - ki - nah glo - ry Now flash forth from with - in.
Rea - dy to have Thee use them, Or not be used at all.
Per - mit - ting Thee to set - tle When Thou hast need of me.

Live out Thy life with-in me, In all things have Thy way!
And all the earth keep si - lence, The bod - y hence-forth be
Held with - out rest - less long - ing, Or strain or stress or fret,
Live out Thy life with-in me, O Je - sus, King of kings!

I, the trans-par-ent me - dium Thy glo - ry to dis - play.
Thy si - lent, do - cile serv - ant, Moved on - ly as by Thee.
Or chaf - ings at Thy deal-ings, Or tho'ts of vain re - gret.
Be Thou the glo - rious an - swer To all my ques - tion - ings. A-MEN.

5

140 Lord, in the Strength of Grace

GREENWOOD. S. M.

CHARLES WESLEY, 1707–1788

JOSEPH E. SWEETSER, 1825–1873

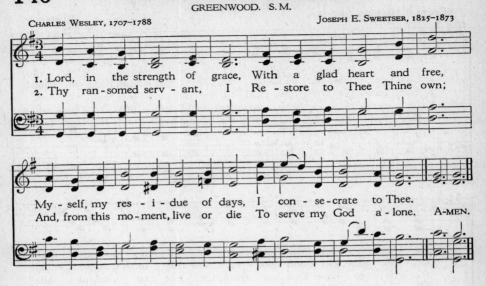

1. Lord, in the strength of grace, With a glad heart and free,
2. Thy ran-somed serv-ant, I Re-store to Thee Thine own;

My-self, my res-i-due of days, I con-se-crate to Thee.
And, from this mo-ment, live or die To serve my God a-lone. A-MEN.

141 Dear God, Our Father

DEEPER LIFE. 11. 10. 11. 10.

KATHARINE LEE BATES, 1859–1929

LINDSAY B. LONGACRE, 1870–

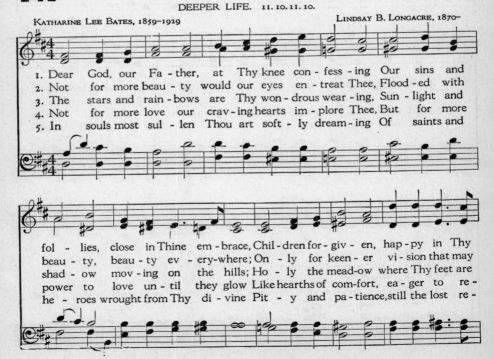

1. Dear God, our Fa-ther, at Thy knee con-fess-ing Our sins and
2. Not for more beau-ty would our eyes en-treat Thee, Flood-ed with
3. The stars and rain-bows are Thy won-drous wear-ing, Sun-light and
4. Not for more love our crav-ing hearts im-plore Thee, But for more
5. In souls most sul-len Thou art soft-ly dream-ing Of saints and

fol-lies, close in Thine em-brace, Chil-dren for-giv-en, hap-py in Thy
beau-ty, beau-ty ev-ery-where; On-ly for keen-er vi-sion that may
shad-ow mov-ing on the hills; Ho-ly the mead-ow where Thy feet are
power to love un-til they glow Like hearths of com-fort, ea-ger to re-
he-roes wrought from Thy di-vine Pit-y and pa-tience, still the lost re-

Dear God, Our Father

bless - ing, Deep-en our spir - its to re - ceive Thy grace.
greet Thee, In all Thy ves - tures of the earth and air.
far - ing, Ho - ly the brook - let that Thy laugh - ter fills.
store Thee, Hid - den in hu - man wretch - ed - ness and woe.
deem - ing, Deep-en our spir - its for a love like Thine. A - MEN.

Words used by permission of Mrs. George S. Burgess.
Music used by permission of Earl E. Harper.

142 Master, Speak! Thy Servant Heareth

AMEN, JESUS HAN SKAL RAADE. 8. 7. 8. 7. 7. 7.

FRANCES R. HAVERGAL, 1836-1879   ANTON P. BERGGREEN, 1801-1880

1. Mas - ter, speak! Thy serv - ant hear - eth, Wait - ing for Thy gra - cious word,
2. Speak to me by name, O Mas - ter, Let me know it is to me;
3. Mas - ter, speak! Tho' least and low - est, Let me not un-heard de - part;
4. Mas - ter, speak! and make me read - y, When Thy voice is tru - ly heard,

Long - ing for Thy voice that cheer - eth; Mas - ter! let it now be heard.
Speak, that I may fol - low fast - er, With a step more firm and free,
Mas - ter, speak! For oh, Thou know - est All the yearn - ing of my heart,
With o - be - dience glad and stead - y Still to fol - low ev - ery word.

I am lis - t'ning, Lord, for Thee: What hast Thou to say to me?
Where the Shep-herd leads the flock, In the shad - ow of the rock.
Know - est all its tru - er need: Speak! and make me blest in - deed.
I am lis - t'ning, Lord, for Thee: Mas - ter, speak! O speak to me! A-MEN.

143 Just As I Am, Thine Own to Be

8. 8. 8. 6.

MARIANNE HEARN, 1834–1909

JOSEPH BARNBY, 1838–1896

1. Just as I am, Thine own to be, Friend of the young, who lov-est me,
2. In the glad morn-ing of my day, My life to give, my vows to pay,
3. I would live ev - er in the light, I would work ev - er for the right,
4. Just as I am, young, strong, and free, To be the best that I can be

Unison

To con - se - crate my-self to Thee, O Je - sus Christ, I come.
With no re - serve and no de - lay, With all my heart I come.
I would serve Thee with all my might; There-fore, to Thee I come.
For truth, and right-eous-ness, and Thee, Lord of my life, I come. A-MEN.

144 Just As I Am

WOODWORTH. L. M.

CHARLOTTE ELLIOTT, 1789–1871

WILLIAM B. BRADBURY, 1816–1868

1. Just as I am, with-out one plea, But that Thy blood was shed for me,
2. Just as I am, and wait - ing not To rid my soul of one dark blot,
3. Just as I am, tho' tossed a-bout With many a con-flict, many a doubt,
4. Just as I am, poor, wretch-ed, blind; Sight, rich-es, heal - ing of the mind,
5. Just as I am—Thou wilt re-ceive, Wilt wel-come, par-don, cleanse, re-lieve;

And that Thou bidd'st me come to Thee, O Lamb of God, I come! I come!
To Thee whose blood can cleanse each spot, O Lamb of God, I come! I come!
Fight-ings and fears with-in, with-out, O Lamb of God, I come! I come!
Yea, all I need in Thee to find, O Lamb of God, I come! I come!
Be-cause Thy prom-ise I be-lieve, O Lamb of God, I come! I come! A-MEN.

145 O God, Our Help in Ages Past

ST. ANNE. C. M.

Isaac Watts, 1674-1748

Probably by William Croft, 1678-1727

1. O God, our help in a-ges past, Our hope for years to come,
2. Un-der the shad-ow of Thy throne Still may we dwell se-cure;
3. Be-fore the hills in or-der stood, Or earth re-ceived her frame,
4. A thou-sand a-ges, in Thy sight, Are like an eve-ning gone;
5. O God, our help in a-ges past, Our hope for years to come;

Our shel-ter from the storm-y blast, And our e-ter-nal home!
Suf-fi-cient is Thine arm a-lone, And our de-fense is sure.
From ev-er-last-ing Thou art God, To end-less years the same.
Short as the watch that ends the night, Be-fore the ris-ing sun.
Be Thou our guide while life shall last, And our e-ter-nal home! A-men.

146 Jesus, Kneel Beside Me

EUDOXIA. 6. 5. 6. 5.

Allen Eastman Cross, 1864-

S. Baring-Gould, 1834-1924

1. Je-sus, kneel be-side me In the dawn of day;
2. Mas-ter, work be-side me In the shin-ing sun;
3. Sav-iour, watch be-side me In the clos-ing light;
4. Birds are wing-ing home-ward, Sun and shad-ow cease;

Thine is prayer e-ter-nal—Teach me how to pray!
Gen-tly guide Thy serv-ant Till the work be done.
Lo, the eve-ning com-eth—Watch with me this night!
Sav-iour, take my spir-it To Thy per-fect peace. A-men.

Words used by permission of Allen Eastman Cross.
Music used by permission of A. W. Ridley & Co.

147 Prayer Is the Soul's Sincere Desire

CAMPMEETING. C. M.

James Montgomery, 1771–1854

Early American melody

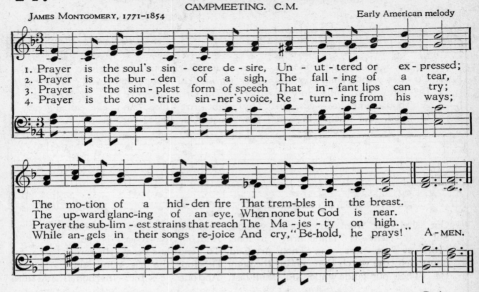

1. Prayer is the soul's sin - cere de - sire, Un - ut - tered or ex - pressed;
2. Prayer is the bur - den of a sigh, The fall - ing of a tear,
3. Prayer is the sim - plest form of speech That in - fant lips can try;
4. Prayer is the con - trite sin - ner's voice, Re - turn - ing from his ways;

The mo-tion of a hid-den fire That trem-bles in the breast.
The up-ward glanc-ing of an eye, When none but God is near.
Prayer the sub-lim - est strains that reach The Ma - jes - ty on high.
While an-gels in their songs re-joice And cry, "Be-hold, he prays!" A - men.

5 Prayer is the Christian's vital breath,
  The Christian's native air,
His watchword at the gates of death;
  He enters heaven with prayer.

6 O Thou, by whom we come to God,
  The Life, the Truth, the Way;
The path of prayer Thyself hast trod:
  Lord, teach us how to pray!

148 Father in Heaven, Hear Us Today

SOUTHAMPTON. Irregular

Charles G. Ames, 1828–1912

Anonymous

1. Fa - ther in heav - en, Hear us to - day; Hal-lowed Thy name be;
2. Fa - ther in heav - en, Hear us to - day; Hal-lowed Thy name be;
3. Fa - ther in heav - en, Hear us to - day; Hal-lowed Thy name be;

Hear us, we pray! O let Thy king-dom come, O let Thy
Hear us, we pray! Giv - er of dai - ly food, Foun - tain of
Hear us, we pray! Lead us in paths of right, Save us from

Father in Heaven, Hear Us Today

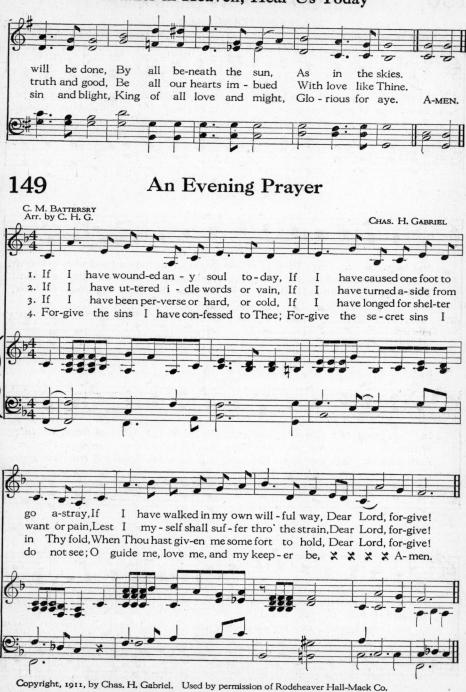

will be done, By all be-neath the sun, As in the skies.
truth and good, Be all our hearts im - bued With love like Thine.
sin and blight, King of all love and might, Glo - rious for aye. A-MEN.

149   An Evening Prayer

C. M. BATTERSRY
Arr. by C. H. G.

CHAS. H. GABRIEL

1. If I have wound-ed an - y soul to-day, If I have caused one foot to
2. If I have ut-tered i - dle words or vain, If I have turned a- side from
3. If I have been per-verse or hard, or cold, If I have longed for shel-ter
4. For-give the sins I have con-fessed to Thee; For-give the se - cret sins I

go a-stray, If I have walked in my own will - ful way, Dear Lord, for-give!
want or pain, Lest I my - self shall suf- fer thro' the strain, Dear Lord, for-give!
in Thy fold, When Thou hast giv-en me some fort to hold, Dear Lord, for-give!
do not see; O guide me, love me, and my keep- er be, ✗ ✗ ✗ ✗ A-men.

150 Sweet Hour of Prayer

SWEET HOUR. L. M. D.

William W. Walford, ?

William B. Bradbury, 1816–1868

1. Sweet hour of prayer! sweet hour of prayer! That calls me from a world of care,
2. Sweet hour of prayer! sweet hour of prayer! The joys I feel, the bliss I share,
3. Sweet hour of prayer! sweet hour of prayer! Thy wings shall my pe-ti-tion bear

And bids me at my Fa-ther's throne Make all my wants and wish-es known;
Of those whose anx-ious spir-its burn With strong de-sires for thy re-turn!
To Him whose truth and faith-ful-ness En-gage the wait-ing soul to bless;

In sea-sons of dis-tress and grief, My soul has oft-en found re-lief;
With such I has-ten to the place Where God my Sav-iour shows His face,
And since He bids me seek His face, Be-lieve His Word and trust His grace,

And oft es-caped the tempt-er's snare, By thy re-turn, sweet hour of prayer!
And glad-ly take my sta-tion there, And wait for thee, sweet hour of prayer!
I'll cast on Him my ev-ery care, And wait for thee, sweet hour of prayer! A-men.

151 Draw Thou My Soul

ST. EDMUND. 6. 4. 6. 4. 6. 6. 6. 4.

LUCY LARCOM, 1826–1893

ARTHUR S. SULLIVAN, 1842–1900

1. Draw Thou my soul, O Christ, Clos - er to Thine;
2. Lead forth my soul, O Christ, One with Thine own,
3. Not for my - self a - lone May my prayer be;

Breathe in - to ev - ery wish Thy will di - vine!
Joy - ful to fol - low Thee Through paths un - known!
Lift Thou Thy world, O Christ, Clos - er to Thee!

Raise my low self a - bove, Won by Thy death-less love;
In Thee my strength re - new; Give me my work to do!
Cleanse it from guilt and wrong; Teach it sal - va - tion's song,

Ev - er, O Christ, through mine Let Thy life shine.
Through me Thy truth be shown, Thy love made known.
Till earth, as heaven, ful - fill God's ho - ly will. A - MEN.

152 God, Who Touchest Earth With Beauty

GENEVA. 8. 5. 8. 5.

Mary S. Edgar

Carl Harold Lowden, 1883–

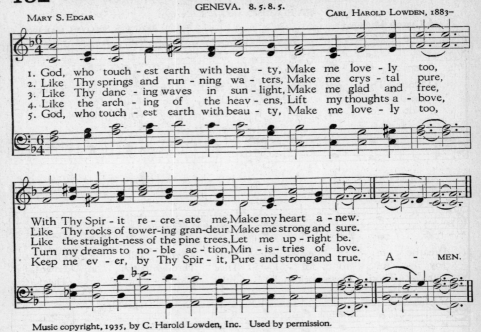

1. God, who touch-est earth with beau-ty, Make me love-ly too,
2. Like Thy springs and run-ning wa-ters, Make me crys-tal pure,
3. Like Thy danc-ing waves in sun-light, Make me glad and free,
4. Like the arch-ing of the heav-ens, Lift my thoughts a-bove,
5. God, who touch-est earth with beau-ty, Make me love-ly too,

With Thy Spir-it re-cre-ate me, Make my heart a-new.
Like Thy rocks of tow-ing gran-deur Make me strong and sure.
Like the straight-ness of the pine trees, Let me up-right be.
Turn my dreams to no-ble ac-tion, Min-is-tries of love.
Keep me ev-er, by Thy Spir-it, Pure and strong and true. A - MEN.

Music copyright, 1935, by C. Harold Lowden, Inc. Used by permission.

153 There Is an Eye That Never Sleeps

WINCHESTER, OLD. C. M.

J. C. Wallace

T. Este

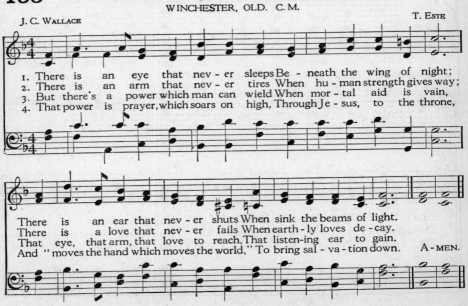

1. There is an eye that nev-er sleeps Be-neath the wing of night;
2. There is an arm that nev-er tires When hu-man strength gives way;
3. But there's a power which man can wield When mor-tal aid is vain,
4. That power is prayer, which soars on high, Through Je-sus, to the throne,

There is an ear that nev-er shuts When sink the beams of light.
There is a love that nev-er fails When earth-ly loves de-cay.
That eye, that arm, that love to reach, That listen-ing ear to gain.
And "moves the hand which moves the world," To bring sal-va-tion down. A-MEN.

154 Moment By Moment

10. 10. 10. 10.

D. W. WHITTLE

MAY WHITTLE MOODY

1. Dy-ing with Je-sus, by death reck-oned mine: Liv-ing with Je-sus, a
2. Nev-er a tri-al that He is not there, Nev-er a bur-den that
3. Nev-er a heart-ache, and nev-er a groan, Nev-er a tear-drop and
4. Nev-er a weak-ness that He doth not feel, Nev-er a sick-ness that

new life di-vine; Look-ing to Je-sus till glo-ry doth shine, Mo-ment by
He doth not bear. Nev-er a sor-row that He doth not share, Mo-ment by
nev-er a moan, Nev-er a dan-ger but there on the throne, Mo-ment by
He can-not heal; Mo-ment by mo-ment, in woe or in weal, Je-sus, my

CHORUS

mo-ment, O Lord, I am Thine. Mo-ment by mo-ment I'm kept in His love;
mo-ment, I'm un-der His care.
mo-ment He thinks of His own.
Sav-iour, a-bides with me still.

Mo-ment by mo-ment, I've life from a-bove; Look-ing to Je-sus till

glo-ry doth shine; Mo-ment by mo-ment, O Lord, I am Thine.

155 When in Twilight

CHESTERVILLE. M. 8. 5. 8. 3.

FRANK W. GUNSAULUS

DANIEL PROTHEROE

1. When in twi-light, foot-sore, bleed-ing, And un-known my way,
2. If my wea-ry heart is fail-ing, Chilled and weak my hand,
3. If I sin in thought or liv-ing, Thro' the day or night,
4. Mov-ing midst time's gloom and splen-dor, Slow-ly wes-tering down,

Lord of light, I ask Thy lead-ing Un - til day.
Let me hear with faith un-quail-ing Love's com - mand.
Grasp me with Thy love for-giv-ing,—Love is light.
Let me find Thee strong and ten - der, And the crown. A-MEN.

156 Lord, For Tomorrow and Its Needs

8. 4. 8. 4. D.

SYBIL F. PARTRIDGE
(SISTER MARY XAVIER)

HORATIO R. PALMER, 1834-1904

1. Lord, for to-mor-row and its needs I do not pray; Keep me, my God, from
2. Let me no wrong or i - dle word Un-think-ing say; Set Thou a seal up-

stain of sin Just for to-day. Help me to la - bor ear-nest-ly,
on my lips Through all to-day. Let me in sea-son, Lord, be grave,

Lord, for Tomorrow and Its Needs

And du-ly pray; Let me be kind in word and deed, Fa - ther, to-day.
In sea-son gay; Let me be faith-ful to Thy grace, Dear Lord, to-day.

157   # In the Hour of Trial

PENITENCE. 6. 5. 6. 5. D.

James Montgomery, 1771–1844
Alt. by Frances A. Hutton, 1811–1877

Spencer Lane, 1843–1903

1. In the hour of tri - al, Je - sus, plead for me; Lest by base de - ni - al,
2. With for-bid-den pleas-ures Would this vain world charm, Or its sor-did treas-ures
3. Should Thy mer-cy send me Sor - row, toil, and woe, Or should pain at-tend me
4. When my last hour com - eth, Fraught with strife and pain, When my dust re-turn-eth

I de-part from Thee. When Thou see'st me wa -ver, With a look re - call,
Spread to work me harm; Bring to my re-mem-brance Sad Geth-sem-a - ne,
On my path be - low, Grant that I may nev - er Fail Thy hand to see;
To the dust a - gain; On Thy truth re - ly - ing, Thro' that mor-tal strife:

Nor for fear or fa - vor Suf - fer me to fall.
Or, in dark - er sem - blance, Cross-crowned Cal-va - ry.
Grant that I may ev - er Cast my care on Thee.
Je - sus, take me, dy - ing, To e - ter - nal life. A - MEN.

158 Thou Didst Leave Thy Throne

MARGARET. (ELLIOTT). Irregular

EMILY E. S. ELLIOTT, 1836–1897

TIMOTHY R. MATTHEWS, 1826–1910

1. Thou didst leave Thy throne and Thy king - ly crown, When Thou
2. Heav - en's arch - es rang when the an - gels sang, Pro -
3. The fox - es found rest, and the birds their nest In the
4. Thou cam'st, O Lord, with the liv - ing word That should
5. When heaven's arch - es shall ring and her choir shall sing At Thy

cam - est to earth for me; But in Beth - le - hem's home there was
claim - ing Thy roy - al de - gree; But in low - ly birth didst Thou
shade of the for - est tree; But Thy couch was the sod, O Thou
set Thy peo - ple free; But with mock - ing scorn, and with
com - ing to vic - to - ry, Let Thy voice call me home, say - ing,

found no room For Thy ho - ly Na - tiv - i - ty. O
come to earth, And in great hu - mil - i - ty. O
Son of God, In the des - erts of Gal - i - lee. O
crown of thorn, They bore Thee to Cal - va - ry. O
"Yet there is room, There is room at my side for thee!" And my

come to my heart, Lord Je - sus, There is room in my heart for Thee.
come to my heart, Lord Je - sus, There is room in my heart for Thee.
come to my heart, Lord Je - sus, There is room in my heart for Thee.
come to my heart, Lord Je - sus, There is room in my heart for Thee.
heart shall re-joice, Lord Je - sus, When Thou com-est and callest for me. A-MEN.

159 O Saviour, Precious Saviour

GREENLAND. 7. 6. 7. 6. D.

FRANCES R. HAVERGAL, 1836–1879

LAUSANNE PSALTER

1. O Sav - iour, pre - cious Sav - iour, Whom yet un - seen we love,
2. O Bring - er of sal - va - tion, Who won - drous - ly hath wrought,
3. In Thee all full - ness dwell - eth, All grace and power di - vine;
4. O grant the con - sum - ma - tion Of this our song a - bove,

O Name of might and fa - vor, All oth - er names a - bove!
Thy - self the rev - e - la - tion Of love be - yond our thought,
The glo - ry that ex - cell - eth, O Son of God, is Thine;
In end - less ad - o - ra - tion, And ev - er - last - ing love;

We wor - ship Thee, we bless Thee, To Thee, O Christ, we sing;
We wor - ship Thee, we bless Thee, To Thee, O Christ, we sing;
We wor - ship Thee, we bless Thee, To Thee, O Christ, we sing;
Then shall we praise and bless Thee Where per - fect prais - es ring,

We praise Thee, and con - fess Thee Our ho - ly Lord and King.
We praise Thee, and con - fess Thee Our gra - cious Lord and King.
We praise Thee, and con - fess Thee Our glo - rious Lord and King.
And ev - er - more con - fess Thee Our Sav - iour and our King. A - MEN.

160 I to the Hills Will Lift Mine Eyes

DUNDEE (FRENCH). C.M.

SCOTTISH PSALTER, 1750   From the SCOTTISH PSALTER, 1615

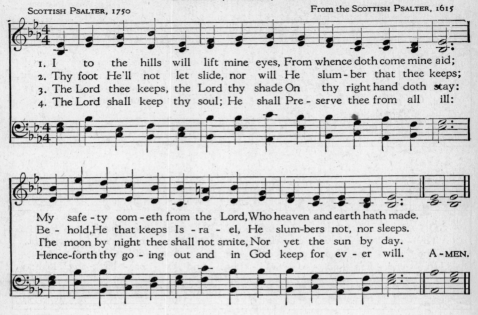

1. I to the hills will lift mine eyes, From whence doth come mine aid;
2. Thy foot He'll not let slide, nor will He slum-ber that thee keeps;
3. The Lord thee keeps, the Lord thy shade On thy right hand doth stay:
4. The Lord shall keep thy soul; He shall Pre-serve thee from all ill:

My safe-ty com-eth from the Lord, Who heaven and earth hath made.
Be-hold, He that keeps Is-ra-el, He slum-bers not, nor sleeps.
The moon by night thee shall not smite, Nor yet the sun by day.
Hence-forth thy go-ing out and in God keep for ev-er will.   A-MEN.

161 Nothing Between, Lord

9. 6. 6. 6. 4.

E.H.H.   J. MOUNTAIN
Plaintively

1. Noth-ing be-tween, Lord, noth-ing be-tween; Let me Thy
2. Noth-ing be-tween, Lord, noth-ing be-tween; Let not earth's
3. Noth-ing be-tween, Lord, noth-ing be-tween; Un-be-lief
4. Noth-ing be-tween, Lord, noth-ing be-tween; Thus may I

glo-ry see, Draw my soul close to Thee, Then speak in
din and noise Sti-fle Thy still small voice; In it let
dis-ap-pear, Van-ish each doubt and fear, Fad-ing when
walk with Thee, Thee on-ly may I see, Thine on-ly

Nothing Between, Lord

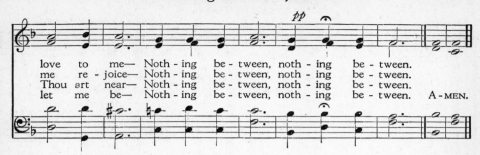

love to me— Noth-ing be-tween, noth-ing be-tween.
me re-joice— Noth-ing be-tween, noth-ing be-tween.
Thou art near— Noth-ing be-tween, noth-ing be-tween.
let me be— Noth-ing be-tween, noth-ing be-tween. A-MEN.

162 No, Not Despairingly Come I to Thee

KEDRON. 6. 4. 6. 4. 6. 6. 4.

HORATIUS BONAR, 1808–1889

ANN B. SPRATT, 1829–?

1. No, not de-spair-ing-ly Come I to Thee; No, not dis-
2. Ah! mine in-i-qui-ty Crim-son hath been, In-fi-nite,
3. Lord, I con-fess to Thee Sad-ly my sin; All I am

trust-ing-ly Bend I the knee: Sin hath gone o-ver me,
in-fi-nite— Sin up-on sin: Sin of not lov-ing Thee,
tell I Thee, All I have been: Purge Thou my sin a-way,

Yet is this still my plea: Je-sus hath died.
Sin of not trust-ing Thee— In-fi-nite sin.
Wash Thou my soul this day: Lord, make me clean. A-MEN.

4 Faithful and just art Thou,
  Forgiving all;
Loving and kind art Thou
  When poor ones call:
Lord, let the cleansing blood
Blood of the Lamb of God,
  Pass o'er my soul.

5 Then all is peace and light
  This soul within;
Thus shall I walk with Thee,
  The loved Unseen;
Leaning on Thee, my God,
Guided along the road,
  Nothing between.

163 O Gracious Father of Mankind

ST. LEONARD. C. M. D.

HENRY HALLAM TWEEDY, 1868–   HENRY HILES, 1826–1904

1. O gra-cious Fa-ther of man-kind, Our spir-its' un-seen Friend,
2. Thou hear-est these, the good and ill, Deep bur-ied in each breast;
3. Our best is but Thy-self in us, Our high-est thought Thy will;
4. Thou seek-est us in love and truth More than our minds seek Thee;

High heav-en's Lord our hearts' dear Guest, To Thee our prayers as-cend.
The se-cret thought, the hid-den plan, Wrought out or un-ex-pressed
To hear Thy voice we need but love, And lis-ten, and be still.
Thro' o-pen gates Thy power flows in Like flood tides from the sea.

Thou dost not wait till hu-man speech Thy gifts di-vine im-plore;
O cleanse our prayers from hu-man dross, At-tune our lives to Thee,
We would not bend Thy will to ours, But blend our wills with Thine;
No more we seek Thee from a-far, Nor ask Thee for a sign,

Our dreams, our aims, our work, our lives Are prayers Thou lov-est more.
Un-til we la-bor for those gifts We ask on bend-ed knee.
Not beat with cries on heav-en's doors, But live Thy life di-vine.
Con-tent to pray in life and love And toil, till all are Thine. A-MEN.

164 Speak, Lord, in the Stillness

6. 5. 6. 5.

E. MAY GRIMES

Slow

H. GREEN

1. Speak, Lord, in the still - ness, While I wait on Thee;
2. Speak, O bless - ed Mas - ter, In this qui - et hour,
3. All to Thee is yield - ed, I am not my own;
4. Fill me with the knowl - edge Of Thy glo - rious will;

Hushed my heart to lis - ten In ex - pec - tan - cy.
Let me see Thy face, Lord, Feel Thy touch of power.
Bliss - ful, glad sur - ren - der— I am Thine a - lone!
All Thine own good pleas - ure In Thy child ful - fill. A - MEN.

165 'Mid All the Traffic of the Ways

ST. AGNES. C. M.

JOHN OXENHAM

JOHN B. DYKES, 1823–1876

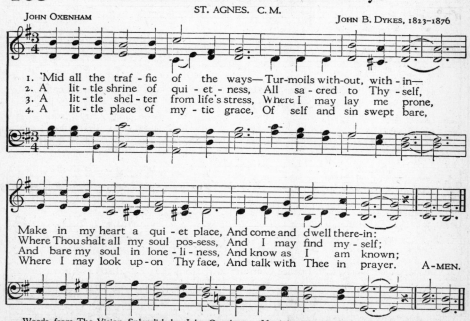

1. 'Mid all the traf - fic of the ways— Tur-moils with-out, with - in—
2. A lit - tle shrine of qui - et - ness, All sa - cred to Thy - self,
3. A lit - tle shel - ter from life's stress, Where I may lay me prone,
4. A lit - tle place of my - tic grace, Of self and sin swept bare,

Make in my heart a qui - et place, And come and dwell there-in:
Where Thou shalt all my soul pos-sess, And I may find my - self;
And bare my soul in lone - li - ness, And know as I am known;
Where I may look up - on Thy face, And talk with Thee in prayer. A - MEN.

Words from The Vision Splendid, by John Oxenham. Used by permission of the author and Messrs. Pinker and Morrison.

166 Wonderful Peace

12. 9. 12. 9. with Chorus

W. D. CORNELL. Alt.

W. G. COOPER

1. Far a-way in the depths of my spir-it to-night Rolls a mel-o-dy sweet-er than psalm; In ce-les-tial-like strains it un-ceas-ing-ly falls O'er my soul like an in-fi-nite calm.

2. What a treas-ure I have in this won-der-ful peace, Bur-ied deep in the heart of my soul! So se-cure that no pow-er can mine it a-way, While the years of e-ter-ni-ty roll.

3. I am rest-ing to-night in this won-der-ful peace, Rest-ing sweet-ly in Je-sus con-trol; For I'm kept from all dan-ger by night and by day, And His glo-ry is flood-ing my soul.

4. And me-thinks when I rise to that Cit-y of peace, Where the Au-thor of peace I shall see, That one strain of the song which the ran-somed will sing, In that heav-en-ly king-dom shall be:

5. Ah! soul, are you here with-out com-fort or rest, March-ing down the rough path-way of time? Make Je-sus your Friend ere the shad-ows grow dark; Oh, ac-cept this sweet peace so sub-lime.

CHORUS

Peace! peace! won-der-ful peace, Com-ing down from the Fa-ther a-bove; Sweep

Wonderful Peace

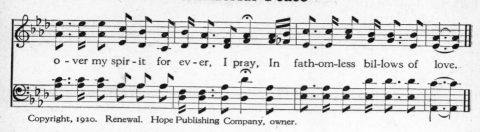

o - ver my spir - it for ev - er, I pray, In fath-om-less bil-lows of love.

167 In Heavenly Love Abiding

AURELIA. 7. 6. 7. 6. D.

Anna L. Waring, 1820–1910

Samuel Wesley, 1810–1876

1. In heav'n - ly love a - bid - ing, No change my heart shall fear,
2. Wher - ev - er He may guide me, No want shall turn me back:
3. Green pas - tures are be - fore me, Which yet I have not seen;

And safe is such con - fid - ing, For noth - ing chang - es here:
My Shep - herd is be - side me, And noth - ing can I lack;
Bright skies will soon be o'er me, Where dark - est clouds have been:

The storm may roar with - out me, My heart may low be laid;
His wis - dom ev - er wak - eth, His sight is nev - er dim;
My hope I can - not meas - ure; My path to life is free;

But God is round a - bout me, And can I be dis-mayed?
He knows the way He tak - eth, And I will walk with Him.
My Sav - iour has my treas - ure, And He will walk with me. A-MEN.

168 Joys Are Flowing Like a River

8. 7. 8. 7.   with Refrain

Anonymous

W. S. MARSHALL
Adapted by JAMES M. KIRK

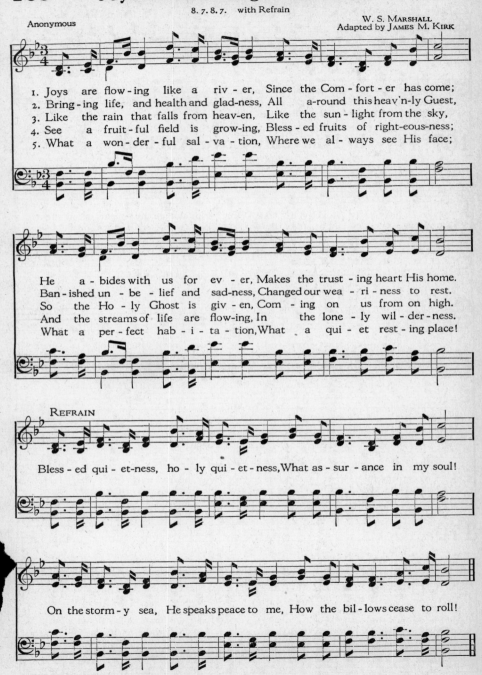

1. Joys are flow-ing like a riv - er, Since the Com - fort - er has come;
2. Bring-ing life, and health and glad-ness, All a-round this heav'n-ly Guest,
3. Like the rain that falls from heav-en, Like the sun - light from the sky,
4. See a fruit-ful field is grow-ing, Bless - ed fruits of right-eous-ness;
5. What a won - der - ful sal - va - tion, Where we al - ways see His face;

He a - bides with us for ev - er, Makes the trust - ing heart His home.
Ban - ished un - be - lief and sad-ness, Changed our wea - ri - ness to rest.
So the Ho - ly Ghost is giv - en, Com - ing on us from on high.
And the streams of life are flow-ing, In the lone - ly wil - der - ness.
What a per - fect hab - i - ta - tion, What a qui - et rest - ing place!

REFRAIN

Bless - ed qui - et-ness, ho - ly qui - et-ness, What as - sur - ance in my soul!

On the storm - y sea, He speaks peace to me, How the bil - lows cease to roll!

169 Jesus, the Calm That Fills My Breast

HESPERUS (QUEBEC). L.M.

FRANK MASON NORTH, 1850–1935

HENRY BAKER, 1835–1910

1. Je - sus, the calm that fills my breast, No oth - er
2. My wea - ry soul has found a charm That turns to
3. In des - ert wastes I feel no dread, Fear - less I
4. O Christ, through change - ful years my Guide, My Com - fort -
5. My time, my powers, I give to Thee; My in - most

heart than Thine can give; This peace un - stirred, this
bless - ed - ness my woe; With - in the shel - ter
walk the track - less sea; I care not where my
er in sor - row's night, My Friend, when friend - less—
soul 'tis Thine to move; I wait for Thy e -

joy of rest, None but Thy loved ones can re - ceive.
of Thine arm, I rest se - cure from storm and foe.
way is led, Since all my life is life with Thee.
still a - bide, My Lord, my Coun - sel - or, my Light.
ter - ni - ty, I wait in peace, in praise, in love. A - MEN.

170 O Love Divine

TO HESPERUS (QUEBEC)

1 O Love divine, that stooped to share
Our sharpest pang, our bitterest tear!
On Thee we cast each earth-born care;
We smile at pain while Thou art near.

2 Though long the weary way we tread,
And sorrow crown each lingering year,
No path we shun, no darkness dread,
Our hearts still whispering, "Thou art near!"

3 When drooping pleasure turns to grief,
And trembling faith is turned to fear,
The murmuring wind, the quivering leaf,
Shall softly tell us Thou art near!

4 On Thee we fling our burdening woe,
O Love divine, for ever dear!
Content to suffer while we know,
Living and dying, Thou art near!

OLIVER W. HOLMES, 1809–1894

171 Not So in Haste, My Heart!

DOLOMITE CHANT. 6. 6. 6. 6.

BRADFORD TORREY, 1843–1912

Austrian melody
Harmonized by JOSEPH T. COOPER, 1819–1870

May be sung in unison

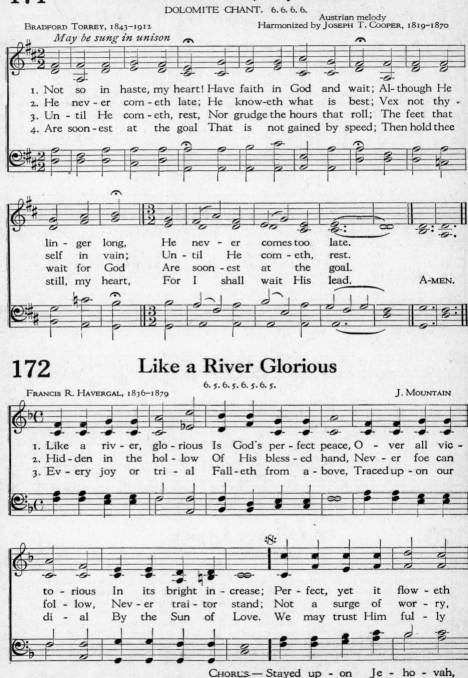

1. Not so in haste, my heart! Have faith in God and wait; Al-though He
2. He nev-er com-eth late; He know-eth what is best; Vex not thy -
3. Un - til He com - eth, rest, Nor grudge the hours that roll; The feet that
4. Are soon-est at the goal That is not gained by speed; Then hold thee

lin - ger long, He nev - er comes too late.
self in vain; Un - til He com - eth, rest.
wait for God Are soon - est at the goal.
still, my heart, For I shall wait His lead.   A-MEN.

172 Like a River Glorious

6. 5. 6. 5. 6. 5. 6. 5.

FRANCIS R. HAVERGAL, 1836–1879

J. MOUNTAIN

1. Like a riv - er, glo - rious Is God's per - fect peace, O - ver all vic -
2. Hid - den in the hol - low Of His bless - ed hand, Nev - er foe can
3. Ev - ery joy or tri - al Fall-eth from a - bove, Traced up - on our

to - rious In its bright in - crease; Per - fect, yet it flow - eth
fol - low, Nev - er trai - tor stand; Not a surge of wor - ry,
di - al By the Sun of Love. We may trust Him ful - ly

CHORUS — Stayed up - on Je - ho - vah,

Like a River, Glorious

Chorus, D.S.

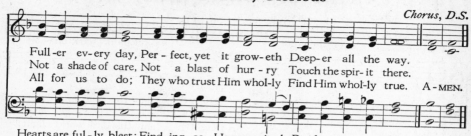

Full-er ev-ery day, Per-fect, yet it grow-eth Deep-er all the way.
Not a shade of care, Not a blast of hur-ry Touch the spir-it there.
All for us to do; They who trust Him whol-ly Find Him whol-ly true. A-MEN.

Hearts are ful-ly blest; Find-ing, as He prom-ised, Per-fect peace and rest.

173 O Thou, in Whose Presence

BELOVED. 11. 8. 11. 8.

JOSEPH SWAIN, 1761–1796

FREEMAN LEWIS, 1780–1859
Arr. by HUBERT P. MAIN, 1839–1926

1. O Thou, in whose pres-ence my soul takes de-light,
2. Where dost Thou, dear Shep-herd, re-sort with Thy sheep,
3. O why should I wan-der, an a-lien from Thee,
4. Ye daugh-ters of Zi-on, de-clare, have you seen
5. He looks! and ten thou-sands of an-gels re-joice,
6. Dear Shep-herd! I hear, and will fol-low Thy call;

On whom in af-flic-tion I call; My com-fort by day and my
To feed them in pas-tures of love; Say, why in the val-ley of
Or cry in the des-ert for bread? Thy foes will re-joice when my
The Star that on Is-ra-el shone? Say, if in your tents my Be-
And myr-i-ads wait for His word; He speaks! and e-ter-ni-ty,
I know the sweet sound of Thy voice; Re-store and de-fend me, for

song in the night, My hope, my sal-va-tion, my all!
death should I weep, Or a-lone in this wil-der-ness rove?
sor-rows they see, And smile at the tears I have shed.
lov-ed has been, And where with His flocks He is gone?
filled with His voice, Re-ech-oes the praise of the Lord.
Thou art my all, And in Thee I will ev-er re-joice. A-MEN.

174 I Heard the Voice of Jesus Say

VOX DILECTI. C. M. D.

HORATIUS BONAR, 1808–1889

JOHN B. DYKES, 1823–1876

1. I heard the voice of Je-sus say, "Come un-to me and rest;
2. I heard the voice of Je-sus say, "Be-hold, I free-ly give
3. I heard the voice of Je-sus say, "I am this dark world's light;

Lay down, thou wea-ry one, lay down Thy head up-on my breast."
The liv-ing wa-ter; thirst-y one, Stoop down, and drink, and live."
Look un-to me, thy morn shall rise, And all thy day be bright."

I came to Je-sus as I was, Wea-ry and worn and sad;
I came to Je-sus, and I drank Of that life-giv-ing stream;
I looked to Je-sus, and I found In Him my star, my sun;

I found in Him a rest-ing place, And He has made me glad.
My thirst was quenched, my soul re-vived, And now I live in Him.
And in that light of life I'll walk, Till trav-el-ing days are done. A-MEN.

175 Lord, Speak to Me, That I May Speak

FRANCES R. HAVERGAL

HOLLEY. L.M.

GEORGE HEWS, 1806–1873

1. Lord, speak to me, that I may speak, In liv - ing
2. O lead me, Lord, that I may lead The wan-dering
3. O strength-en me, that while I stand Firm on the
4. O teach me, Lord, that I may teach The pre - cious

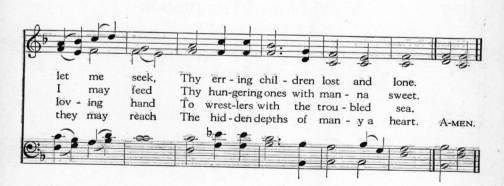

ech - oes of Thy tone; As Thou hast sought, so
and the wav - ering feet; O feed me, Lord, that
Rock, and strong in Thee, I may stretch out a
things Thou dost im - part; And wing my words, that

let me seek, Thy err - ing chil - dren lost and lone.
I may feed Thy hun-gering ones with man - na sweet.
lov - ing hand To wrest-lers with the trou - bled sea.
they may reach The hid-den depths of man - y a heart. A-MEN.

5 O give Thine own sweet rest to me,
  That I may speak with soothing power
A word in season, as from Thee,
  To weary ones in needful hour.

6 O fill me with Thy fullness, Lord,
  Until my very heart o'erflow
In kindling thought and glowing word
  Thy love to tell, Thy praise to show.

7 O use me, Lord, use even me,
  Just as Thou wilt, and when, and where;
Until Thy blessèd face I see,
  Thy rest, Thy joy, Thy glory share.

176 O For a Heart to Praise My God

BELMONT. C.M.

CHARLES WESLEY, 1707-1788

From WILLIAM GARDINER'S SACRED MELODIES, 1812

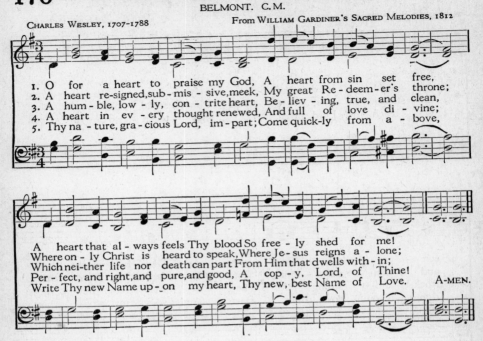

1. O for a heart to praise my God, A heart from sin set free,
2. A heart re-signed, sub-mis-sive, meek, My great Re-deem-er's throne;
3. A hum-ble, low-ly, con-trite heart, Be-liev-ing, true, and clean,
4. A heart in ev-ery thought renewed, And full of love di-vine;
5. Thy na-ture, gra-cious Lord, im-part; Come quick-ly from a-bove,

A heart that al-ways feels Thy blood So free-ly shed for me!
Where on-ly Christ is heard to speak, Where Je-sus reigns a-lone;
Which nei-ther life nor death can part From Him that dwells with-in;
Per-fect, and right, and pure, and good, A cop-y, Lord, of Thine!
Write Thy new Name up-on my heart, Thy new, best Name of Love.

A-MEN.

177 Yield Not to Temptation

FREDERICK. 11. 11. 11. 11.

HORATIO R. PALMER, 1834-1907

GEORGE KINGSLEY, 1811-1884

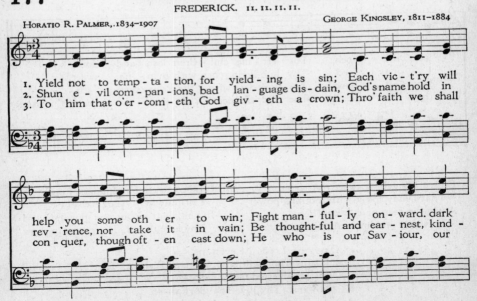

1. Yield not to temp-ta-tion, for yield-ing is sin; Each vic-t'ry will
2. Shun e-vil com-pan-ions, bad lan-guage dis-dain, God's name hold in
3. To him that o'er-com-eth God giv-eth a crown; Thro' faith we shall

help you some oth-er to win; Fight man-ful-ly on-ward, dark
rev-'rence, nor take it in vain; Be thought-ful and ear-nest, kind-
con-quer, though oft-en cast down; He who is our Sav-iour, our

Yield Not to Temptation

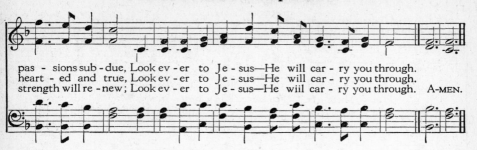

pas - sions sub - due, Look ev - er to Je - sus—He will car - ry you through.
heart - ed and true, Look ev - er to Je - sus—He will car - ry you through.
strength will re - new; Look ev - er to Je - sus—He will car - ry you through. A-MEN.

178 Keep Thyself Pure!

PENTECOST. L.M.

Adelaide M. Plumptre

William Boyd, 1847–1928

1. Keep thy - self pure! Christ's sol - dier, hear, Through life's loud
2. Keep thy - self pure! Thrice bless - ed he Whose heart from
3. Keep thy - self pure! For He who died, Him - self for
4. O Ho - ly Spir - it, keep us pure, Grant us Thy

strife the call rings clear. Thy Cap - tain speaks; His
taint of sin is free. His feet shall stand where
thy sake sanc - ti - fied. Then hear Him speak - ing
strength when sins al - lure; Our bod - ies are Thy

word o - bey; So shall thy strength be as thy day.
saints have trod, He with rapt eyes shall see his God.
from the skies; And vic - tor o'er temp - ta - tion rise.
tem - ple, Lord; Be Thou in thought and act a - dored A - MEN.

179 Lord Jesus, I Love Thee

GORDON. 11. 11. 11. 11.

William Ralf Featherstone, 1842–1878
From The London Hymn Book, 1864

Adoniram J. Gordon, 1836–1895

1. Lord Je - sus, I love Thee, I know Thou art mine,
2. I love Thee, be - cause Thou hast first lov - ed me,
3. In man - sions of glo - ry and end - less de - light,

For Thee all the fol - lies of sin I re - sign;
And pur - chased my par - don on Cal - va - ry's tree;
I'll ev - er a - dore Thee in heav - en so bright;

My gra - cious Re - deem - er, my Sav - iour art Thou;
I love Thee for wear - ing the thorns on Thy brow;
I'll sing with the glit - ter - ing crown on my brow

If ev - er I lov'd Thee, Lord Je - sus, 'tis now.
If ev - er I lov'd Thee, Lord Je - sus, 'tis now.
If ev - er I lov'd Thee, Lord Je - sus, 'tis now. A - men.

180 Lift Up Your Hearts!

BIRMINGHAM. 10. 10. 10. 10.

HENRY MONTAGUE BUTLER, 1833–1918

A Selection of Psalm Tunes, 1834

1. Lift up your hearts! We lift them, Lord, to Thee;
2. A - bove the lev - el of the form - er years,
3. A - bove the swamps of sub - ter - fuge and shame,
4. Then, as the trum - pet - call, in af - ter years:

Here at Thy feet none oth - er may we see;
The mire of sin, the slough of guilt - y fears,
The deeds, the thoughts that hon - or may not name,
Lift up your hearts, rings peal - ing in our ears,

Lift up your hearts! E'en so, with one ac - cord,
The mist of doubt, the blight of love's de - cay,
The halt - ing tongue that dares not tell the whole,
Still shall those hearts re - spond, with full ac - cord:

We lift them up, we lift them to the Lord.
O Lord of Light, lift all our hearts to - day!
O Lord of Truth, lift ev - - ery Chris - tian soul!
We lift them up, we lift them to the Lord! A-MEN.

Heralds of Christ, Who Bear

NATIONAL HYMN. 10. 10. 10. 10.

LAURA S. COPENHAVER, 1868–   GEORGE W. WARREN, 1828–1902

Trumpets, before each verse

1. Her - alds of Christ, who bear the King's com-mands,
2. Thro' des - ert ways, dark fen, and deep mo - rass,
3. Lord, give us faith and strength the road to build,

Im - mor - tal ti - dings in your mor - tal hands,
Through jun - gles, slug - gish seas, and moun - tain pass,
To see the prom - ise of the day ful - filled,

Pass on and car - ry swift the news ye bring:
Build ye the road, and fal - ter not, nor stay;
When war shall be no more and strife shall cease

Make straight, make straight the high - way of the King.
Pre - pare a - cross the earth the King's high - way.
Up - on the high - way of the Prince of Peace. A - MEN.

Words used by permission of Mrs. H. W. Parker

182 Be Strong! We Are Not Here to Play

FORTITUDE. 2. 10. 10. 10.

MALTBIE D. BABCOCK, 1858-1901

DAVID S. SMITH, 1877-

1. Be strong! We are not here to play, to dream, to drift: We have hard work to do and loads to lift; Shun not the strug - gle: face it— tis God's gift. Be strong, be strong!

2. Be strong! Say not the days are e - vil— who's to blame? And fold the hands and ac - qui - esce— O shame! Stand up, speak out, and brave - ly, in God's Name, Be strong, be strong!

3. Be strong! It mat - ters not how deep en - trenched the wrong, How hard the bat - tle goes, the day, how long; Faint not, fight on! To - mor - row comes the song. Be strong, be strong!

A - MEN.

Be strong, be

183 My Master Was a Worker

ELLACOMBE. 7.6.7.6.D.

WILLIAM G. TARRANT, 1853–1928

GESANGBUCH DER HERZOGL. WIRTEMBURGISCHEN KATHOLISCHEN HOFKAPELLE, 1784

1. My Mas-ter was a work-er, With dai-ly work to do,
2. My Mas-ter was a com-rade, A trust-y friend and true,
3. My Mas-ter was a help-er, The woes of life He knew,
4. Then, broth-ers brave and man-ly, To-geth-er let us be,

And he who would be like Him Must be a work-er too.
And he who would be like Him Must be a com-rade too;
And he who would be like Him Must be a help-er too;
And He, who is our Mas-ter, The Man of men was He;

Then wel-come hon-est la-bor And hon-est la-bor's fare,
In hap-py hours of sing-ing, In si-lent hours of care,
The bur-den will grow light-er, If each will take a share,
The men who would be like Him Are want-ed ev-ery-where,

For where there is a work-er The Mas-ter's man is there.
Where goes a loy-al com-rade, The Mas-ter's man is there.
And where there is a help-er The Mas-ter's man is there.
And where they love each oth-er The Mas-ter's men are there. A-MEN.

184   "Are Ye Able?" said the Master

BEACON HILL. Irregular

EARL MARLATT, 1892–

HARRY S. MASON, 1881–

1. "Are ye a - ble," said the Mas - ter, "To be cru - ci - fied with me?—"
2. "Are ye a - ble" to re - mem - ber, When a thief lifts up his eyes,
3. "Are ye a - ble" when the shad - ows Close a - round you with the sod,
4. "Are ye a - ble?" Still the Mas - ter Whis-pers down e - ter - ni - ty,

"Yea," the sturd - y dream-ers an-swered, "To the death we fol - low Thee."
That his par-doned soul is wor - thy Of a place in par - a - dise?
To be - lieve that spir - it tri-umphs, To com-mend your soul to God?
And he - ro - ic spir - its an - swer Now, as then, in Gal - i - lee.

REFRAIN

"Lord, we are a - ble." Our spir - its are Thine. Re - mold them,

make us, Like Thee, di - vine. Thy guid - ing ra - diance A - bove us shall

be A bea - con to God, To faith and loy - al - ty. A - MEN.

Words used by permission of Earl Marlatt
Music used by permission of Harry S. Mason

185 Hark, the Voice of Jesus Calling

LUX EOI. 8.7.8.7.D.

Daniel March, 1816–1909

Arthur Seymour Sullivan, 1842–1900

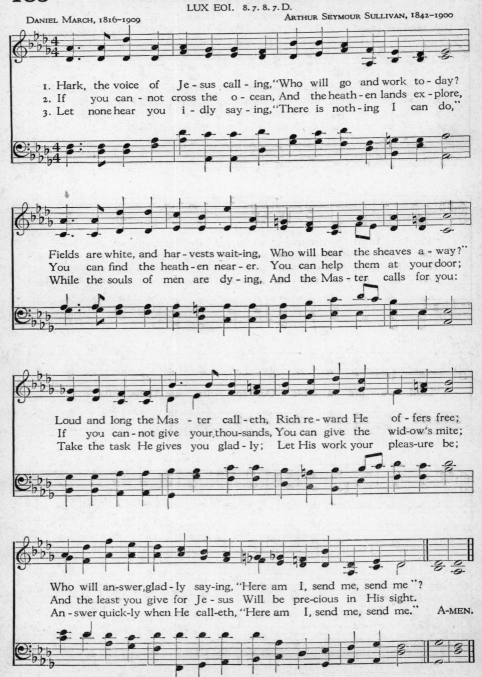

1. Hark, the voice of Je-sus call-ing, "Who will go and work to-day?
2. If you can-not cross the o-cean, And the heath-en lands ex-plore,
3. Let none hear you i-dly say-ing, "There is noth-ing I can do,"

Fields are white, and har-vests wait-ing, Who will bear the sheaves a-way?"
You can find the heath-en near-er. You can help them at your door;
While the souls of men are dy-ing, And the Mas-ter calls for you:

Loud and long the Mas-ter call-eth, Rich re-ward He of-fers free;
If you can-not give your thou-sands, You can give the wid-ow's mite;
Take the task He gives you glad-ly; Let His work your pleas-ure be;

Who will an-swer, glad-ly say-ing, "Here am I, send me, send me"?
And the least you give for Je-sus Will be pre-cious in His sight.
An-swer quick-ly when He call-eth, "Here am I, send me, send me." A-men.

186   A Charge to Keep I Have

BOYLSTON. S. M.

CHARLES WESLEY, 1707–1788

LOWELL MASON, 1792–1872

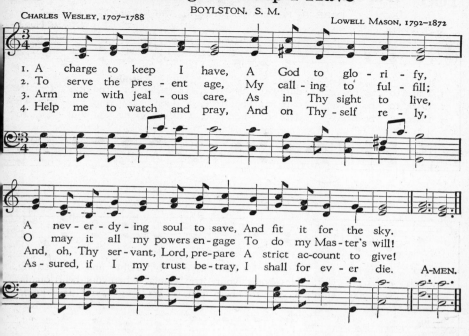

1. A charge to keep I have, A God to glo - ri - fy,
2. To serve the pres - ent age, My call - ing to ful - fill;
3. Arm me with jeal - ous care, As in Thy sight to live,
4. Help me to watch and pray, And on Thy - self re - ly,

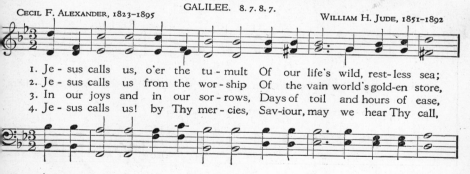

A nev - er - dy - ing soul to save, And fit it for the sky.
O may it all my powers en - gage To do my Mas - ter's will!
And, oh, Thy ser - vant, Lord, pre - pare A strict ac - count to give!
As - sured, if I my trust be - tray, I shall for ev - er die.   A-MEN.

187   Jesus Calls Us, O'er the Tumult

GALILEE. 8. 7. 8. 7.

CECIL F. ALEXANDER, 1823–1895

WILLIAM H. JUDE, 1851–1892

1. Je - sus calls us, o'er the tu - mult Of our life's wild, rest - less sea;
2. Je - sus calls us from the wor - ship Of the vain world's gold-en store,
3. In our joys and in our sor - rows, Days of toil and hours of ease,
4. Je - sus calls us! by Thy mer - cies, Sav-iour, may we hear Thy call,

Day by day His sweet voice sound-eth, Say-ing, "Chris-tian, fol-low me!"
From each i - dol that would keep us, Say-ing, "Chris-tian, love me more!"
Still He calls, in cares and pleas-ures, "Christian, love me more than these!"
Give our hearts to Thine o - be-dience, Serve and love Thee best of all!   A-MEN.

188 Dare to Be Brave, Dare to Be True

DARE TO BE BRAVE. 8. 10. 9. 10. With Refrain

W. J. ROOPER

DUNCAN HUME

1. Dare to be brave, dare to be true, Strive for the right, for the Lord is with you; Fight with sin brave - ly, fight and be strong, Christ is your Cap - tain, fear on - ly what's wrong. Fight then, good sol - diers, fight and be brave, Christ is your Cap - tain, might - y to save. A - MEN.

2. Dare to be brave, dare to be true, God is your Fa - ther, He watch - es o'er you; He knows your tri - als; when your heart quails, Call Him to res - cue, His grace nev - er fails.

3. Dare to be brave, dare to be true, God grant you cour - age to car - ry you thro'; Try to help oth - ers, ev - er be kind, Let the op - press'd a strong friend in you find.

REFRAIN

189 Give of Your Best to the Master

8. 7. 8. 7. D.

REV. HOWARD B. GROSE

MRS. CHARLES BARNARD

1. Give of your best to the Mas - ter; Give of the strength of your youth;
2. Give of your best to the Mas - ter; Give Him first place in your heart;
3. Give of your best to the Mas - ter; Naught else is wor - thy His love;

REF. Give of your best to the Mas - ter; Give of the strength of your youth;

Throw your soul's fresh, glow-ing ar - dor In - to the bat-tle for truth.
Give Him first place in your serv - ice, Con - se - crate, ev - ery part.
He gave Him - self for your ran - som, Gave up His glo - ry a - bove;

Clad in sal - va - tion's full ar - mor, Join in the bat-tle for truth.

Fine

Je - sus has set the ex - am - ple; Daunt-less was He, young and brave;
Give, and to you shall be giv - en; God His be - lov - ed Son gave;
Laid down His life with-out mur - mur, You from sin's ru - in to save;

Give Him your loy - al de - vo - tion, Give Him the best that you have.
Grate-ful - ly seek-ing to serve Him, Give Him the best that you have.
Give Him your heart's ad - o - ra - tion, Give Him the best that you have.

rall. D.C.

190 O Young Mariner

SUNDOWN. Irregular

ALFRED TENNYSON, 1809–1892

JOHN H. GOWER, 1855–1922

In unison

1. O young mar - in - er, you from the ha - ven Un - der the
2. Not of the sun - light, not of the moon - light, Not of the

Voices in Harmony

sea - cliff, you who are watch - ing Broad - er and bright - er the
star - light, O young mar - in - er, Down to the ha - ven

Gleam fly - ing on - ward, So to the land's last lim - it I came,
call your com - pan - ions, Launch your ves - sel, and crowd your can - vas,

Unison

There on the bor - der of bound - less o - cean, And
And, ere it van - ish - es o - ver the mar - gin,

Harmony

all but in heav - en, hov - ers the Gleam.
Af - ter it, fol - low it, fol - low the Gleam. A-MEN.

191 Forward! Be Our Watchword

WATCHWORD. 6. 5. 6. 5. 12 lines

HENRY ALFORD, 1810–1871

HENRY SMART, 1813–1879

1. For-ward! be our watch-word, Steps and voic-es joined; Seek the
2. Glo-ries up-on glo-ries Hath our God pre-pared, By the
3. Far o'er yon ho-ri-zon Rise the cit-y tow'rs, Where our

things be-fore us, Not a look be-hind. Burns the fi-ery pil-lar
souls that love Him One day to be shared; Eye hath not be-held them,
God a-bid-eth; That fair home is ours. Flash the streets with jas-per,

At our ar-mies' head, Who shall dream of shrink-ing, By our Cap-tain
Ear hath nev-er heard; Nor of these hath ut-tered Tho't or speech a
Shine the gates with gold! Flows the glad-'ning riv-er, Shed-ding joys un-

led? For-ward thro' the des-ert, Thro' the toil and fight!
word; For-ward, march-ing east-ward, Where the heav'n is bright,
told; Thith-er, on-ward thith-er, In the Spir-it's might,

Jor-dan flows be-fore us; Zi-on beams with light.
Till the veil be lift-ed, Till our faith be sight.
Pil-grims, to your coun-try, For-ward in-to light. A-MEN.

192 March On, O Soul, With Strength!

ARTHUR'S SEAT. 6. 6. 6. 6. 8. 8.

George T. Coster, 1835–1912

Arr. from John Goss, 1800–1880

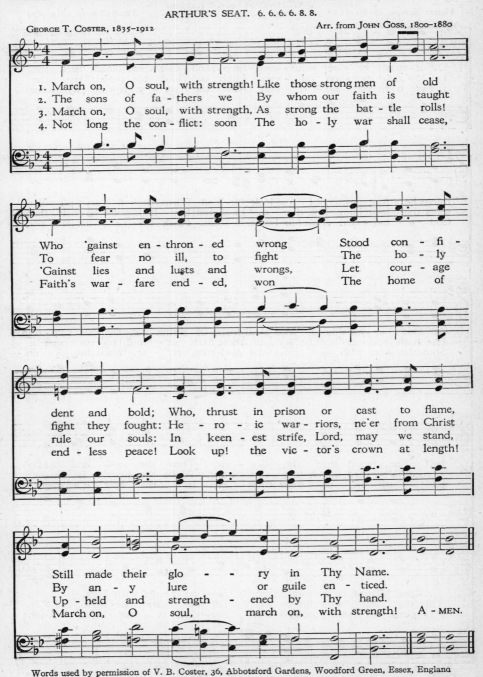

1. March on, O soul, with strength! Like those strong men of old
2. The sons of fa-thers we By whom our faith is taught
3. March on, O soul, with strength, As strong the bat-tle rolls!
4. Not long the con-flict: soon The ho-ly war shall cease,

Who 'gainst en-thron-ed wrong Stood con-fi-
To fear no ill, to fight The ho-ly
'Gainst lies and lusts and wrongs, Let cour-age
Faith's war-fare end-ed, won The home of

dent and bold; Who, thrust in prison or cast to flame,
fight they fought: He-ro-ic war-riors, ne'er from Christ
rule our souls: In keen-est strife, Lord, may we stand,
end-less peace! Look up! the vic-tor's crown at length!

Still made their glo-ry in Thy Name.
By an-y lure or guile en-ticed.
Up-held and strength-ened by Thy hand.
March on, O soul, march on, with strength! A-men.

Words used by permission of V. B. Coster, 36, Abbotsford Gardens, Woodford Green, Essex, England

193 Onward, Christian Soldiers!

ST. GERTRUDE. 6. 5. 6. 5. D. with Refrain

Sabine Baring-Gould, 1834-1924

Arthur S. Sullivan, 1842-1900

1. On - ward, Chris-tian sol - diers! March-ing as to war, With the cross of
2. Like a might - y arm - y Moves the Church of God; Broth-ers, we are
3. Crowns and thrones may per - ish, King-doms rise and wane, But the Church of
4. On - ward, then, ye peo - ple, Join our hap - py throng, Blend with ours your

Je - sus Go - ing on be - fore. Christ, the roy - al Mas - ter,
tread-ing Where the saints have trod; We are not di - vid - ed,
Je - sus Con - stant will re - main; Gates of hell can nev - er
voic - es In the tri - umph-song; Glo - ry, laud, and hon - or

Leads a - gainst the foe; For-ward in - to bat - tle, See His ban-ners go!
All one bod - y we, One in hope and doc - trine, One in char - i - ty.
'Gainst that Church pre-vail; We have Christ's own prom-ise, And that can - not fail.
Un - to Christ the King; This thro' count-less a - ges Men and an - gels sing.

REFRAIN

On - ward, Chris - tian sol - diers, March - ing as to war,

With the cross of Je - sus Go - ing on be - fore. A - MEN.

194 Stand Up, Stand Up for Jesus

GEIBEL. 7. 6. 7. 6. D. with Refrain

GEORGE DUFFIELD, JR., 1818–1888

ADAM GEIBEL, 1855–

In unison

1. Stand up, stand up for Je - sus, Ye sol - diers of the cross;
2. Stand up, stand up for Je - sus, The trum - pet call o - bey;
3. Stand up, stand up for Je - sus, Stand in His strength a - lone;
4. Stand up, stand up for Je - sus, The strife will not be long;

Lift high His roy - al ban - ner, It must not suf - fer loss:
Forth to the might - y con - flict, In this His glo - rious day;
The arm of flesh will fail you, Ye dare not trust your own;
This day the noise of bat - tle, The next, the vic - tor's song;

From vic - t'ry un - to vic - t'ry His ar - my shall He lead,
Ye that are men now serve Him A - gainst un - num-bered foes;
Put on the gos - pel ar - mor, Each piece put on with prayer;
To him that o - ver - com - eth, A crown of life shall be;

Till ev - ery foe is van - quished, And Christ is Lord in - deed.
Let cour - age rise with dan - ger, And strength to strength op - pose.
Where du - ty calls or dan - ger, Be nev - er want - ing there.
He with the King of Glo - ry Shall reign e - ter - nal - ly

Stand Up, Stand Up for Jesus

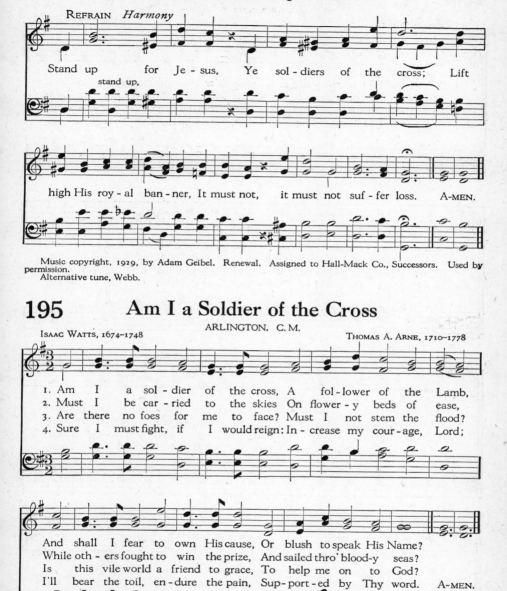

Stand up for Je-sus, Ye sol-diers of the cross; Lift
stand up,

high His roy-al ban-ner, It must not, it must not suf-fer loss. A-MEN.

Alternative tune, Webb.

195 Am I a Soldier of the Cross

ARLINGTON. C. M.

ISAAC WATTS, 1674-1748

THOMAS A. ARNE, 1710-1778

1. Am I a sol-dier of the cross, A fol-lower of the Lamb,
2. Must I be car-ried to the skies On flower-y beds of ease,
3. Are there no foes for me to face? Must I not stem the flood?
4. Sure I must fight, if I would reign: In-crease my cour-age, Lord;

And shall I fear to own His cause, Or blush to speak His Name?
While oth-ers fought to win the prize, And sailed thro' blood-y seas?
Is this vile world a friend to grace, To help me on to God?
I'll bear the toil, en-dure the pain, Sup-port-ed by Thy word. A-MEN.

5 Thy saints in all this glorious war
  Shall conquer, though they die;
They see the triumph from afar,
  By faith they bring it nigh.

6 When that illustrious day shall rise,
  And all Thy armies shine
In robes of victory through the skies,
  The glory shall be Thine.

196 For the Man of Galilee

8. 7. 8. 7. 7. 7. 7. 7.

S. J. Duncan-Clark

I. H. Meredith, 1872–

1. Shout a-loud the stir-ring sum-mons O'er the land from sea to sea,
2. Men are want-ed, men of pur-pose, Men of high or low de-gree,
3. From the count-ing house and col-lege, From the forge and fac-to-ry,
4. On-ward! are His march-ing or-ders, He who leads to vic-to-ry,

Men are want-ed, men of cour-age, For the Man of Gal-i-lee.
Each to be a fel-low-work-er With the Man of Gal-i-lee.
Lo, there throngs a loy-al le-gion For the Man of Gal-i-lee.
On-ward! till the world is tak-en For the Man of Gal-i-lee.

Rall.

O thou Man of Gal-i-lee! Thou who died to set men free,
O thou Man of Gal-i-lee! In the fight to set men free,
O thou Man of Gal-i-lee! We will fol-low on-ly Thee,
O thou Man of Gal-i-lee! We will fol-low on-ly Thee,

a tempo

We will fol-low on-ly Thee, Bless-ed Man of Gal-i-lee!
We will fol-low on-ly Thee, Glo-rious Man of Gal-i-lee!
In a life of faith and serv-ice, Bless-ed Man of Gal-i-lee!
O Thou fear-less, peer-less Lead-er, Glo-rious Man of Gal-i-lee!

197 The World's Astir! The Clouds of Storm

ALL SAINTS, NEW. C. M. D.

FRANK MASON NORTH, 1850–1935

HENRY S. CUTLER, 1824–1902

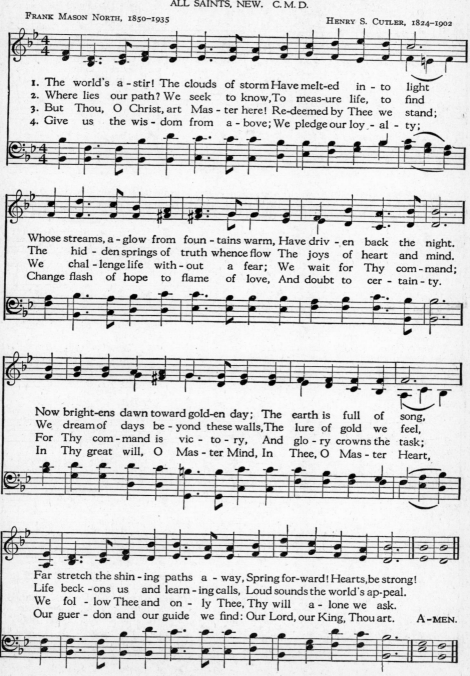

1. The world's a-stir! The clouds of storm Have melt-ed in-to light
2. Where lies our path? We seek to know, To meas-ure life, to find
3. But Thou, O Christ, art Mas-ter here! Re-deemed by Thee we stand;
4. Give us the wis-dom from a-bove; We pledge our loy-al-ty;

Whose streams, a-glow from foun-tains warm, Have driv-en back the night.
The hid-den springs of truth whence flow The joys of heart and mind.
We chal-lenge life with-out a fear; We wait for Thy com-mand;
Change flash of hope to flame of love, And doubt to cer-tain-ty.

Now bright-ens dawn toward gold-en day; The earth is full of song,
We dream of days be-yond these walls, The lure of gold we feel,
For Thy com-mand is vic-to-ry, And glo-ry crowns the task;
In Thy great will, O Mas-ter Mind, In Thee, O Mas-ter Heart,

Far stretch the shin-ing paths a-way, Spring for-ward! Hearts, be strong!
Life beck-ons us and learn-ing calls, Loud sounds the world's ap-peal.
We fol-low Thee and on-ly Thee, Thy will a-lone we ask.
Our guer-don and our guide we find: Our Lord, our King, Thou art.

A-MEN.

198 Men of the Soil!

HOESTEN. Irregular

HAROLD M. HILDRETH

Danish Harvest Song

1. Men of the soil! We have la - bored un - end - ing:
2. Men of the soil! Now the torch we have light - ed;
3. Men of the soil! We are com - ing in judg - ment,

We have fed the world up - on the grain that we have grown.
Kin - dle fires in ev - ery land where rings the har - vest song!
To tell the world till jus - tice rules there is no lib - ér - ty.

Now with the star of the new day as - cend - ing,
Shoul - der to shoul - der in cour - age u - nit - ed
We in our strength are a - ris - ing as proph - ets,

Gi - ants of the earth, at last we rise to claim our own.
From every race we come to join the til - ler's might - y throng.
March - ing on to show the world the dawn that is to be.

Jus - tice through-out the land, Hap - pi - ness as God has planned,
Earth ne'er shall eat a - gain Bread gain'd through blood of men.
There's a light -ning in the sky, There's a thun - der shout - ing high;

Men of the Soil!

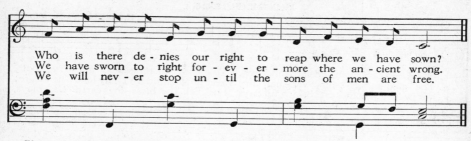

Who is there de-nies our right to reap where we have sown?
We have sworn to right for-ev-er-more the an-cient wrong.
We will nev-er stop un-til the sons of men are free.

Written during the Chicago milk strike by one of the group of theological students who were working with the farmers. Sung to the Danish folk tune at Ashland College, Grant, Michigan.

199 We are Living, We are Dwelling

AUSTRIA. 8.7.8.7.D.

ARTHUR CLEVELAND COXE, 1840

FRANZ JOSEPH HAYDN, 1732-1809

1. We are liv-ing, we are dwell-ing In a grand and aw-ful time;
In an age on a-ges tell-ing; To be liv-ing is sub-lime.
2. Worlds are charg-ing, heaven be-hold-ing; Thou hast but an hour to fight;
Now the bla-zoned cross un-fold-ing, On—right on-ward for the right!

Hark! the stir-ring of the na-tions, Right and wrong are in ar-ray.
On! let all the soul with-in you, For the truth's sake go a-broad!

Hark! what sound-eth? Is cre-a-tion Groan-ing for its lat-ter day?
Strike! let ev-ery nerve and sin-ew Tell on a-ges—tell for God! A-MEN.

200 O Lord of Heaven and Earth and Sea

OLDBRIDGE. 8. 8. 8. 4.

CHRISTOPHER WORDSWORTH, 1807–1885

ROBERT N. QUAILE, 1867–

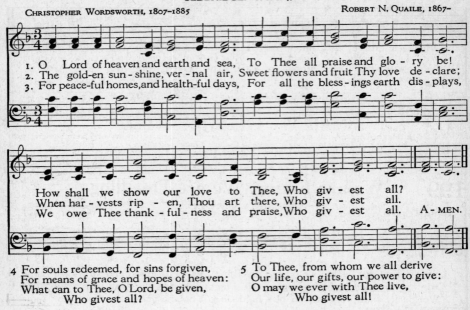

1. O Lord of heaven and earth and sea, To Thee all praise and glo - ry be!
2. The gold-en sun - shine, ver - nal air, Sweet flowers and fruit Thy love de - clare;
3. For peace-ful homes, and health-ful days, For all the bless-ings earth dis - plays,

How shall we show our love to Thee, Who giv - est all?
When har - vests rip - en, Thou art there, Who giv - est all.
We owe Thee thank - ful - ness and praise, Who giv - est all. A - MEN.

4 For souls redeemed, for sins forgiven,
For means of grace and hopes of heaven:
What can to Thee, O Lord, be given,
Who givest all?

5 To Thee, from whom we all derive
Our life, our gifts, our power to give:
O may we ever with Thee live,
Who givest all!

201 Sweetly, Lord, Have We Heard Thee Calling

9. 4. 9. 4. with Chorus

MARY B. C. SLADE, 1826–1882

ASA B. EVERETT, 1828–1875

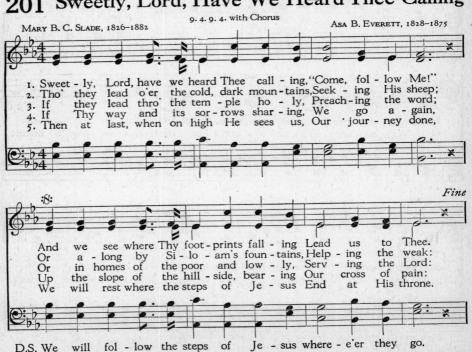

1. Sweet - ly, Lord, have we heard Thee call - ing, "Come, fol - low Me!"
2. Tho' they lead o'er the cold, dark moun - tains, Seek - ing His sheep;
3. If they lead thro' the tem - ple ho - ly, Preach - ing the word;
4. If Thy way and its sor - rows shar - ing, We go a - gain,
5. Then at last, when on high He sees us, Our jour - ney done,

Fine

And we see where Thy foot - prints fall - ing Lead us to Thee.
Or a - long by Si - lo - am's foun - tains, Help - ing the weak:
Or in homes of the poor and low - ly, Serv - ing the Lord:
Up the slope of the hill - side, bear - ing Our cross of pain:
We will rest where the steps of Je - sus End at His throne.

D.S. We will fol - low the steps of Je - sus where - e'er they go.

Sweetly, Lord, Have We Heard Thee Calling

CHORUS

D.S.

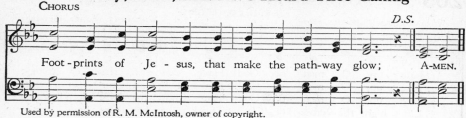

Foot-prints of Je-sus, that make the path-way glow; A-MEN.

Used by permission of R. M. McIntosh, owner of copyright.

202   I Bind My Heart This Tide

FEALTY. 6. 7. 7. 7. 6. 7. 7. 7.

LAUCHLAN MACLEAN WATT, 1867–   GRACE WILBUR CONANT

1. I bind my heart this tide To the Gal - i - le - an's side,
2. I bind my heart in thrall To the God, the Lord of All,

To the wounds of Cal - va - ry, To the Christ who died for me.
To the God, the poor man's Friend, And the Christ whom He did send.

I bind my soul this day To the broth - er far a - way,
I bind my - self to peace, To make strife and en - vy cease,

And the broth-er near at hand, In this town, and in this land.
God! knit Thou sure the cord Of my thral-dom to my Lord. A - MEN.

Tune used by permission of The Century Co., owners of copyright.

203 Rise Up, O Men of God!

FESTAL SONG. S. M.

William Pierson Merrill, 1867–

William H. Walter, 1825–1893

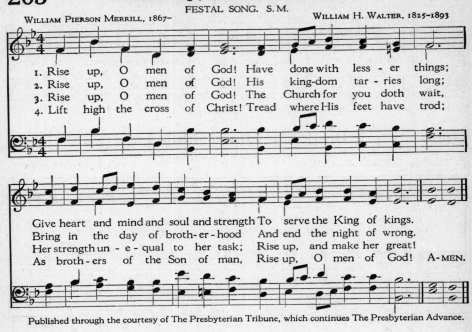

1. Rise up, O men of God! Have done with less-er things;
2. Rise up, O men of God! His king-dom tar-ries long;
3. Rise up, O men of God! The Church for you doth wait,
4. Lift high the cross of Christ! Tread where His feet have trod;

Give heart and mind and soul and strength To serve the King of kings.
Bring in the day of broth-er-hood And end the night of wrong.
Her strength un-e-qual to her task; Rise up, and make her great!
As broth-ers of the Son of man, Rise up, O men of God! A-men.

Published through the courtesy of The Presbyterian Tribune, which continues The Presbyterian Advance.

204 Fight the Good Fight

PENTECOST. L. M.

John S. B. Monsell, 1811–1875

William Boyd, 1847–1928

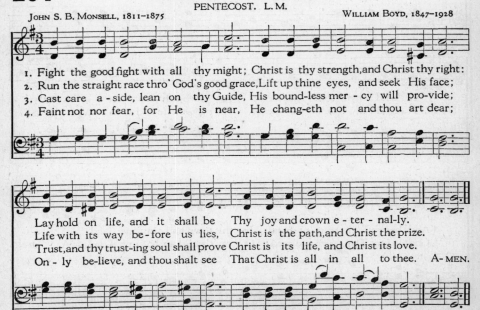

1. Fight the good fight with all thy might; Christ is thy strength,and Christ thy right:
2. Run the straight race thro' God's good grace,Lift up thine eyes, and seek His face;
3. Cast care a-side, lean on thy Guide, His bound-less mer-cy will pro-vide;
4. Faint not nor fear, for He is near, He chang-eth not and thou art dear;

Lay hold on life, and it shall be Thy joy and crown e-ter-nal-ly.
Life with its way be-fore us lies, Christ is the path,and Christ the prize.
Trust,and thy trust-ing soul shall prove Christ is its life, and Christ its love.
On-ly be-lieve, and thou shalt see That Christ is all in all to thee. A-men.

205 The Voice of God Is Calling

MEIRIONYDD. 7. 6. 7. 6. D.

JOHN HAYNES HOLMES, 1879–

Welsh hymn melody

1. The voice of God is call - ing Its sum-mons un - to men;
2. I hear my peo - ple cry - ing In cot and mine and slum;
3. We heed, O Lord, Thy sum-mons, And an - swer: Here are we!
4. From ease and plen - ty save us; From pride of place ab - solve;

As once He spake in Zi - on, So now He speaks a - gain.
No field or mart is si - lent, No cit - y street is dumb.
Send us up - on Thine er - rand, Let us Thy serv -ants be.
Purge us of low de - sire; Lift us to high re - solve;

Whom shall I send to suc - cor My peo - ple in their need?
I see my peo - ple fall - ing In dark -ness and de - spair.
Our strength is dust and ash - es, Our years a pass - ing hour;
Take us, and make us ho - ly; Teach us Thy will and way.

Whom shall I send to loos - en The bonds of shame and greed?
Whom shall I send to shat - ter The fet - ters which they bear?
But Thou canst use our weak -ness To mag - ni - fy Thy power.
Speak, and, be - hold! we an - swer; Com-mand, and we o - bey! A-MEN.

206 We Thank Thee, Lord

FIELD. 10. 10. 10. 10.

CALVIN W. LAUFER, 1874–

CALVIN W. LAUFER, 1874–

1. We thank Thee, Lord, Thy paths of serv - ice lead
2. We've sought and found Thee in the se - cret place
3. We've felt Thy touch in sor - row's dark - ened way
4. We've seen Thy glo - ry like a man - tle spread

To bla - zoned heights and down the slopes of need;
And mar - veled at the ra - diance of Thy face;
A - bound with love and sol - ace for the day;
O'er hill and dale in saf - fron flame and red;

They reach Thy throne, en - com - pass land and sea,
But of - ten in some far - off Gal - i - lee
And, 'neath the bur - dens there, Thy sov - reign - ty
But in the eyes of men, re - deemed and free,

And he who jour - neys in them walks with Thee.
Be - held Thee fair - er yet while serv - ing Thee.
Has held our hearts en - thralled while serv - ing Thee.
A splen - dor great - er yet while serv - ing Thee. A - MEN.

207 Now in the Days of Youth

FROM STRENGTH TO STRENGTH. 6. 6. 8. 6. D.

WALTER J. MATHAMS
In unison

EDWARD WOODALL NAYLOR, 1867–

1. Now in the days of youth, When life flows fresh and free, Thou Lord of all our hearts and lives, We give our-selves to Thee; Our fer-vent gift re-ceive, And fit us to ful-fill, Thro' all our days, in all our ways, Our Heav'n-ly Fa-ther's will.

2. Teach us wher-e'er we live, To act as in Thy sight, And do what Thou wouldst have us do With ra-di-ant de-light; Not choos-ing what is great, Nor spurn-ing what is small, But take as from Thy hands our tasks, And glo-ri-fy them all.

3. Teach us to love the true, The beau-ti-ful and pure, And let us not for one short hour An e-vil thought en-dure; But give us grace to stand De-cid-ed, brave, and strong, The lov-ers of all ho-ly things, The foes of all things wrong.

4. Spir-it of Christ, do Thou Our first bright days in-spire That we may live the life of love And loft-i-est de-sire; And be by Thee pre-pared For larg-er years to come, And for the life in-ef-fa-ble With-in the Fa-ther's home. A-MEN.

208 Lord and Saviour, True and Kind

BOYCE (SHARON). 7.7.7.7.

HANDLEY C. G. MOULE, 1841–1920

WILLIAM BOYCE, 1710–1779

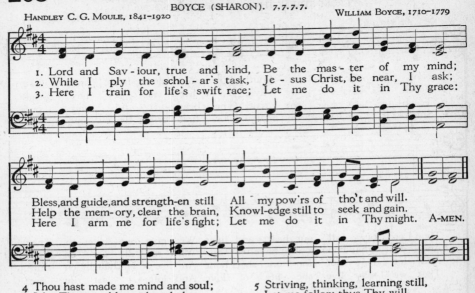

1. Lord and Sav-iour, true and kind, Be the mas-ter of my mind;
2. While I ply the schol-ar's task, Je-sus Christ, be near, I ask;
3. Here I train for life's swift race; Let me do it in Thy grace:

Bless, and guide, and strength-en still All my pow'rs of tho't and will.
Help the mem-ory, clear the brain, Knowl-edge still to seek and gain.
Here I arm me for life's fight; Let me do it in Thy might. A-MEN.

4 Thou hast made me mind and soul;
 I for Thee would use the whole:
 Thou hast died that I might live;
 All my powers to Thee I give.

5 Striving, thinking, learning still,
 Let me follow thus Thy will,
 Till my whole glad nature be
 Trained for duty and for Thee.

209 Blest Be the Tie That Binds

DENNIS. S. M.

JOHN FAWCETT, 1740–1817

From HANS G. NÄGELI, 1768–1836
Arr. by LOWELL MASON, 1792–1872

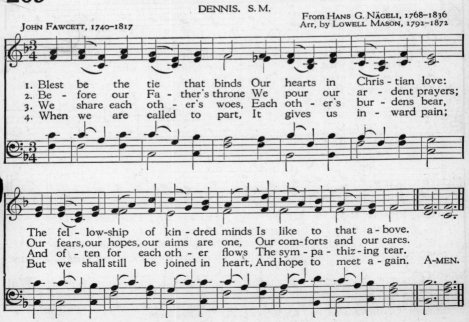

1. Blest be the tie that binds Our hearts in Chris-tian love:
2. Be-fore our Fa-ther's throne We pour our ar-dent prayers;
3. We share each oth-er's woes, Each oth-er's bur-dens bear,
4. When we are called to part, It gives us in-ward pain;

The fel-low-ship of kin-dred minds Is like to that a-bove.
Our fears, our hopes, our aims are one, Our com-forts and our cares.
And of-ten for each oth-er flows The sym-pa-thiz-ing tear.
But we shall still be joined in heart, And hope to meet a-gain. A-MEN.

210 Lead On, O King Eternal

LANCASHIRE. 7.6.7.6.D.

Ernest W. Shurtleff, 1862–1917

Henry Smart, 1813–1879

1. Lead on, O King E-ter-nal, The day of march has come;
2. Lead on, O King E-ter-nal, Till sin's fierce war shall cease,
3. Lead on, O King E-ter-nal, We fol-low, not with fears;

Hence-forth in fields of con-quest Thy tents shall be our home.
And ho-li-ness shall whis-per The sweet A-men of peace;
For glad-ness breaks like morn-ing Wher-e'er Thy face ap-pears;

Thro' days of prep-a-ra-tion Thy grace has made us strong,
For not with swords loud clash-ing, Nor roll of stir-ring drums;
Thy cross is lift-ed o'er us; We jour-ney in its light:

And now, O King e-ter-nal, We lift our bat-tle song.
With deeds of love and mer-cy, The heav'n-ly king-dom comes.
The crown a-waits the con-quest; Lead on, O God of might. A-men.

To the Knights in the Days of Old

FOLLOW THE GLEAM. Irregular

Bryn Mawr College

SALLIE HUME DOUGLAS

In unison

1. To the knights in the days of old, Keep-ing watch on the
2. And we who would serve the King And loy-al-ly

moun-tain heights, Came a vi-sion of Ho-ly Grail,
Him o-bey, In the con-se-crate si-lence know

And a voice thro' the wait-ing night. Fol-low, fol-low,
That the chal-lenge still holds to-day. Fol-low, fol-low,

fol-low the gleam, Ban-ners un-furled o'er all the world. Fol-low, fol-
fol-low the gleam, Stand-ards of worth o'er all the earth, Fol-low, fol-

low, fol-low the gleam Of the chal-ice that is the Grail.
low, fol-low the gleam Of the light that shall bring the dawn.

212 O Young and Fearless Prophet

BLAIRGOWRIE (Dykes). 13. 13. 13. 13

S. RALPH HARLOW, 1885–

JOHN B. DYKES, 1823–1876

1. O young and fear-less Proph-et of an-cient Gal-i-lee:
2. We mar-vel at the pur-pose that held Thee to Thy course
3. O help us stand un-swerv-ing a-gainst war's blood-y way,
4. Cre-ate in us the splen-dor that dawns when hearts are kind,
5. O young and fear-less Proph-et, we need Thy pres-ence here,

Thy life is still a sum-mons to serve hu-man-i-ty,
While ev-er on the hill-top be-fore Thee loomed the cross;
Where hate and lust and false-hood hold back Christ's ho-ly sway;
That knows not race nor sta-tion as boun-daries of the mind;
A-mid our pride and glo-ry to see Thy face ap-pear;

To make our thoughts and ac-tions less prone to please the crowd,
Thy stead-fast face set for-ward where love and du-ty shone,
For-bid false love of coun-try, that blinds us to His call
That learns to val-ue beau-ty, in heart, or brain, or soul,
Once more to hear Thy chal-lenge a-bove our noi-sy day,

To stand with hum-ble cour-age for Truth with hearts un-cowed.
While we be-tray so quick-ly and leave Thee there a-lone.
Who lifts a-bove the na-tion the broth-er-hood of all.
And longs to bind God's chil-dren in-to one per-fect whole.
A-gain to lead us for-ward a-long God's ho-ly way. A-MEN.

8 Words used by permission of S. Ralph Harlow

213 The Light of God Is Falling

LAUFER. 7. 6. 7. 6. D.

Louis F. Benson, 1855–1930

Emily S. Perkins, 1866–

1. The light of God is fall - ing Up - on life's com-mon way;
2. Who shares his life's pure pleas - ures, And walks the hon - est road,
3. Where hu - man lives are throng - ing In toil and pain and sin,
4. Thy ran-somed host in glo - ry, All souls that sin and pray,

The Mas - ter's voice still call - ing, "Come, walk with me to - day;"
Who trades with heap - ing meas - ures, And lifts his broth - er's load,
While clois - tered hearts are long - ing To bring the king-dom in,
Turn toward the cross that bore Thee; "Be - hold the man!" they say;

No du - ty can seem low - ly To him who lives with Thee,
Who turns the wrong down blunt - ly, And lends the right a hand,
O Christ, the Eld - er Broth - er Of proud and beat - en men,
And while Thy Church is plead - ing For all who would do good,

And all of life grows ho - ly, O Christ of Gal - i - lee!
He dwells in God's own coun - try, He tills the Ho - ly Land.
When they have found each oth - er, Thy king-dom will come then.
We hear Thy true voice lead - ing Our song of broth - er-hood. A - MEN.

Words used by permission of Mrs. Robert F. Jefferys
Music copyright, 1924, by Emily S. Perkins. Used by permission

214 Where Cross the Crowded Ways of Life

GERMANY. L. M.

FRANK MASON NORTH, 1850–1935

From WILLIAM GARDINER'S
SACRED MELODIES, 1815

1. Where cross the crowd - ed ways of life, Where sound the
2. In haunts of wretch - ed - ness and need, On shad - owed
3. From ten - der child - hood's help - less - ness, From wo - man's
4. The cup of wa - ter given for Thee Still holds the

cries of race and clan, A - bove the noise of
thresh - olds dark with fears, From paths where hide the
grief, man's bur - dened toil, From fam - ished souls, from
fresh - ness of Thy grace; Yet long these mul - ti -

self - ish strife, We hear Thy voice, O Son of man!
lures of greed, We catch the vi - sion of Thy tears.
sor - row's stress, Thy heart has nev - er known re - coil.
tudes to see The sweet com - pas - sion of Thy face. A - MEN.

5 O Master, from the mountain side,
   Make haste to heal these hearts of pain;
Among these restless throngs abide,
   O tread the city's streets again.

6 Till sons of men shall learn Thy love
   And follow where Thy feet have trod;
Till, glorious from Thy heaven above,
   Shall come the city of our God!

215 We've a Story to Tell

MESSAGE. 10. 8. 8. 7. 7. with Refrain

Colin Sterne, 1862–

H. Ernest Nichol, 1862–1928. Adapted

1. We've a sto - ry to tell to the na - tions That shall
2. We've a song to be sung to the na - tions, That shall
3. We've a mes - sage to give to the na - tions, That the
4. We've a Sav - iour to show to the na - tions, Who the

turn their hearts to the right, A sto - ry of truth and mer - cy,
lift their hearts to the Lord; A song that shall con - quer e - vil
Lord who reign - eth a - bove, Hath sent us His Son to save us,
path of sor - row has trod, That all of the world's great peo - ples

A sto - ry of peace and light, A sto - ry of peace and light.
And shat - ter the spear and sword, And shat - ter the spear and sword.
And show us that God is love, And show us that God is love.
Might come to the truth of God, Might come to the truth of God!

Refrain

For the dark-ness shall turn to dawn - ing, And the dawn-ing to noon-day bright,

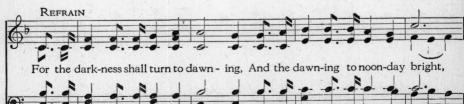

We've a Story to Tell

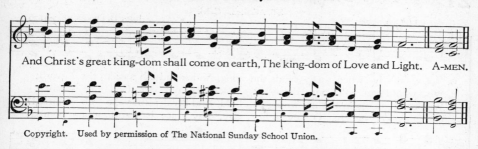

And Christ's great king-dom shall come on earth, The king-dom of Love and Light. A-MEN.

216 Lord of Health, Thou Life Within Us

WORK. 8. 7. 8. 7. 7.

Percy Dearmer, 1867–1936

Chas. C. Washburn

1. Lord of health, Thou life with-in us, Strength of all that
2. Praise for all our work and lei-sure, Mirth and games and
3. Praise for joys, for sor-rows e-ven, All that leads us
4. Help us now, each mo-ment fill-ing, Keep us true to

lives and grows, Love that meets our hearts to win us, Beau-ty that a-
jol-li-ty, Stu-dy, sci-ence, all the treas-ure That is stored by
up to Thee; Most of all that out from heav-en Came Thy Son to
Thee, and wise; May our work be keen and will-ing, Power and ser-vice

round us glows, Take the praise that brims and flows!
mem-o-ry, Skill of mind and hand and eye;
set us free, Came to show us what to be.
be our prize— Till to Thy far hills we rise!

217 Not Only When Ascends the Song

ST. AGNES. C.M.

THOMAS H. GILL

JOHN B. DYKES, 1823–1876

1. Not on-ly when as-cends the song, And sound-eth sweet the word;
2. We would not to our dai-ly task With-out our God re-pair;
3. Would we a-gainst some wrong be bold, And break some yoke ab-horred?
4. O ev-ery-where, O ev-ery day, Thy grace is still out-poured;

Not on-ly 'midst the Sab-bath throng Our souls would seek the Lord.
But in the world Thy pres-ence ask, And seek Thy glo-ry there.
A-midst the strife and stir be-hold The seek-ers of the Lord!
We work, we watch, we strive, we pray; Be-hold Thy seek-ers, Lord!   A-MEN.

218 Love Thyself Last

LANHERNE. 11. 10. 11. 10.

Anonymous

HENRY HAYMAN, 1820–1894

1. Love thy-self last. Look near, be-hold thy du-ty To those who
2. Love thy-self last. Look far, and find the stran-ger Who stag-gers
3. Love thy-self last. The vast-ness-es a-bove thee Are filled with
4. Love thy-self last; And thou shalt grow in spir-it To see, to

walk be-side thee down life's road; Make glad their days by lit-tle acts of
'neath his sin and his de-spair; Go lend a hand and lead him out of
spir-it forc-es, strong and pure; And fer-vent-ly these faith-ful friends shall
hear, to know and un-der-stand. The mes-sage of the stars, lo, thou shalt

Love Thyself Last

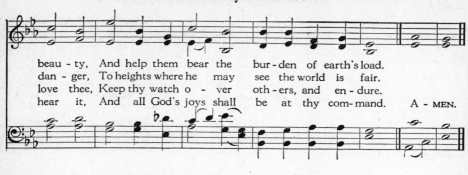

beau - ty, And help them bear the bur - den of earth's load.
dan - ger, To heights where he may see the world is fair.
love thee, Keep thy watch o - ver oth - ers, and en - dure.
hear it, And all God's joys shall be at thy com - mand. A - MEN.

219   Speed Thy Servants, Saviour

DISMISSAL. 8. 7. 8. 7. 8. 7.

WILLIAM LETTON VINER, 1790–1867

1. Speed Thy ser - vants, Sav - iour, speed them! Thou art Lord of winds and waves:
2. Friends, and home, and all for - sak - ing, Lord! they go at Thy com - mand;
3. Where no fruit ap - pears to cheer them, And they seem to toil in vain,
4. In the midst of op - po - si - tion Let them trust, O Lord, in Thee;

They were bound, but Thou hast freed them; Now they go to free the slaves.
As their stay Thy prom - ise tak - ing, While they trav - erse sea and land:
Then in mer - cy, Lord, draw near them, Then their sink - ing hopes sus - tain:
When suc - cess at - tends their mis - sion, Let Thy ser - vants hum - bler be:

Be Thou with them! Be Thou with them! 'Tis Thine arm a - lone that saves!
Oh, be with them! Oh, be with them! Lead them safe - ly by the hand!
Thus sup - port - ed, Thus sup - port - ed, Let their zeal re - vive a - gain!
Nev - er leave them, Nev - er leave them, Till Thy face in heav'n they see!

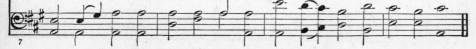

220 Jesus Shall Reign Where'er the Sun

RIMINGTON. L. M.

ISAAC WATTS, 1674–1748

FRANCIS DUCKWORTH, 1862–

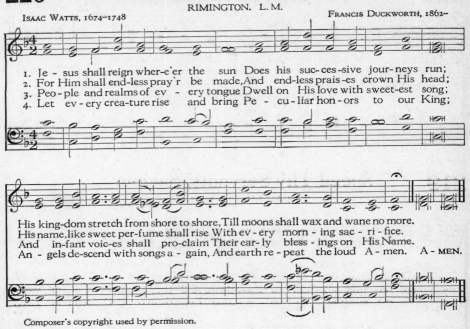

1. Je - sus shall reign wher-e'er the sun Does his suc-ces-sive jour-neys run;
2. For Him shall end-less pray'r be made, And end-less prais-es crown His head;
3. Peo - ple and realms of ev - ery tongue Dwell on His love with sweet-est song;
4. Let ev - ery crea-ture rise and bring Pe - cu - liar hon - ors to our King;

His king-dom stretch from shore to shore, Till moons shall wax and wane no more.
His name, like sweet per-fume shall rise With ev - ery morn - ing sac - ri - fice.
And in-fant voic-es shall pro-claim Their ear - ly bless - ings on His Name.
An - gels de-scend with songs a - gain, And earth re - peat the loud A - men. A - MEN.

Composer's copyright used by permission.

221 In Christ There Is No East or West

ST. PETER. C. M.

JOHN OXENHAM

ALEXANDER R. REINAGLE, 1799–1877

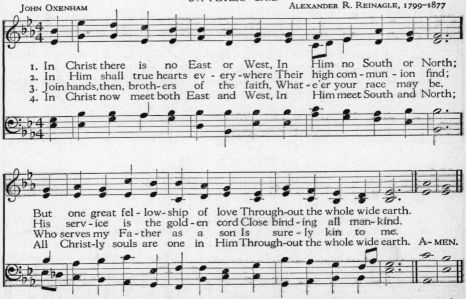

1. In Christ there is no East or West, In Him no South or North;
2. In Him shall true hearts ev - ery-where Their high com - mun - ion find;
3. Join hands, then, broth-ers of the faith, What - e'er your race may be.
4. In Christ now meet both East and West, In Him meet South and North;

But one great fel - low-ship of love Through-out the whole wide earth.
His serv - ice is the gold - en cord Close bind - ing all man-kind.
Who serves my Fa - ther as a son Is sure - ly kin to me.
All Christ-ly souls are one in Him Through-out the whole wide earth. A - MEN.

222 O Zion, Haste

TIDINGS. 11. 10. 11. 10. with Refrain

MARY A. THOMSON, 1834–1923

JAMES WALCH, 1837–1901

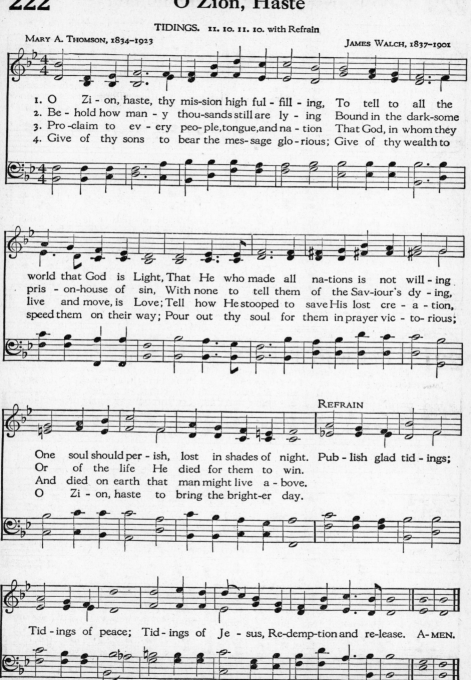

1. O Zi - on, haste, thy mis-sion high ful - fill - ing, To tell to all the
2. Be - hold how man - y thou-sands still are ly - ing Bound in the dark-some
3. Pro -claim to ev - er - y peo-ple, tongue, and na - tion That God, in whom they
4. Give of thy sons to bear the mes-sage glo-rious; Give of thy wealth to

world that God is Light, That He who made all na-tions is not will - ing
pris - on-house of sin, With none to tell them of the Sav-iour's dy - ing,
live and move, is Love; Tell how He stooped to save His lost cre - a - tion,
speed them on their way; Pour out thy soul for them in prayer vic - to- rious;

REFRAIN

One soul should per - ish, lost in shades of night. Pub - lish glad tid - ings;
Or of the life He died for them to win.
And died on earth that man might live a - bove.
O Zi - on, haste to bring the bright-er day.

Tid - ings of peace; Tid - ings of Je - sus, Re-demp-tion and re-lease. A - MEN.

223 Christ Shall Have Dominion

11. 11. 11. 11. with Chorus

Arr. by JOHN GOSS, 1800–1880

1. Christ shall have do - min - ion o - ver land and sea, Earth's re - mot - est
2. When the need - y seek Him, He will mer - cy show; Yea, the weak and
3. Ev - er and for ev - er shall His Name en - dure, Long as suns con -
4. Un - to God Al - might - y joy - ful Zi - on sings; He a - lone is

re - gions shall His em - pire be; They that wilds in - hab - it shall their
help - less shall His pit - y know; He will sure - ly save them from op -
tin - ue it shall stand se - cure; And in Him for ev - er all men
glo - rious, do - ing won-drous things. Ev - er - more, ye peo - ple, bless His

wor - ship bring, Kings shall ten - der trib - ute, na - tions serve our King.
pres-sion's might, For their lives are pre-cious in His ho - ly sight.
shall be blest, And all na - tions hail Him King of kings con - fessed.
glo - rious Name, His e - ter - nal glo - ry through the earth pro - claim.

CHORUS

Christ shall have do - min - ion O - ver land and sea;

Earth's re - mot - est re - gions Shall His em - pire be.

224 Watchman, Tell Us of the Night

WATCHMAN. 7. 7. 7. 7. D.

John Bowring, 1792–1872

Lowell Mason, 1792–1872

1. Watch-man, tell us of the night, What its signs of prom-ise are.
2. Watch-man, tell us of the night; High-er yet that star as-cends.
3. Watch-man, tell us of the night, For the morn-ing seems to dawn.

Trav-eler, o'er yon moun-tain's height See that glo-ry-beam-ing star!
Trav-eler, bless-ed-ness and light, Peace and truth, its course por-tends.
Trav-eler, dark-ness takes its flight; Doubt and ter-ror are with-drawn.

Watch-man, doth its beau-teous ray Aught of joy or hope fore-tell?
Watch-man, will its beams a-lone Gild the spot that gave them birth?
Watch-man, let thy wan-dering cease; Hie thee to thy qui-et home!

Trav-eler, yes; it brings the day, Prom-ised day of Is-ra-el.
Trav-eler, a-ges are its own; See, it bursts o'er all the earth!
Trav-eler, lo, the Prince of Peace, Lo, the Son of God is come! A-MEN.

225 Eternal God, Whose Power Upholds

SARAH. 8. 6. 8. 6. D.

Henry H. Tweedy, 1868–

Rhys Thomas, 1867–1932

1. E - ter - nal God, whose pow'r up - holds Both flow'r and flam - ing star,
2. O God of love, whose spir - it wakes In ev - ery hu - man breast,
3. O God of truth, whom sci - ence seeks And rev - erent souls a - dore,

To whom there is no here nor there, No time, no near nor far,
Whom love, and love a - lone can know, In whom all hearts find rest,
Who light - est ev - ery earn - est mind Of ev - ery clime and shore,

No a - lien race, no for - eign shore, No child un - sought, un - known,
Help us to spread Thy gra - cious reign Till greed and hate shall cease,
Dis - pel the gloom of er - ror's night, Of ig - no - rance and fear,

Oh! send us forth, Thy proph - ets true, To make all lands Thine own!
And kind - ness dwell in hu - man hearts, And all the earth find peace!
Un - til true wis - dom from a - bove Shall make life's path - way clear!   A-MEN.

4 O God of beauty, oft revealed
      In dreams of human art,
   In speech that flows to melody,
      In holiness of heart,
   Teach us to ban all ugliness
      That blinds our eyes to Thee,
   Till all shall know the loveliness
      Of lives made fair and free.

5 O God of righteousness and grace,
      Seen in the Christ, Thy Son,
   Whose life and death reveal Thy face,
      By whom Thy will was done,
   Inspire Thy heralds of good news
      To live Thy life divine,
   Till Christ is formed in all mankind
      And every land is Thine!

226 God of Our Fathers

NATIONAL HYMN. 10. 10. 10. 10.

Daniel C. Roberts, 1841-1907   George W. Warren, 1828-1902

Trumpets, before
each stanza

1. God of our fa - thers, whose al-might-y hand
2. Thy love di-vine hath led us in the past;
3. From war's a-larms, from dead-ly pes - ti-lence,
4. Re - fresh Thy peo - ple on their toil-some way;

Leads forth in beau - ty all the star - ry band
In this free land by Thee our lot is cast;
Be Thy strong arm our ev - er sure de - fense;
Lead us from night to nev - er - end - ing day;

Of shin - ing worlds in splen - dor through the skies,
Be Thou our Rul - er, Guard-ian, Guide, and Stay,
Thy true re - li - gion in our hearts in - crease,
Fill all our lives with love and grace di - vine,

Our grate - ful songs be - fore Thy throne a - rise.
Thy Word our law, Thy paths our cho - sen way
Thy boun - teous good - ness nour - ish us in peace
And glo - ry, laud, and praise be ev - er Thine.

A - MEN.

227 O Master of the Waking World

MELITA. 8. 8. 8. 8. 8. 8.

Frank Mason North, 1850–1935

John B. Dykes, 1823–1876

1. O Mas-ter of the wak-ing world, Who hast the na-tions in Thy heart—The heart that bled and broke to send God's love to earth's re-mot-est part: Show us a-new in Cal-va-ry The won-drous power that makes men free.

2. On ev-ery side the walls are down, The gates swing wide to ev-ery land, The rest-less tribes and rac-es feel The pres-sure of Thy pierc-ed hand; Thy way is in the sea and air, Thy world is o-pen ev-ery-where.

3. We hear the throb of surg-ing life, The clank of chains, the curse of greed, The moan of pain, the fu-tile cries Of su-per-sti-tion's cru-el creed; The peo-ples hun-ger for Thee, Lord, The isles are wait-ing for Thy word.

4. Thy wit-ness in the souls of men, Thy Spir-it's cease-less, brood-ing power, In lands where shad-ows hide the light, A-wait a new cre-a-tive hour: O might-y God, set us a-flame To show the glo-ry of Thy Name. A-men.

228 America the Beautiful

MATERNA. C. M. D.

KATHARINE LEE BATES, 1859-1929

SAMUEL A. WARD, 1847-1903

1. O beau - ti - ful for spa - cious skies, For am - ber waves of grain,
2. O beau - ti - ful for pil - grim feet, Whose stern, im - pas - sioned stress
3. O beau - ti - ful for he - roes proved In lib - er - at - ing strife,
4. O beau - ti - ful for pa - triot dream That sees, be - yond the years,

For pur - ple moun - tain maj - es - ties A - bove the fruit - ed plain!
A thor - ough - fare for free - dom beat A - cross the wil - der - ness!
Who more than self their coun - try loved, And mer - cy more than life!
Thine al - a - bas - ter cit - ies gleam, Un - dimmed by hu - man tears!

A - mer - i - ca! A - mer - i - ca! God shed His grace on thee,
A - mer - i - ca! A - mer - i - ca! God mend thine ev - ery flaw,
A - mer - i - ca! A - mer - i - ca! May God thy gold re - fine,
A - mer - i - ca! A - mer - i - ca! God shed His grace on thee,

And crown thy good with broth - er - hood From sea to shin - ing sea.
Con - firm thy soul in self - con - trol, Thy lib - er - ty in law.
Till all suc - cess be no - ble - ness, And ev - ery gain di - vine.
And crown thy good with broth - er - hood From sea to shin - ing sea. A - MEN.

229   O God Creator, in Whose Hand

BYRD. C.M.

HARRY WEBB FARRINGTON, 1880-1931   ROB ROY PEERY, 1900-

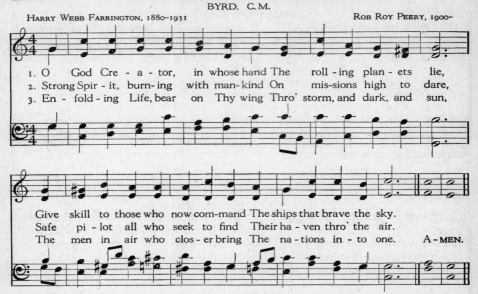

1. O God Cre - a - tor, in whose hand The roll - ing plan - ets lie,
2. Strong Spir - it, burn - ing with man - kind On mis-sions high to dare,
3. En - fold - ing Life, bear on Thy wing Thro' storm, and dark, and sun,

Give skill to those who now com-mand The ships that brave the sky.
Safe pi - lot all who seek to find Their ha - ven thro' the air.
The men in air who clos - er bring The na - tions in - to one. A-MEN.

Words copyright, 1928, by Harry Webb Farrington. Used by permission of Dora Davis Farrington.
Music copyright, 1929, by Rob Roy Peery. Used by permission.

230   These Things Shall Be: A Loftier Race

TRURO. L.M.

J. ADDINGTON SYMONDS, 1840-1893   From T. WILLIAMS'S PSALMODIA EVANGELICA, 1789

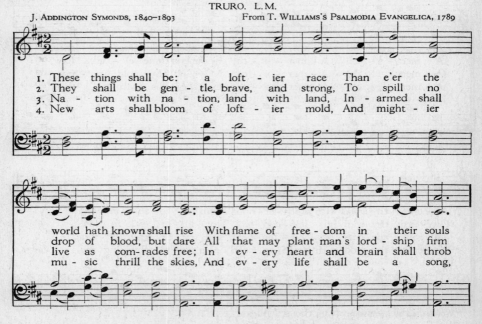

1. These things shall be: a loft - ier race Than e'er the
2. They shall be gen - tle, brave, and strong, To spill no
3. Na - tion with na - tion, land with land, In - armed shall
4. New arts shall bloom of loft - ier mold, And might - ier

world hath known shall rise With flame of free - dom in their souls
drop of blood, but dare All that may plant man's lord - ship firm
live as com - rades free; In ev - ery heart and brain shall throb
mu - sic thrill the skies, And ev - ery life shall be a song,

These Things Shall Be: A Loftier Race

And light of knowl - edge in their eyes.
On earth, and fire, and sea, and air.
The pulse of one fra - ter - ni - ty.
When all the earth is par - a - dise. A - MEN.

231 My Country, 'Tis of Thee

AMERICA. 6. 6. 4. 6. 6. 4.

S. F. SMITH   HENRY CAREY, c. 1690–1743

1. My coun - try, 'tis of thee, Sweet land of lib - er - ty,
2. My na - tive coun - try, thee, Land of the no - ble free,
3. Let mu - sic swell the breeze, And ring from all the trees
4. Our fa - thers' God, to Thee, Au - thor of lib - er - ty

Of thee I sing; Land where my fa - thers died, Land of the
Thy name I love; I love thy rocks and rills, Thy woods and
Sweet free - dom's song: Let mor - tal tongues a - wake; Let all that
To Thee we sing; Long may our land be bright With free - dom's

pil - grim's pride, From ev - ery moun - tain side Let free - dom ring.
tem - pled hills; My heart with rap - ture thrills Like that a - bove.
breathe par - take; Let rocks their si - lence break, The sound pro - long.
ho - ly light; Pro - tect us by Thy might, Great God, our King. A - MEN.

232 Peace in Our Time, O Lord

DIADEMATA. S. M. D.

JOHN OXENHAM

GEORGE J. ELVEY, 1816–1893

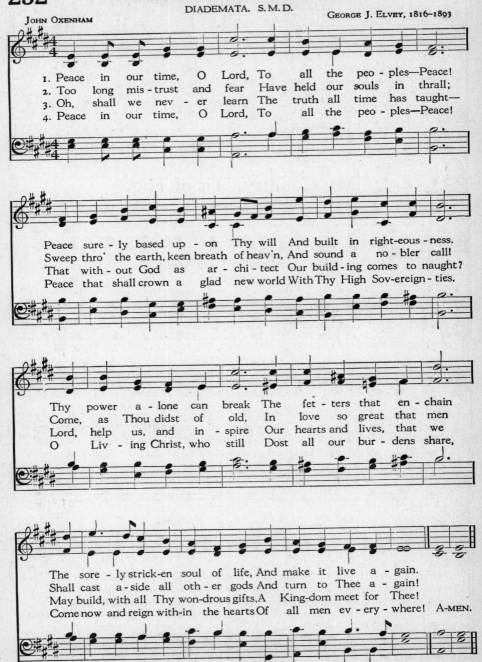

1. Peace in our time, O Lord, To all the peo - ples—Peace!
2. Too long mis - trust and fear Have held our souls in thrall;
3. Oh, shall we nev - er learn The truth all time has taught—
4. Peace in our time, O Lord, To all the peo - ples—Peace!

Peace sure - ly based up - on Thy will And built in right-eous - ness.
Sweep thro' the earth, keen breath of heav'n, And sound a no - bler call!
That with - out God as ar - chi - tect Our build-ing comes to naught?
Peace that shall crown a glad new world With Thy High Sov-ereign - ties.

Thy power a - lone can break The fet - ters that en - chain
Come, as Thou didst of old, In love so great that men
Lord, help us, and in - spire Our hearts and lives, that we
O Liv - ing Christ, who still Dost all our bur - dens share,

The sore - ly strick-en soul of life, And make it live a - gain.
Shall cast a - side all oth - er gods And turn to Thee a - gain!
May build, with all Thy won-drous gifts, A King-dom meet for Thee!
Come now and reign with-in the hearts Of all men ev - ery - where! A-MEN.

233 Our Spirit's Home

FINLANDIA. 11. 10. 11. 10. 11. 10.

ROLLAND W. SCHLOERB

JEAN SIBELIUS, 1865–

1. O Church of God, our sol - i - tude for - sak - ing, We now u-
2. O Church of God, like bells at noon-day peal - ing, Thy call has
3. Our spir - it's home, with joy to thee re - turn - ing, Our voic - es

nite with all who seek Thy way— With those who sing, with
come to us that we may bring Our strength to serve, to
join to sing our high - est praise, For hours of cheer, where

those whose hearts are break-ing, We lift our spir - its as to God we
all the Christ re - veal - ing In deeds of love and when our hopes take
friend-ship's fires are burn-ing, For strength and peace which glad-den all our

pray. O Church of God, our love for thee is wak - ing,
wing. O Church of God, where sin and pain find heal - ing,
days. O Church of God, for thee our hearts are yearn - ing,

We bring our al - le - lu - i - as to day.
To thee our al - le - lu - i - as we sing.
To thee our al - le - lu - i - as we raise.

A-MEN.

Words used by permission of Rolland W. Schloerb.

234 The Church's One Foundation

AURELIA. 7. 6. 7. 6. D.

SAMUEL J. STONE, 1839-1900

SAMUEL S. WESLEY, 1810-1876

1. The Church-'s one foun - da - tion Is Je - sus Christ her Lord;
2. E - lect from ev - ery na - tion, Yet one o'er all the earth,
3. 'Mid toil and trib - u - la - tion, And tu - mult of her war,
4. Yet she on earth hath un - ion With God the Three in One,

She is His new cre - a - tion By wa - ter and the word:
Her char - ter of sal - va - tion, One Lord, one faith, one birth;
She waits the con - sum - ma - tion Of peace for ev - er - more;
And mys - tic sweet com - mun - ion With those whose rest is won:

From heaven He came and sought her To be His ho - ly bride;
One ho - ly Name she bless - es, Par - takes one ho - ly food,
Till, with the vi - sion glo - rious, Her long - ing eyes are blest,
O hap - py ones and ho - ly! Lord, give us grace that we,

With His own blood He bought her, And for her life He died.
And to one hope she press - es, With ev - ery grace en - dued.
And the great Church vic - to - rious Shall be the Church at rest.
Like them, the meek and low - ly, On high may dwell with Thee. A - MEN.

235 Break Thou the Bread of Life

BREAD OF LIFE. 6. 4. 6. 4. D.

MARY A. LATHBURY, 1841–1913

WILLIAM F. SHERWIN, 1826–1888

1. Break Thou the bread of life, Dear Lord, to me,
2. Bless Thou the truth, dear Lord, To me — to me,

As Thou didst break the loaves Be - side the sea;
As Thou didst bless the bread By Gal - i - lee;

Be - yond the sa - cred page I seek Thee, Lord;
Then shall all bond - age cease, All fet - ters fall;

My spir - it pants for Thee, O liv - ing Word!
And I shall find my peace, My All - in - All. A - MEN.

236 Thy Word Is Like a Garden, Lord

SERAPH. 8.6.8.6.D.

EDWIN HODDER, 1837-1904

GOTTFRIED W. FINK, 1783-1846

1. Thy Word is like a gar-den, Lord, With flow-ers bright and fair;
2. Thy Word is like a star-ry host; A thou-sand rays of light
3. O may I love Thy pre-cious Word, May I ex-plore the mine,

And ev-ery one who seeks may pluck A love-ly clus-ter there.
Are seen to guide the trav-el-er, And makes his path-way bright.
May I its fra-grant flow-ers glean, May light up-on me shine.

Thy Word is like a deep, deep mine; And jew-els rich and rare
Thy Word is like an ar-mor-y, Where sol-diers may re-pair,
O may I find my ar-mor there, Thy Word my trust-y sword;

Are hid-den in its might-y depths For ev-ery search-er there.
And find, for life's long bat-tle-day, All need-ful weap-ons there.
I'll learn to fight with ev-ery foe The bat-tle of the Lord. A-MEN.

237 Wonderful Words of Life

8. 6. 8. 6. 6. 6. with Refrain

PHILIP P. BLISS, 1838–1876

PHILIP P. BLISS, 1838–1876

1. Sing them o - ver a - gain to me, Won - der - ful words of life,
2. Christ, the bless - ed One, gives to all Won - der - ful words of life,
3. Sweet - ly ech - o the gos - pel call Won - der - ful words of life,

Let me more of their beau - ty see, Won - der - ful words of life.
List, O list to His lov - ing call, Won - der - ful words of life.
Of - fer par - don and peace to all, Won - der - ful words of life.

Words of life and beau - ty, Teach me faith and du - ty;
All so free - ly giv - en, Tell - ing us of heav - en,
Je - sus, on - ly Sav - iour, Be our Guide for ev - er,

REFRAIN

Beau - ti - ful words, won - der - ful words, Won - der - ful words of life,

Beau - ti - ful words, won - der - ful words, Won - der - ful words of life.

238 A Parting Hymn We Sing

BOYLSTON. S. M.

AARON R. WOLFE, 1858–

LOWELL MASON, 1792–1872

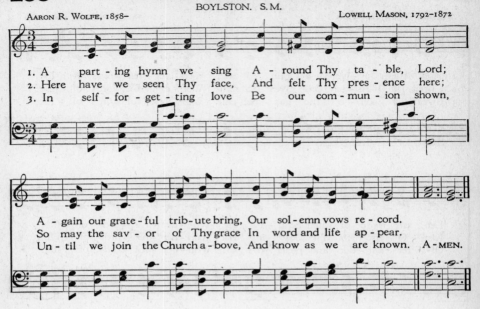

1. A part - ing hymn we sing A - round Thy ta - ble, Lord;
2. Here have we seen Thy face, And felt Thy pres - ence here;
3. In self - for - get - ting love Be our com - mun - ion shown,

A - gain our grate - ful trib - ute bring, Our sol - emn vows re - cord.
So may the sav - or of Thy grace In word and life ap - pear.
Un - til we join the Church a - bove, And know as we are known. A - MEN.

239 The King of Heaven His Table Spreads

DUNDEE (FRENCH). C. M.

PHILIP DODDRIDGE, 1702–1751

SCOTTISH PSALTER, 1615

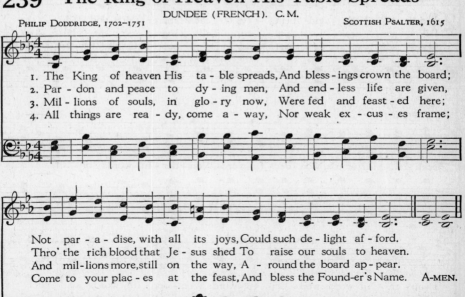

1. The King of heaven His ta - ble spreads, And bless - ings crown the board;
2. Par - don and peace to dy - ing men, And end - less life are given,
3. Mil - lions of souls, in glo - ry now, Were fed and feast - ed here;
4. All things are rea - dy, come a - way, Nor weak ex - cus - es frame;

Not par - a - dise, with all its joys, Could such de - light af - ford.
Thro' the rich blood that Je - sus shed To raise our souls to heaven.
And mil - lions more, still on the way, A - round the board ap - pear.
Come to your plac - es at the feast, And bless the Found - er's Name. A-MEN.

240 Bread of the World in Mercy Broken

EUCHARISTIC HYMN. 9.8.9.8.

REGINALD HEBER, 1783–1826

JOHN S. B. HODGES, 1830–1915

1. Bread of the world in mer-cy bro-ken, Wine of the soul in mer-cy shed,
2. Look on the heart by sor-row bro-ken, Look on the tears by sin-ners shed;

By whom the words of life were spo-ken, And in whose death our sins are dead;
And be Thy feast to us the to-ken That by Thy grace our souls are fed. A-MEN.

241 Be Known to Us in Breaking Bread

DUNDEE (FRENCH). C. M.

JAMES MONTGOMERY, 1771–1854

SCOTTISH PSALTER, 1615

1. Be known to us in break-ing bread, But do not then de-part;
2. There sup with us in love di-vine; Thy bod-y and Thy blood,

Sav-iour, a-bide with us, and spread Thy ta-ble in our heart.
That liv-ing bread, that heaven-ly wine, Be our im-mor-tal food. A-MEN.

242 Happy the Home When God Is There

ST. AGNES. C. M.

HENRY WARE, the younger, 1794–1843

JOHN B. DYKES, 1823–1876

1. Hap - py the home when God is there, And love fills ev - ery breast;
2. Hap - py the home where Je - sus' Name Is sweet to ev - ery ear;
3. Hap - py the home where prayer is heard, And praise is wont to rise;
4. Lord, let us in our homes a - gree This bless-ed peace to gain;

When one their wish, and one their pray'r, And one their heav'n-ly rest.
Where chil-dren ear - ly lisp His fame, And par-ents hold Him dear.
Where par - ents love the sa - cred Word And all its wis-dom prize.
U - nite our hearts in love to Thee, And love to all will reign. A-MEN.

243 Lord, When We Have Not Any Light

LYTHAM. C. M.

ANNIE MATHESON, 1853–1924

JAMES T. LIGHTWOOD, 1856–

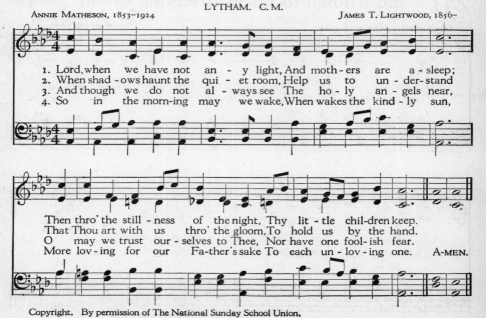

1. Lord, when we have not an - y light, And moth - ers are a - sleep;
2. When shad - ows haunt the qui - et room, Help us to un - der-stand
3. And though we do not al - ways see The ho - ly an - gels near,
4. So in the morn-ing may we wake, When wakes the kind - ly sun,

Then thro' the still - ness of the night, Thy lit - tle chil-dren keep.
That Thou art with us thro' the gloom, To hold us by the hand.
O may we trust our - selves to Thee, Nor have one fool-ish fear.
More lov - ing for our Fa-ther's sake To each un - lov-ing one. A-MEN.

244 I Think When I Read

SWEET STORY. Irregular

Jemima T. Luke, 1813-1906

Arr. by William B. Bradbury, 1816-1868

A Greek melody

1. I think when I read that sweet sto-ry of old,
2. I wish that His hands had been placed on my head,
3. Yet still to His foot-stool in prayer I may go,

When Je-sus was here a-mong men,
That His arms had been thrown a-round me,
And ask for a share in His love;

How He called lit-tle chil-dren as lambs to His fold,
And that I might have seen His kind look when He said,
And if I thus ear-nest-ly seek Him be-low,

I should like to have been with them then.
"Let the lit-tle ones come un-to me."
I shall see Him and know Him a-bove. A-men.

245 Saviour, Teach Me Day by Day

INNOCENTS. 7.7.7.7.

JANE ELIZABETH LEESON, 1807–1882

From THE PARISH CHOIR, 1850

1. Sav - iour, teach me, day by day, Love's sweet les - son to o - bey;
2. With a child's glad heart of love At Thy bid - ding may I move,
3. Teach me thus Thy steps to trace, Strong to fol - low in Thy grace,
4. Thus may I re - joice to show That I feel the love I owe;

Sweet - er les - son can - not be, Lov - ing Him who first loved me.
Prompt to serve and fol - low Thee, Lov - ing Him who first loved me.
Learn - ing how to love from Thee, Lov - ing Him who first loved me.
Sing - ing, till Thy face I see, Of His love who first loved me. A-MEN.

246 Holy Spirit, Lord of Love

DIX. 7.7.7.7.7.7.

RICHARD REDHEAD, 1853–

Abridged from a chorale by
CONRAD KOCHER, 1786–1872

1. Ho - ly Spir - it, Lord of Love, Thou who cam - est from a - bove,
2. From their bright bap - tis - mal day, Thro' their child-hood's on - ward way,
3. Give them light Thy truth to see, Give them life to live for Thee,
4. When the ho - ly vow is made, When the hands are on them laid,

Gifts of bless - ing to be - stow, On Thy wait - ing Church be - low;
Thou hast been their con-stant Guide, Watch-ing ev - er by their side;
Dai - ly pow'r to con - quer sin, Pa - tient faith the crown to win;
Come, in this most sol - emn hour, With Thy seven-fold gifts of pow'r,

Holy Spirit, Lord of Love

Once a-gain in love draw near To Thy chil-dren gath-ered here.
May they now till life shall end, Choose and know Thee as their Friend.
Shield them from temp-ta-tions' breath, Keep them faith-ful un - to death.
Come, Thou bless-ed Spir-it, come, Make each heart Thy hap - py home. A-MEN.

247 O Father, Thou Who Givest All

JEWISH TUNE. L. M.

JOHN HAYNES HOLMES, 1879–

Traditional Jewish

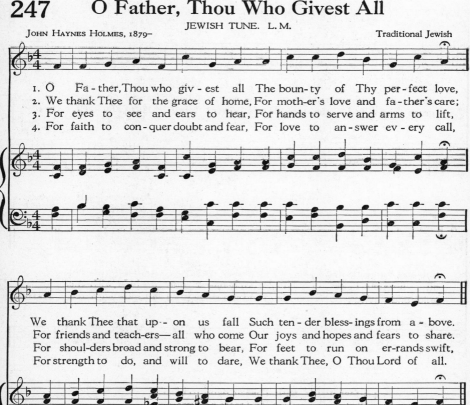

1. O Fa-ther, Thou who giv-est all The boun-ty of Thy per-fect love,
2. We thank Thee for the grace of home, For moth-er's love and fa-ther's care;
3. For eyes to see and ears to hear, For hands to serve and arms to lift,
4. For faith to con-quer doubt and fear, For love to an-swer ev-ery call,

We thank Thee that up--on us fall Such ten-der bless-ings from a-bove.
For friends and teach-ers—all who come Our joys and hopes and fears to share.
For shoul-ders broad and strong to bear, For feet to run on er-rands swift,
For strength to do, and will to dare, We thank Thee, O Thou Lord of all.

248

Abide With Me

EVENTIDE. 10. 10. 10. 10.

HENRY F. LYTE, 1793-1847

WILLIAM H. MONK, 1823-1889

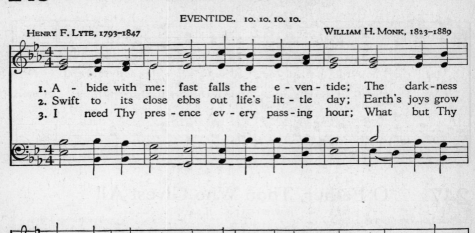

1. A - bide with me: fast falls the e - ven - tide; The dark-ness
2. Swift to its close ebbs out life's lit - tle day; Earth's joys grow
3. I need Thy pres - ence ev - ery pass-ing hour; What but Thy

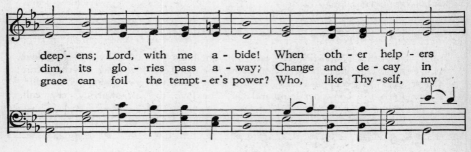

deep - ens; Lord, with me a - bide! When oth - er help - ers
dim, its glo - ries pass a - way; Change and de - cay in
grace can foil the tempt - er's power? Who, like Thy - self, my

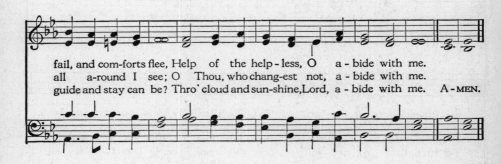

fail, and com-forts flee, Help of the help - less, O a - bide with me.
all a-round I see; O Thou, who chang-est not, a - bide with me.
guide and stay can be? Thro' cloud and sun-shine, Lord, a - bide with me. A - MEN.

4 I fear no foe, with Thee at hand to bless;
 Ills have no weight, and tears no bitterness.
 Where is death's sting? where, grave, thy victory
 I triumph still, if Thou abide with me.

5 Hold Thou Thy cross before my closing eyes;
 Shine through the gloom and point me to the skies;
 Heaven's morning breaks, and earth's vain shadows flee;
 In life, in death, O Lord, abide with me.

249 The Sands of Time Are Sinking

7. 6. 7. 6. 7. 6. 7. 5.

ANNE R. COUSIN

CHRÉTIEN D'URHAN
Har. E. F. RIMBAULT, 1816–1876

1. The sands of time are sink - ing, The dawn of heav - en breaks,
2. Oh, Christ, He is the foun - tain, The deep, sweet well of love!
3. With mer - cy and with judg - ment My web of time He wove,
4. The bride eyes not her gar - ment, But her dear bride-groom's face;

The sum - mer morn I've sighed for, The fair, sweet morn a - wakes.
The streams of earth I've tast - ed; More deep I'll drink a - bove.
And aye the dews of sor - row Were lus - tered with His love:
I will not gaze at glo - ry, But on my King of grace;

O dark hath been the mid - night, But day - spring is at hand,
There to an o - cean full - ness His mer - cy doth ex - pand,
I'll bless the hand that guid - ed, I'll bless the heart that planned
Not at the crown He giv - eth, But on His pierc - ed hand:

And glo - ry, glo - ry dwell - eth In Em - man - uel's land.
And glo - ry, glo - ry dwell - eth In Em - man - uel's land.
When throned where glo - ry dwell - eth In Em - man - uel's land.
The Lamb is all the glo - ry Of Em - man - uel's land.

250 For All the Saints

SARUM. 10. 10. 10. 4.

W. W. How, 1823–1897

Joseph Barnby, 1838–1896

1. For all the saints who from their la-bors rest, Who Thee by
2. Thou wast their rock, their for-tress, and their might; Thou, Lord, their
3. O may Thy sol-diers, faith-ful, true, and bold, Fight as the
4. O blest com-mun-ion, fel-low-ship di-vine! We fee-bly

faith be-fore the world con-fessed, Thy name, O Je-sus,
Cap-tain in the well-fought fight; Thou, in the dark-ness
saints who no-bly fought of old, And win with them the
strug-gle, they in glo-ry shine; Yet all are one in

be for ev-er blest. Al-le-lu-ia! Al-le-lu-ia!
drear, their one true Light. Al-le-lu-ia! Al-le-lu-ia!
vic-tor's crown of gold. Al-le-lu-ia! Al-le-lu-ia!
Thee, for all are Thine. Al-le-lu-ia! Al-le-lu-ia!

5 And when the strife is fierce, the warfare long,
   Steals on the ear the distant triumph song,
   And hearts are brave again, and arms are strong.

6 The golden evening brightens in the west;
   Soon, soon to faithful warriors comes Thy rest;
   Sweet is the calm of paradise the blest.

7 But lo! there breaks a yet more glorious day;
   The saints triumphant rise in bright array;
   The King of Glory passes on His way.

8 From earth's wide bounds, from ocean's farthest coast,
   Through gates of pearl streams in the countless host,
   Singing to Father, Son, and Holy Ghost.

251 God Be With You Till We Meet Again

GOD BE WITH YOU. 9. 8. 8. 9. with Refrain

JEREMIAH E. RANKIN, 1828–1904

WILLIAM G. TOMER, 1832–1896

1. God be with you till we meet again! By His coun-sels guide, up-
2. God be with you till we meet again! 'Neath His wings se - cure - ly
3. God be with you till we meet again! When life's per - ils thick con-
4. God be with you till we meet again! Keep love's ban-ner float - ing

hold you, With His sheep se-cure - ly fold you; God be with you till we
hide you, Dai - ly man-na still pro-vide you; God be with you till we
found you, Put His arms un - fail - ing round you; God be with you till we
o'er you, Smite death's threat-'ning wave be-fore you; God be with you till we

REFRAIN

meet a - gain! Till we meet! Till we meet!
Till we meet! Till we meet a - gain!

Till we meet at Je - sus' feet; Till we meet! . . .
Till we meet! Till we meet!

Till we meet! God be with you till we meet a - gain! A - MEN.
Till we meet a - gain!

May be sung without the Refrain

252 Hark, Hark, My Soul!

PILGRIMS. 11. 10. 11. 10. with Refrain

FREDERICK W. FABER, 1814-1863

HENRY SMART, 1812-1879

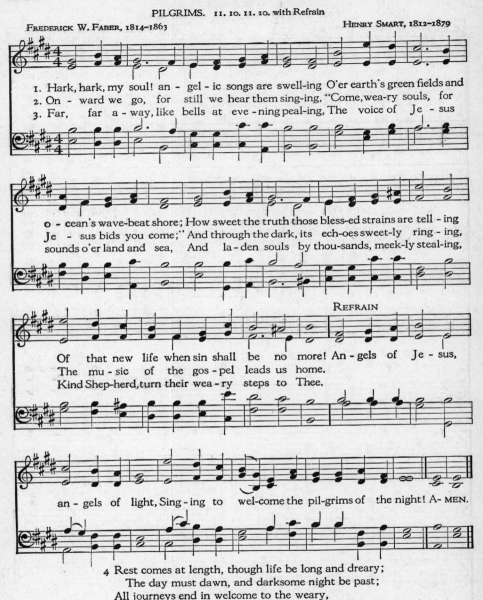

1. Hark, hark, my soul! an-gel-ic songs are swell-ing O'er earth's green fields and o-cean's wave-beat shore; How sweet the truth those bless-ed strains are tell-ing Of that new life when sin shall be no more! An-gels of Je-sus, an-gels of light, Sing-ing to wel-come the pil-grims of the night! A-MEN.

2. On-ward we go, for still we hear them sing-ing, "Come, wea-ry souls, for Je-sus bids you come;" And through the dark, its ech-oes sweet-ly ring-ing, The mu-sic of the gos-pel leads us home.

3. Far, far a-way, like bells at eve-ning peal-ing, The voice of Je-sus sounds o'er land and sea, And la-den souls by thou-sands, meek-ly steal-ing, Kind Shep-herd, turn their wea-ry steps to Thee.

4 Rest comes at length, though life be long and dreary;
   The day must dawn, and darksome night be past;
   All journeys end in welcome to the weary,
   And heaven, the heart's true home, will come at last.

5 Angels, sing on! your faithful watches keeping;
   Sing us sweet fragments of the songs above;
   Till morning's joy shall end the night of weeping,
   And life's long shadows break in cloudless love.

253 I Will Sing You a Song

ELLEN H. GATES, 1835-1920   HOME OF THE SOUL. Irregular   PHILIP PHILLIPS, 1834-1875

1. I will sing you a song of that beau-ti-ful land, The
2. O that home of the soul! In my vi-sions and dreams Its
3. That un-change-a-ble home is for you and for me, Where
4. O how sweet it will be in that beau-ti-ful land, So

far - a - way home of the soul, Where no storms ev - er beat on the
bright, jas-per walls I can see; Till I fan-cy but thin-ly the
Je - sus of Naz - a - reth stands; The King of all king-doms for
free from all sor - row and pain, With songs on our lips and with

glit - ter-ing strand, While the years of e-ter-ni-ty roll, While the
veil in - ter-venes Be - tween the fair cit - y and me, Be -
ev - er is He, And He hold-eth our crowns in His hands, And He
harps in our hands, To meet one an-oth-er a - gain! To

years of e-ter-ni-ty roll; Where no storms ev-er beat on the
tween the fair cit - y and me; Till I fan-cy but thin-ly the
hold - eth our crowns in His hands; The King of all king-doms for
meet one an-oth-er a - gain; With songs on our lips and with

glit - ter-ing strand, While the years of e-ter-ni-ty roll.
veil in - ter-venes Be - tween the fair cit - y and me.
ev - er is He, And He hold-eth our crowns in His hands.
harps in our hands, To meet one an-oth-er a - gain! A - MEN.

254 Praise to the Living God!

LEONI (YIGDAL). 6.6.8.4.D.

Jewish Doxology (Medieval);
Tr. by MAX LANDSBERG, 1845-1928 and NEWTON MANN, 1836-

1. Praise to the liv-ing God! All prais-ed be His name
2. Form-less, all love-ly forms De-clare His love-li-ness;
3. His Spir-it flow-eth free, High surg-ing where it will:
4. E-ter-nal life hath He Im-plant-ed in the soul;

Who was, and is, and is to be, For aye the same!
Ho-ly, no ho-li-ness of earth Can His ex-press.
In pro-phet's word He spake of old, He speak-eth still.
His love shall be our strength and stay While a-ges roll.

The One E-ter-nal God Ere aught that now ap-pears:
Lo, He is Lord of all! Cre-a-tion speaks His praise,
Es-tab-lished is His law, And change-less it shall stand,
Praise to the liv-ing God! All prais-ed be His name,

The First, the Last, be-yond all thought His time-less years!
And ev-ery-where, a-bove, be-low, His will o-beys.
Deep writ up-on the hu-man heart, On sea, on land.
Who was, and is, and is to be, For aye the same. A-MEN.

255 The Prince of Peace His Banner Spreads

ST. LEONARD. C. M. D.

HARRY EMERSON FOSDICK, 1878–

HENRY HILES, 1826–1904

1. The Prince of Peace His ban-ner spreads, His way-ward folk to lead
2. Lead on, O Christ! That haunt-ing song No cen-tu-ries can dim,
3. Thy par-don, Lord, for war's dark shame, Its death-strewn, blood-y fields!
4. Cleanse all our hearts from our dis-grace—We love not world, but clan!

From war's em-bat-tled hates and dreads, Its bul-warked ire and greed.
Which long a-go the heaven-ly throng Sang o-ver Beth-le-hem.
Yet thanks to Thee for souls a-flame Who dared with swords and shields!
Make clear our eyes to see our race One fam-i-ly of man.

O mar-shal us, the sons of sires Who braved the can-non's roar,
Cast down our ran-cor, fear, and pride, Ex-alt good will a-gain!
O Christ, who died to give men life, Bring that vic-to-rious hour,
Rend Thou our lit-tle tem-ple veils That cloak the truth di-vine.

To ven-ture all that peace re-quires As they dared death for war.
Our wor-ship doth Thy name de-ride, Bring we not peace to men.
When man shall use for peace, not strife, His val-or, skill, and power.
Un-til Thy might-y word pre-vails, That cries, "All souls are mine." A-MEN.

256 Hail to the Brightness

WESLEY. 11. 10. 11. 10.

THOMAS HASTINGS, 1784–1872

LOWELL MASON, 1792–1872

1. Hail to the bright-ness of Zi-on's glad morn-ing,
2. Hail to the bright-ness of Zi-on's glad morn-ing,
3. Lo, in the des-ert rich flow-ers are spring-ing,
4. See, from all lands, from the isles of the o-cean,

Joy to the lands that in dark-ness have lain!
Long by the proph-ets of Is-rael fore-told!
Streams ev-er co-pious are glid-ing a-long;
Praise to Je-ho-vah as-cend-ing on high;

Hushed be the ac-cents of sor-row and mourn-ing,
Hail to the mil-lions from bond-age re-turn-ing,
Loud from the moun-tain-tops ech-oes are ring-ing,
Fall'n are the en-gines of war and com-mo-tion,

Zi-on in tri-umph be-gins her mild reign.
Gen-tiles and Jews the blest vi-sions be-hold.
Wastes rise in ver-dure and min-gle in song.
Shouts of sal-va-tion are rend-ing the sky. A-MEN.

257 Thy Kingdom Come, O Lord

BLESSED HOME. 6. 6. 6. 6. D.

Frederick L. Hosmer, 1840–1929

John Stainer, 1840–1901

1. Thy king-dom come, O Lord, Wide-cir-cling as the sun;
2. Speed, speed the longed-for time Fore-told by rap-tured seers,

Ful-fill of old Thy word, And make the na-tions one;
The proph-e-cy sub-lime, The hope of all the years,

One in the bond of peace, The ser-vice glad and free Of
Till rise at last, to span Its firm foun-da-tions broad, The

truth and right-eous-ness, Of love and eq-ui-ty.
com-mon-wealth of man, The cit-y of our God. A-MEN.

258 I Seek Not Life's Ease and Pleasures

8. 7. 8. 7. with Chorus

Tr. by REES HARRIS, 1874–

JOHN HUGHES, 1872–1914

1. I seek not life's ease and pleas-ures, Earth-ly rich-es, pearls, nor
2. If I cher-ish earth-ly treas-ures, Swift they flee and all is
3. Morn and eve-ning my pe-ti-tion Wings its flight to heaven in

gold; Give to me a heart made hap-py, Clean and hon-est to un-fold.
vain; A clean heart en-riched with vir-tues Brings to me e-ter-nal gain.
song; In the name or my Re-deem-er, Make my heart clean, pure, and strong.

CHORUS

A clean heart o'er-flown with good-ness, Fair-er than the li-lies

bright; A clean heart for ev-er sing-ing, Sing-ing thro' the day and night. A-MEN.

Words used by permission of Rees Harris.

259 As With Gladness Men of Old

DIX. 7. 7. 7. 7. 7. 7.

WILLIAM C. DIX, 1837–1898

Abridged from a chorale by
CONRAD KOCHER, 1786–1872

1. As with glad-ness men of old Did the guid-ing star be-hold; As with joy they hailed its light, Lead-ing on-ward, beam-ing bright; So, most gra-cious Lord, may we Ev-er-more be led to Thee.

2. As with joy-ous steps they sped To that low-ly man-ger bed, There to bend the knee be-fore Him whom heaven and earth a-dore; So may we with will-ing feet Ev-er seek Thy mer-cy-seat.

3. As they of-fered gifts most rare At that man-ger rude and bare, So may we with ho-ly joy, Pure, and free from sin's al-loy, All our cost-liest treas-ures bring, Christ, to Thee, our Heaven-ly King.

4. Ho-ly Je-sus, ev-ery day Keep us in the nar-row way; And, when earth-ly things are past, Bring our ran-somed souls at last Where they need no star to guide, Where no clouds Thy glo-ry hide.

A-MEN.

260 O God, in Restless Living

RUTHERFORD. 7. 6. 7. 6. 7. 6. 7. 5.

HARRY EMERSON FOSDICK, 1878–

Adapted from CHRÉTIEN URHAN
by EDWARD F. RIMBAULT

1. O God, in rest-less liv-ing We lose our spir-its' peace.
2. Teach us, be-yond our striv-ing, The rich re-wards of rest.
3. Re-cep-tive make our spir-its, Our need is to be still;
4. We grow not wise by strug-gling, We gain but things by strain.

Calm our un-wise con-fu-sion, Bid Thou our cla-mor cease.
Who does not live se-rene-ly Is nev-er deep-ly blest.
As dawn fades flick-ering can-dle So dim our anx-ious will.
We cease to wa-ter gar-dens, When comes Thy plen-teous rain.

Let anx-ious hearts grow qui-et, Like pools at eve-ning still,
O tran-quil, ra-diant Sun-light, Bring Thou our lives to flower,
Re-veal Thy ra-diance through us, Thine am-ple strength re-lease.
O beau-ti-fy our spir-its In rest-ful-ness from strife;

Till Thy re-flect-ed heav-ens All our spir-its fill.
Less wea-ried with our ef-fort More a-ware of power.
Not ours but Thine the tri-umph, In the power of peace.
En-rich our souls in se-cret With a-bun-dant life. A-MEN.

261 God of the Nations

NATIONAL HYMN. 10. 10. 10. 10.

WALTER RUSSELL BOWIE, 1882–   GEORGE W. WARREN, 1828–1902

Trumpets, before
each verse

1. God of the Na - tions, who from dawn of days
2. Thine an - cient might re-buked the Pha-raoh's boast,
3. Thy hand has led a - cross the hun - gry sea
4. Then, for Thy grace to grow in broth -er - hood

Hast led Thy peo - ple in their widen - ing ways,
Thou wast the shield for Is - rael's march - ing host,
The ea - ger peo - ples flock - ing to be free,
For hearts a - flame to serve Thy des - tined good,

Thro' whose deep pur - pose stran - ger thou - sands stand
And, all the a - ges through, past crumb - ling throne
And from the breeds of earth, Thy si - lent sway
For faith, and will to win what faith shall see,

Here in the bor - ders of our prom - ised land.
And bro - ken fet - ter, Thou hast brought Thine own.
Fash - ions the Na - tion of the broaden - ing day.
God of Thy peo - ple, hear us cry to Thee! A - MEN.

Words used by permission of Walter Russell Bowie.

262 Christian, Rise, and Act Thy Creed

INNOCENTS. 7. 7. 7. 7.

F. A. ROLLO RUSSELL

Arr. from an old French melody,
xiii C., and G. F. HANDEL

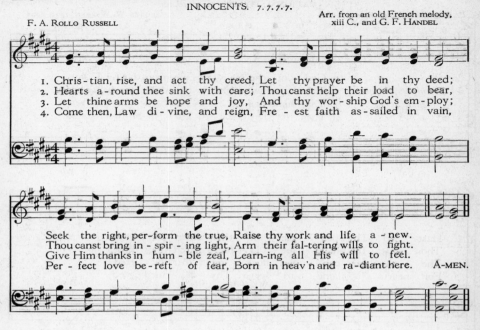

1. Chris - tian, rise, and act thy creed, Let thy prayer be in thy deed;
2. Hearts a - round thee sink with care; Thou canst help their load to bear,
3. Let thine arms be hope and joy, And thy wor - ship God's em - ploy;
4. Come then, Law di - vine, and reign, Fre - est faith as - sailed in vain,

Seek the right, per - form the true, Raise thy work and life a - new.
Thou canst bring in - spir - ing light, Arm their fal - tering wills to fight.
Give Him thanks in hum - ble zeal, Learn - ing all His will to feel.
Per - fect love be - reft of fear, Born in heav'n and ra - diant here. A-MEN.

263 Father of Lights

ANCIENT OF DAYS. 11. 10. 11. 10.

ELIZABETH WILSON and HELEN THOBURN

J. ALBERT JEFFERY, 1851-1928

1. Fa - ther of lights, in whom there is no shad - ow,
2. Glad for the cause that binds our lives to - geth - er,
3. Light of the world, through whom we know the Fa - ther!
4. Thou art the Christ! To Thee we own al - le - giance.

Giv - er of ev - ery good and per - fect gift! With one ac - cord we
Thro' Thee u - nit - ed, wor - ship - ing as one: Glad for the crown - ing
Pour out up - on us Thine a - bid - ing love, That we may know its
May our de - vo - tion sweep from sea to sea, Ev - en as we, the

Father of Lights

seek Thy ho - ly pres-ence, Glad-ly our hearts to Thee in praise we lift.
gift that Thou hast giv - en, Send-ing, to light the world, Thine on - ly Son.
depth and height and splen-dor, That heaven may come to earth from heaven above.
gift from Thee re-ceiv-ing, Joy-ful-ly min - is - ter that gift for Thee. A-MEN.

264 Lord, I Have Shut the Door

SANCTUARY. 6 4 6 4 D.

W. M. R.

WILLIAM M. RUNYAN, 1870–

1. Lord, I have shut the door, Speak now the word Which, in the
2. Lord, I have shut the door, Here do I bow; Speak, for my
3. In this blest qui - et - ness Clam - or - ings cease; Here in Thy
4. Lord, I have shut the door, Strength-en my heart; Yon - der a -

din and throng, Could not be heard. Hushed now my in - ner heart,
soul, at - tent, Turns to Thee now. Re - buke Thou what is vain,
pres - ence dwells In - fi - nite peace; Yon - der the strife and cry,
waits the task— I share a part. On - ly thro' grace be-stowed

Whis - per Thy will, While I have come a - part, While all is still.
Coun - sel my soul, Thy ho - ly will re - veal, My will con - trol.
Yon - der the sin: Lord, I have shut the door, Thou art with - in!
May I be true; Here, while a - lone with Thee, My strength re - new.

265 By Cool Siloam's Shady Rill

SILOAM. C.M.

REGINALD HEBER, 1783–1826

ISAAC B. WOODBURY, 1819–1858

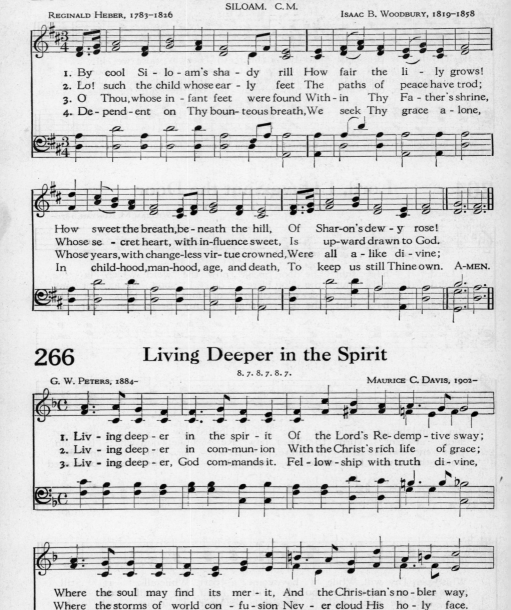

1. By cool Si - lo - am's sha - dy rill How fair the li - ly grows!
2. Lo! such the child whose ear - ly feet The paths of peace have trod;
3. O Thou, whose in - fant feet were found With - in Thy Fa - ther's shrine,
4. De - pend - ent on Thy boun - teous breath, We seek Thy grace a - lone,

How sweet the breath, be - neath the hill, Of Shar - on's dew - y rose!
Whose se - cret heart, with in - fluence sweet, Is up - ward drawn to God.
Whose years, with change - less vir - tue crowned, Were all a - like di - vine;
In child - hood, man - hood, age, and death, To keep us still Thine own. A - MEN.

266 Living Deeper in the Spirit

8. 7. 8. 7. 8. 7.

G. W. PETERS, 1884–

MAURICE C. DAVIS, 1902–

1. Liv - ing deep - er in the spir - it Of the Lord's Re - demp - tive sway;
2. Liv - ing deep - er in com - mun - ion With the Christ's rich life of grace;
3. Liv - ing deep - er, God com - mands it. Fel - low - ship with truth di - vine,

Where the soul may find its mer - it, And the Chris - tian's no - bler way,
Where the storms of world con - fu - sion Nev - er cloud His ho - ly face.
Hope for na - tions e'er de - mand it; Love's true way of life to find.

Living Deeper in the Spirit

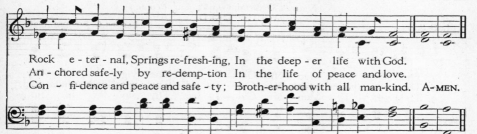

Rock e - ter - nal, Springs re-fresh-ing, In the deep - er life with God.
An - chored safe-ly by re-demp-tion In the life of peace and love.
Con - fi-dence and peace and safe - ty; Broth-er-hood with all man-kind. A-MEN.

Words used by permission of G. W. Peters.
Music used by permission of Maurice C. Davis.

267   O Thou God of My Salvation

REGENT SQUARE. 8s. 7s. 6l.

THOMAS OLIVER

HENRY SMART, 1813–1879

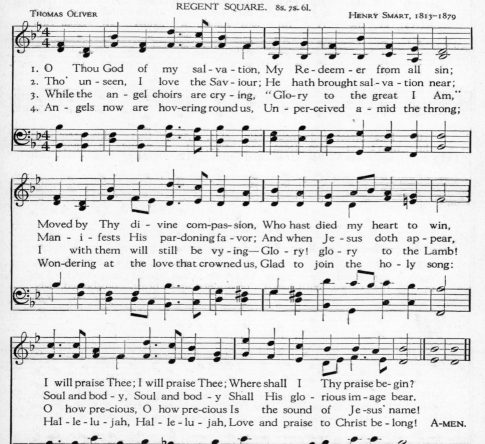

1. O Thou God of my sal - va - tion, My Re - deem - er from all sin;
2. Tho' un - seen, I love the Sav - iour; He hath brought sal - va - tion near;
3. While the an - gel choirs are cry - ing, "Glo - ry to the great I Am,"
4. An - gels now are hov-ering round us, Un - per-ceived a - mid the throng;

Moved by Thy di - vine com-pas-sion, Who hast died my heart to win,
Man - i - fests His par-doning fa - vor; And when Je - sus doth ap - pear,
I with them will still be vy - ing—Glo - ry! glo - ry to the Lamb!
Won-dering at the love that crowned us, Glad to join the ho - ly song:

I will praise Thee; I will praise Thee; Where shall I Thy praise be-gin?
Soul and bod - y, Soul and bod - y Shall His glo - rious im - age bear.
O how pre-cious, O how pre-cious Is the sound of Je-sus' name!
Hal - le - lu - jah, Hal - le - lu - jah, Love and praise to Christ be-long! A-MEN.

268 Thou Strong Young Man of Galilee

(A Hymn of Dedication for Young People)
YOUTH. L. M. D.

L. G. S.

LLOYDE G. STROUSE, 1898–

1. Thou strong young Man of Gal - i - lee, The vig - or of Thy
2. Thou wise young Man of Gal - i - lee, Thy wis - dom stands to
3. Thou ho - ly Man of Gal - i - lee, Thy sin - less life in -

youth I see, As Thou didst walk with man - ly stride The
chal - lenge me. As Thou didst shed the truth of God, And
spires in me A val - iant stand a - gainst all wrong, And

vil - lage street and moun - tain side. And, that this teem - ing
lift man's vi - sion from the clod, I would e - quip my
cour - age to be true and strong De - spite temp - ta - tions

power of mine Be set to no - ble works, like Thine, My
open - ing mind To guide and lift con - fused man - kind; This
of the crowd. With hands un - stained and heart un - bowed, My

strength I con - se - crate to Thee, Thou strong young Man of Gal - i - lee.
mind I con - se - crate to Thee, Thou wise young Man of Gal - i - lee.
life I con - se - crate to Thee, Di - vine young Man of Gal - i - lee.

269 We Thank Thee for the Brawny Arm

8s. 6s.

W. M. R.

WILLIAM M. RUNYAN, 1870–

1. We thank Thee for the brawn-y arm, And for the fer-tile brain,
2. We thank Thee for cre-a-tive hands That serve a na-tion's need,
3. Thee do we praise for all the strong Who bat-tle brave-ly on,

For nerves that quake not in the storm, That mock at stress and strain;
That scat-ter seed, that reap the lands For that on which we feed;
Who stand a-gainst the false, the wrong, And shall, till life is done.

We thank Thee for the thews that bear, With rug-ged strength, the
We thank Thee for the val-iant mind That brave-ly seeks Thy
Thy-self, the God of strength and power, Art giv-er of Thy

weight of care, That wea-ri-ness dis-dain.
paths to find, And, find-ing, dares to lead.
grace each hour— To Thee be praise a-lone. A - MEN.

270 It May Not Be on the Mountain's Height

FIDELITY. P. M.

MARY BROWN

CARRIE E. ROUNSEFELL

1. It may not be on the moun-tain's height, Or o - ver the storm-y sea;
2. Per-haps to-day there are lov - ing words Which Je-sus would have me speak;
3. There's sure-ly some-where a low - ly place In earth's har-vest field so wide,

It may not be at the bat - tle's front, My Lord will have need of me;
There may be now in the paths of sin Some wan-d'rer whom I should seek;
Where I may la - bor thro' life's short day, For Je - sus the Cru - ci - fied;

But if by a still small voice He calls To paths that I do not know,
O Sav - iour, if Thou wilt be my guide, Tho' dark and rug-ged the way,
So trust-ing my all to Thy ten - der care, And know-ing Thou lov-est me,

I'll an-swer, dear Lord, with my hand in Thine, I'll go where you want me to go.
My voice shall ech - o Thy mes-sage sweet, I'll say what you want me to say.
I'll do Thy will with a heart sin-cere, I'll be what you want me to be.

271 Not I, But Christ

A. A. F.

A. B. Simpson

1. Not I but Christ, be hon-ored, loved, ex-alt-ed; Not I, but
2. Not I but Christ, to gen-tly soothe in sor-row; Not I, but
3. Christ, on-ly Christ, no i-dle word e'er fall-ing; Christ, on-ly
4. Not I but Christ, my ev-ery need sup-ply-ing; Not I, but

Christ, be seen, be known, be heard; Not I, but Christ, in
Christ, to wipe the fall-ing tear: Not I, but Christ, to
Christ, no need-less bust-ling sound; Christ, on-ly Christ, no
Christ, my strength and health to be; Christ, on-ly Christ, for

ev-ery look and ac-tion, Not I, but Christ, in ev-ery tho't and word.
lift the wea-ry bur-den; Not I, but Christ, to hush a-way all fear.
self-im-por-tant bear-ing; Christ, on-ly Christ, no trace of "I" be found.
bod-y, soul, and spir-it; Christ, on-ly Christ, live then Thy life in me.

CHORUS. *Slower*

O to be saved from my-self, dear Lord, O to be lost in Thee,

O that it might be no more I, but Christ, that lives in me.

272 Tell Me the Old, Old Story

7.6.7.6. D.

Katherine Hankey, 1834–1911

William H. Doane, 1832–1916

1. Tell me the old, old story, Of un-seen things a - bove,
2. Tell me the story slow - ly, That I may take it in—
3. Tell me the story soft - ly, With ear - nest tones and grave;
4. Tell me the same old sto - ry, When you have cause to fear

Of Je - sus and His glo - ry, Of Je - sus and His love;
That won-der - ful re - demp-tion, God's rem - e - dy for sin;
Re -mem - ber I'm the sin - ner Whom Je - sus came to save;
That this world's emp - ty glo - ry Is cost - ing me too dear;

Tell me the sto - ry sim - ply, As to a lit - tle child,
Tell me the sto - ry oft - en, For I for - get so soon,
Tell me the sto - ry al - ways, If you would real - ly be,
Yes, and when that world's glo - ry Is dawn-ing on my soul,

For I am weak and wea - ry, And help - less and de - filed.
The "ear - ly dew" of morn-ing Has passed a - way at noon.
In an - y time of trou - ble, A com - fort - er to me.
Tell me the old, old sto - ry: "Christ Je - sus makes thee whole."

Tell Me the Old, Old Story

CHORUS

Tell me the old, old sto - ry, Tell me the old, old sto - ry,

Tell me the old, old sto - ry Of Je - sus and His love.

273 Rise, Crowned With Light

10. 10. 10. 10.

ALEXANDER POPE, 1688–1744
Stanza 3, line 4, alt.
With majesty

Russian Hymn
ALEXIS T. LWOFF

1. Rise, crowned with light, im - pe - rial cit - y, rise! Ex - alt thy
2. See a long race thy spa - cious courts a - dorn: See fu - ture
3. The seas shall waste, the skies in smoke de - cay, Rocks fall to

tow - ering head and lift thine eyes! See heaven its spar - kling por - tals
sons, and daugh-ters yet un - born, In crowd-ing ranks on ev - ery
dust, and moun-tains melt a - way; But fixed His word, His sav - ing

wide dis - play, And break up - on thee in a flood of day!
side a - rise, De - mand-ing life, im-pa-tient for the skies.
power re - mains; Thy realm shall last, Thy own Mes-si - ah reigns! A-MEN.

274 O Christ, My Lord, Whose Perfect Life

FLEMMING. 8.8.8.6.

FRANK MASON NORTH, 1850–1935   FRIEDRICH F. FLEMMING, 1778–1813

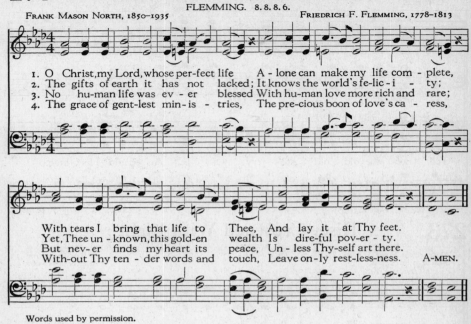

1. O Christ, my Lord, whose per-fect life   A - lone can make my life com - plete,
2. The gifts of earth it has not   lacked; It knows the world's fe-lic-i - ty;
3. No   hu-man life was ev - er   blessed With hu-man love more rich and   rare;
4. The grace of gent-lest min-is - tries,   The pre-cious boon of love's ca - ress,

With tears I   bring that life to   Thee, And lay it   at Thy feet.
Yet, Thee un - known, this gold-en   wealth Is   dire-ful pov-er - ty.
But nev-er   finds my heart its   peace, Un - less Thy-self art there.
With-out Thy ten - der words and   touch, Leave on-ly rest-less-ness.   A-MEN.

Words used by permission.

275 Lord, Through Changing Days, Unchanging

REGENT SQUARE. 8.7.8.7.8.7.

WALTER RUSSELL BOWIE   HENRY SMART, 1813–1879

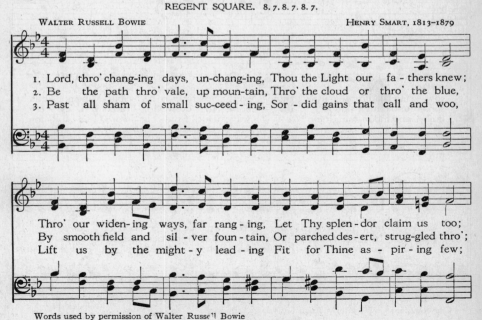

1. Lord, thro' chang-ing days, un-chang-ing, Thou the Light our   fa - thers knew;
2. Be   the path thro' vale, up moun-tain, Thro' the cloud or   thro' the blue,
3. Past   all sham of small suc-ceed - ing, Sor - did gains that call and woo,

Thro' our widen-ing   ways, far rang - ing, Let Thy splen-dor claim us   too;
By smooth field and   sil - ver foun - tain, Or parched des - ert, strug-gled thro';
Lift   us   by the might - y   lead - ing Fit for Thine as - pir - ing few;

Words used by permission of Walter Russell Bowie

Lord, Through Changing Days, Unchanging

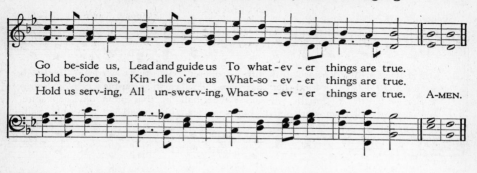

Go be-side us, Lead and guide us To what-ev - er things are true.
Hold be-fore us, Kin-dle o'er us What-so - ev - er things are true.
Hold us serv-ing, All un-swerv-ing, What-so - ev - er things are true. A-MEN.

276 Take Thou Our Minds, Dear Lord

10. 10. 10. 10.

WILLIAM H. FOULKES, 1877–   CALVIN W. LAUFER, 1874–

In moderate time

1. Take Thou our minds, dear Lord, we hum-bly pray; Give us the
2. Take Thou our hearts, O Christ, they are Thine own; Come Thou with-
3. Take Thou our wills, Most High! Hold Thou full sway; Have in our
4. Take Thou our-selves, O Lord, heart, mind, and will; Thro' our sur-

mind of Christ each pass-ing day; Teach us to know the truth
in our souls and claim Thy throne; Help us to shed a - broad
in - most souls Thy per - fect way; Guard Thou each sa - cred hour
ren - dered souls Thy plans ful - fill. We yield our-selves to Thee—

that sets us free; Grant us in all our tho'ts to hon - or Thee.
Thy death-less love; Use us to make the earth like heaven a - bove.
from self - ish ease; Guide Thou our or-dered lives as Thou dost please.
time, tal - ents, all; We hear, and hence-forth heed, Thy sov-ereign call. A-MEN.

277 Forward Still! With Face Full Forward

8. 7. 8. 7. D.

W. M. R.

WILLIAM M. RUNYAN, 1870–

1. For-ward still! With face full for-ward, Let us press tow'rd yon-der height,
2. For-ward still! A kind-lier pas-sion, Shall earth's trou-bled bos-om warm;
3. For-ward still! A might-y con-clave Shall in that great day con-spire
4. For-ward still! Tho' dark-some hours Seem to spread a sa-ble pall—

There to view a fair-er morn-ing Ban-ish-ing op-pres-sion's night.
Weap-ons wrought for hurt and slaugh-ter Shall no long-er fling a-larm.
Forth to pour its hal-lowed an-them, Kin-dled by love's ho-ly fire.
Morn-ing breaks, 'tis sure-ly com-ing, When the pow'rs of night shall fall.

For-ward still, for day is dawn-ing When the reign of hate shall cease—
Seeds of love shall yield a har-vest That shall ev-er-more in-crease
Hate and all its brood of sor-rows—All the earth shall frown on these
Morn-ing breaks, its won-drous heal-ing Shall of sor-row mean sur-cease,

Not thro' might of sword-girt mon-archs, But thro' Christ, the Prince of Peace.
Bless-ed hope, we dare to claim it, Thro' our Christ, the Prince of Peace.
In that ho-ly, hap-py mor-row—Day of Christ, the Prince of Peace.
And the world shall hail the glo-ry Of our Christ, the Prince of Peace. A-MEN.

278   I Hear Thy Welcome Voice

WELCOME VOICE. S. M. with Refrain

L. H.

Moderate

LEWIS HARTSOUGH, 1828–1919

1. I hear Thy wel-come voice That calls me, Lord, to Thee,
2. 'Tis Je - sus calls me on To per - fect faith and love,
3. 'Tis Je - sus who con - firms The bless - ed work with - in,
4. And He the wit - ness gives To loy - al hearts and free,

For cleans - ing in Thy pre-cious blood That flowed on Cal - va - ry.
To per - fect hope, and peace, and trust, For earth and heaven a - bove.
By add - ing grace to wel-comed grace, Where reigned the power of sin.
That ev - ery prom - ise is ful-filled, If faith but brings the plea.

REFRAIN

I am com - ing, Lord! Com - ing now to Thee! Wash me, cleanse me,

in the blood That flowed on Cal - va - ry. A - MEN.

279 O God, the Rock of Ages

GREENLAND. 7. 6. 7. 6. D.

EDWARD H. BICKERSTETH

LAUSANNE PSALTER

1. O God, the Rock of A - ges, Who ev - er - more hast been,
2. Our years are like the shad - ows On sun - ny hills that lie,
3. O Thou, who dost not slum - ber, Whose light grows nev - er pale,

What time the tem - pest ra - ges, Our dwell - ing place se - rene;
Or grass - es in the mead - ows That blos - som but to die:
Teach us a - right to num - ber Our years be - fore they fail.

Be - fore Thy first cre - a - tions, O Lord, the same as now,
A sleep, a dream, a sto - ry By stran - gers quick - ly told,
On us Thy mer - cy light - en, On us Thy good - ness rest,

To end - less gen - er - a - tions The ev - er - last - ing Thou!
An un - re - main - ing glo - ry Of things that soon are old.
And let Thy Spir - it bright - en The hearts Thy - self hath blessed. A-MEN.

280 Show Us Thy Way, O God

LAKE ENON. S. M.

JOHN HAYNES HOLMES, 1879–

ISAAC B. WOODBURY, 1819–1858

1. Show us Thy way, O God! Our feet have wan-dered far.
2. Teach us Thy word, O God! Sub-due earth's rack-ing din;
3. Tell us Thy will, O God! Our own we can-not trust.
4. Thy way, Thy word, Thy will— These are our sur-est guides

We seek the path Thy saints have trod, Where peace and beau-ty are.
That we may hear at home, a-broad, The still small voice with-in.
We seek the sum-mons of Thy rod To raise us from the dust.
To bring us where Thy spir-it still In ho-li-ness a-bides. A-MEN.

Words used by permission of John Haynes Holmes.

281 God of the Searching Mind

MORNINGTON. S. M.

JOHN HAYNES HOLMES, 1879–

Arr. from a chant by
GARRET WELLESLEY, 1735–1781

1. God of the search-ing mind, Help us Thy Truth to find,
2. God of the lov-ing heart, Teach us our hum-ble part—
3. God of th' as-pir-ing soul, Point on-ward to Thy goal,
4. Our Teach-er and our Friend, More of Thy wis-dom lend,

That we may gaze, from er-ror free, With sin-gle eye on Thee.
To live in kind-ness un-to all Thy crea-tures great and small.
That we, with ea-ger strength and grace, May run the spir-it's race.
That we in vir-tue may in-crease, And find at last Thy peace. A-MEN.

Words used by permission of John Haynes Holmes.

282 Swing Low, Sweet Chariot

Fine

Swing low, sweet char-i-ot, Com-ing for to car-ry me home, Swing low, sweet char-i-ot, Com-ing for to car-ry me home.

1. I looked o - - ver Jor - dan, and what did I see,
2. If you get there be - fore I do,
3. I'm some - - times up, I'm some - times down,

Com - ing for to car - ry me home? A band of an - gels
Com - ing for to car - ry me home; Tell all my friends I'm
Com - ing for to car - ry me home; But still my soul feels

com - ing af - ter me, Com-ing for to car - ry me home.
com - ing too, Com-ing for to car - ry me home.
heav - en - ly bound, Com-ing for to car - ry me home.

Musical arrangement used by permission of John W. Work.

283 They Led My Lord Away

Doloroso

They led my Lord a-way, a-way, a-way; They
led my Lord a-way, O tell me where to find Him. find Him.

1. The Jews and Ro-mans, in - a one band, Tell me where to find Him;
2. They led Him up to Pi - late's bar, Tell me where to find Him;
3. Old Pi - late said, "I wash my hands," Tell me where to find Him;

They cru - ci - fied the Son of man, Tell me where to find Him.
But the Jews could not con-demn Him there, Tell me where to find Him.
"I find no fault in this just Man," Tell me where to find Him.

Musical arrangement used by permission of John W. Work.

284   Lord, I Want to Be a Christian

1. Lord, I want to be a Chris-tian In-a my heart, in-a my heart,Lord, I want to be a Chris-tian In-a my heart.
2. Lord, I want to be more lov-ing In-a my heart, in-a my heart,Lord, I want to be more lov-ing In-a my heart.
3. Lord, I want to be more ho-ly In-a my heart, in-a my heart,Lord, I want to be more ho-ly In-a my heart.
4. I don't want to be like Ju-das In-a my heart, in-a my heart, I don't want to be like Ju-das In-a my heart.
5. Lord, I want to be like Je-sus In-a my heart, in-a my heart,Lord, I want to be like Je-sus In-a my heart.

REFRAIN

In-a my heart, ... In-a my heart, ...
In-a my heart,   In-a my heart,

Lord, I want to be a Chris-tian In-a my heart.

285 Balm in Gilead

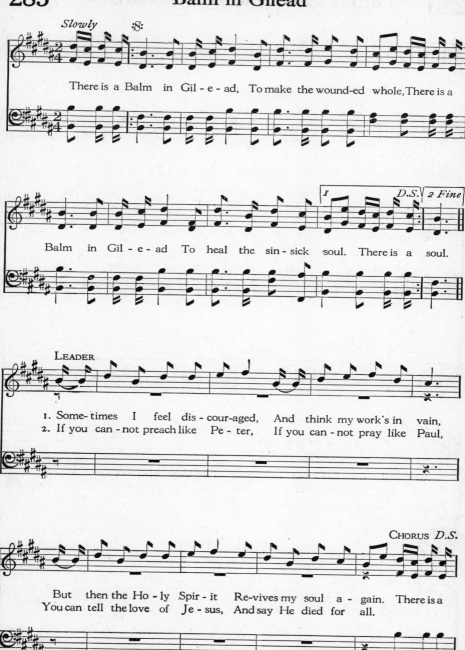

There is a Balm in Gil - e - ad, To make the wound-ed whole, There is a Balm in Gil - e - ad To heal the sin - sick soul. There is a soul.

LEADER

1. Some-times I feel dis - cour-aged, And think my work's in vain,
2. If you can-not preach like Pe - ter, If you can-not pray like Paul,

CHORUS D.S.

But then the Ho - ly Spir - it Re-vives my soul a - gain. There is a
You can tell the love of Je - sus, And say He died for all.

Musical arrangement used by permission of John W. Work.

286 Let Us Cheer the Weary Traveler

Let us cheer the wea-ry trav-el-er, Cheer the wea-ry trav-el-er,

Let us cheer the wea-ry trav-el-er, A-long the heav-en-ly way.

Fine

1. I'll take my gos-pel trum-pet, And I'll be-gin to blow,
2. And if you meet with cross-es And tri-als on the way,

D.C.

And if my Sav-iour helps me, I'll blow wher-ev-er I go.
Just put your trust in Je-sus, And don't for-get to pray.

Musical arrangement used by permission of John W. Work.

287 Steal Away

Irregular

Negro Melody

mp CHORUS

mp

Steal a-way, steal a-way, Steal a-way to Je-sus. Steal a-way, steal a-way home,

Steal Away

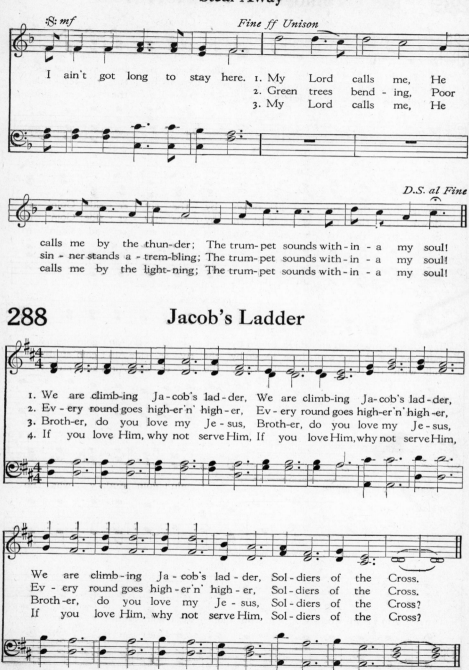

:S: mf   *Fine ff Unison*

I ain't got long to stay here.
1. My Lord calls me, He
2. Green trees bend-ing, Poor
3. My Lord calls me, He

D.S. al Fine

calls me by the thun-der; The trum-pet sounds with-in - a my soul!
sin - ner stands a - trem-bling; The trum-pet sounds with-in - a my soul!
calls me by the light-ning; The trum-pet sounds with-in - a my soul!

288 Jacob's Ladder

1. We are climb-ing Ja-cob's lad-der, We are climb-ing Ja-cob's lad-der,
2. Ev - ery round goes high-er'n' high-er, Ev - ery round goes high-er'n' high-er,
3. Broth-er, do you love my Je - sus, Broth-er, do you love my Je - sus,
4. If you love Him, why not serve Him, If you love Him, why not serve Him,

We are climb-ing Ja-cob's lad - der, Sol-diers of the Cross.
Ev - ery round goes high-er'n' high - er, Sol-diers of the Cross.
Broth-er, do you love my Je - sus, Sol-diers of the Cross?
If you love Him, why not serve Him, Sol-diers of the Cross?

Musical arrangement used by permission of John W. Work.

289 Study War No More

LEADER   CHORUS

1. Goin' to lay down my sword an' shield Down by the riv-er-side,
2. Goin' to put on my long white robe Down by the riv-er-side,
3. Goin' to talk with the Prince of Peace Down by the riv-er-side,

down by the riv-er-side, down by the riv-er-side; Goin' to
down by the riv-er-side, down by the riv-er-side; Goin' to
down by the riv-er-side, down by the riv-er-side; Goin' to

lay down my sword an' shield Down by the riv-er-side, Ain't goin' stud-y
put on my long white robe Down by the riv-er-side, Ain't goin' stud-y
talk with the Prince of Peace Down by the riv-er-side, Ain't goin' stud-y

war no more, ... I ain't goin' stud-y war no

stud-y war no more,

more, Ain't goin' stud-y war no more, ain't goin' stud-y war no

Musical arrangement used by permission of John W. Work.

Study War No More

more. . . . . . ., I ain't goin' stud-y war no more, Ain't goin'

stud-y war no more,

stud-y war no more, Ain't goin' stud-y war no more.

290

All I Want

All I want, All I want, All I want is a lit-tle more faith in

Je-sus. 1. Rise up, ser-vant, get your crown, Lit-tle more faith in Je-sus.
2. Tho' you see me going a-long so, Lit-tle more faith in Je-sus.

By your Sav-iour's side sit down, Lit-tle more faith in Je-sus.
I have my trials here be-low, Lit-tle more faith in Je-sus.

Musical arrangement used by permission of John W. Work.

291 Were You There?

1. Were you there when they cru - ci - fied my Lord? Were you there? Were you
2. Were you there when they nailed Him to the tree? Were you there? Were you
3. Were you there when they pierc'd Him in the side? Were you there? Were you
4. Were you there when they laid Him in the tomb? Were you there? Were you

there when they cru - ci - fied my Lord? Oh . . . .
there when they nailed Him to the tree? Oh . . . .
there when they pierced Him in the side? Oh . . . .
there when they laid Him in the tomb? Oh . . . .

some - times it caus - es me to trem - ble, trem - ble,
some - times it caus - es me to trem - ble, trem - ble,
some - times it caus - es me to trem - ble, trem - ble,
some - times it caus - es me to trem - ble, trem - ble,

trem - ble, Were you there when they cru - ci - fied my Lord?
trem - ble, Were you there when they nailed Him to the tree?
trem - ble, Were you there when they pierced Him in the side?
trem - ble, Were you there when they laid Him in the tomb?

Musical arrangement used by permission of John W. Work.

292 This Is My Story

This is my sto - ry, this is my song, Prais - ing my

Sav - iour all the day long; This is my sto - ry, this is my

song, Prais - ing my Sav - iour all the day long. A - MEN.

293 His Yoke Is Easy

R. E. HUDSON

His yoke is eas - y, His bur - den is light, I've found it so, I've found it so;

He lead - eth me, by day and by night, Where liv - ing wa - ters flow.

294 Let the Beauty of Jesus Be Seen in Me

ALBERT ORSBORN

TOM JONES

Let the beau-ty of Je-sus be seen in me, All His won-der-ful pas-sion and pu - ri - ty; O Thou Spir - it di - vine, All my na-ture re-fine, Till the beau-ty of Je-sus be seen in me.

Copyright property of the Rev. Tom Jones. (Hall-Mack Co., agent.)

295 O Lord and Master of Us All

SERENITY. C.M.

JOHN G. WHITTIER, 1807–1892

WILLIAM V. WALLACE, 1814–1865

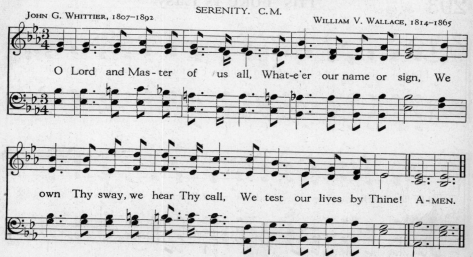

O Lord and Mas-ter of us all, What-e'er our name or sign, We own Thy sway, we hear Thy call, We test our lives by Thine! A-MEN.

296 Gloria in Excelsis Deo

REFRAIN

Glo - - - - - ri - a in ex-cel-sis De - o, Glo - - - - - - - ri - a in ex - cel - sis De - o!

297 Holy, Holy, Holy

Ho - ly, ho - ly, ho - ly, Lord God of Hosts!

Heaven and earth are full of Thee! Heaven and earth are

prais - ing Thee, O Lord most High! A - MEN.

298 The Lord Is in His Holy Temple

KARL P. HARRINGTON, 1861–

In unison or harmony

The Lord is in His ho-ly tem-ple; let all the earth keep si-lence be-fore Him.

299 The Lord Bless Thee and Keep Thee

LUCY RIDER MEYER

The Lord bless thee and keep thee! The Lord make His face shine up-

on thee, and be gra-cious un-to thee, And be

gra-cious un-to thee: The Lord lift up His coun-te-nance, His

And give thee peace.

coun-te-nance up-on thee, and give thee peace.

300

Holy, Holy, Holy

SANCTUS

From "The Holy City"
Alfred R. Gaul, 1837–1913

Ho - ly, ho - ly, ho - ly, Lord of hosts:

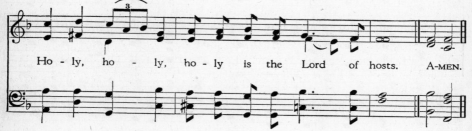

Ho - ly, ho - ly, ho - ly is the Lord of hosts. A-MEN.

301

All Things Come of Thee, O Lord

Offertory Sentence

Arr. from Beethoven

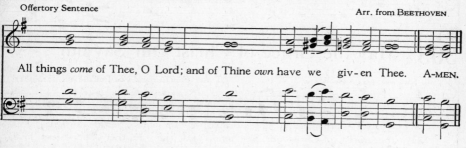

All things *come* of Thee, O Lord; and of Thine *own* have we giv-en Thee. A-MEN.

302

DRESDEN AMEN

303

THREEFOLD AMEN

A - men, A - men.

A - men, A - men, A - men.

304 Praise God, from Whom All Blessings Flow

DOXOLOGY

Thomas Ken, 1637-1711

Melody from Genevan Psalter, 1551

Praise God, from whom all bless - ings flow; Praise

Him, all crea - tures here be - low; Praise Him a - bove, ye

heaven - ly host; Praise Fa - ther, Son, and Ho - ly Ghost!

305 May the Grace of Christ Our Saviour

SARDIS. 8. 7. 8. 7.

John Newton, 1725-1807

Arr. from Ludwig van Beethoven, 1770-1827

May the grace of Christ our Sav - iour And the Fa - ther's bound-less love,

With the Ho - ly Spir - it's fa - vor, Rest up - on us from a - bove. A - MEN.

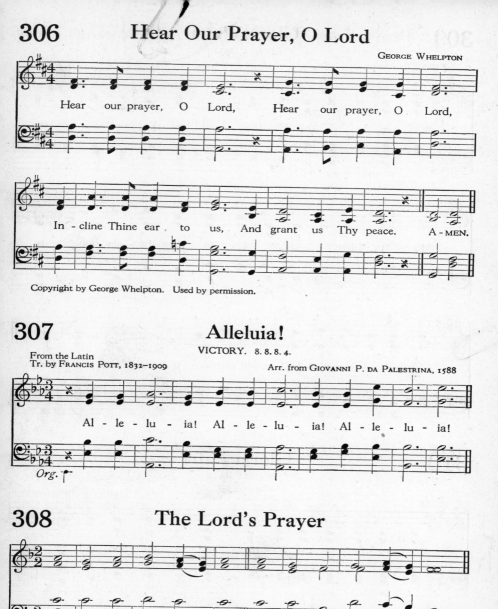

306   # Hear Our Prayer, O Lord

GEORGE WHELPTON

Hear our prayer, O Lord, Hear our prayer, O Lord,

In-cline Thine ear to us, And grant us Thy peace. A-MEN.

307   # Alleluia!

VICTORY. 8. 8. 8. 4.

From the Latin
Tr. by FRANCIS POTT, 1832–1909

Arr. from GIOVANNI P. DA PALESTRINA, 1588

Al - le - lu - ia! Al - le - lu - ia! Al - le - lu - ia!

Org.

308   # The Lord's Prayer

1 Our Father, who art in heaven, | hallowed | be thy | name; ‖ thy kingdom come, thy will be done on | earth, as it | is in | heaven;

2 Give us this | day our | daily | bread; ‖ and forgive us our trespasses, as we forgive | them that | trespass a- | gainst us.

3 And lead us not into temptation, but de- | liver | us from | evil; ‖ for thine is the king-dom, and the power, and the | glory, for | ever. A- | men.

309

Gloria Patri
GLORIA PATRI
(First Tune)

CHARLES MEINEKE, 1782–1850

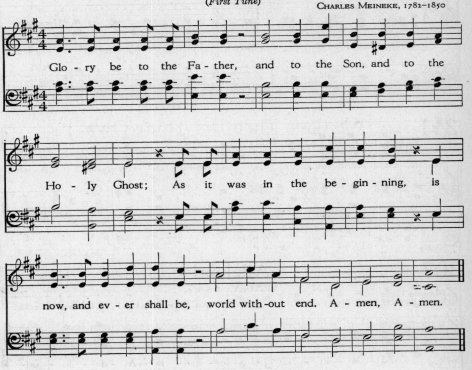

Glo - ry be to the Fa - ther, and to the Son, and to the

Ho - ly Ghost; As it was in the be - gin - ning, is

now, and ev - er shall be, world with - out end. A - men, A - men.

310

Gloria Patri
GLORIA PATRI
(Second Tune)

HENRY W. GREATOREX

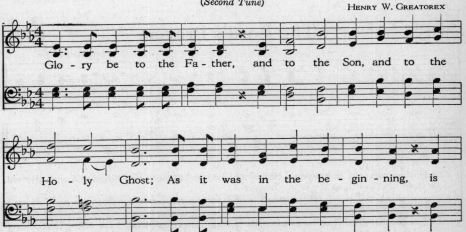

Glo - ry be to the Fa - ther, and to the Son, and to the

Ho - ly Ghost; As it was in the be - gin - ning, is

Gloria Patri

now and ev - er shall be, world with-out end. A men, A men.

311 We Give Thee But Thine Own

ST. ANDREW. 6. 6. 8. 6.

William W. How, 1823–1897

Joseph Barnby, 1838–1896

We give Thee but Thine own, What-e'er the gift may be; All

that we have is Thine a - lone, A trust, O Lord, from Thee. A-MEN.

312 Let the Words of My Mouth

From Psalm xix

Adolph Baumbach

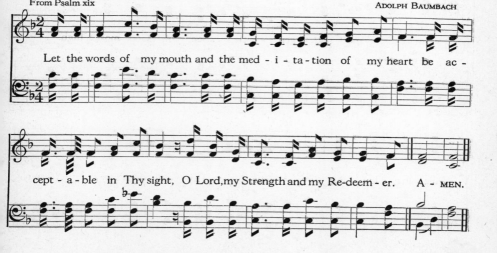

Let the words of my mouth and the med - i - ta - tion of my heart be ac -

cept - a - ble in Thy sight, O Lord, my Strength and my Re-deem - er. A - MEN.

313 Jesus, Stand Among Us

VESPER (MANN). 6. 5. 6. 5.

WILLIAM PENNEFATHER, 1816-1873

FREDERICK A. MANN, ?

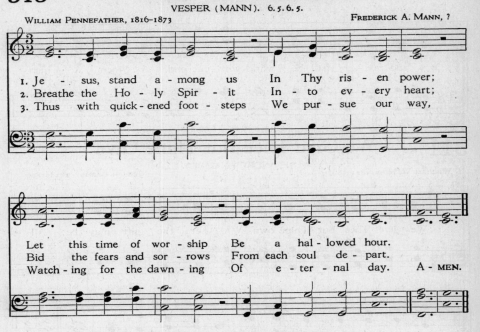

1. Je - sus, stand a - mong us In Thy ris - en power;
2. Breathe the Ho - ly Spir - it In - to ev - ery heart;
3. Thus with quick - ened foot - steps We pur - sue our way,

Let this time of wor - ship Be a hal - lowed hour.
Bid the fears and sor - rows From each soul de - part.
Watch - ing for the dawn - ing Of e - ter - nal day. A - MEN.

314 Jesus, Meek and Gentle

RESPONSE TO PRAYER

Rev. G. R. PRYNNE, 1856-

WARNER M. HAWKINS

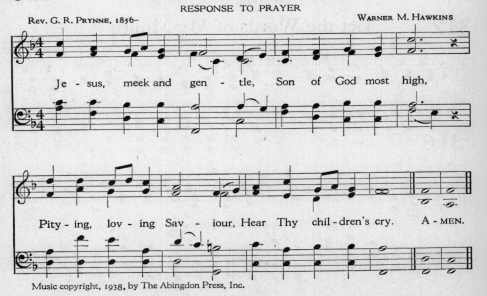

Je - sus, meek and gen - tle, Son of God most high,

Pity - ing, lov - ing Sav - iour, Hear Thy chil - dren's cry. A - MEN.

315 Saviour, Hear Us, We Pray

LUCY. 6. 6. 6. 6. with Refrain

W. W. Ellsworth

Arr. from Johannes Brahms, 1833–1897

1. Sav - iour, hear us, we pray: Keep us safe through this
2. Be our Guard - ian and Guide; May we walk by Thy

day; Keep our lives free from sin And our hearts pure with - in.
side Till the eve - ning shades fall O - ver us— o - ver all.

Refrain

Je - sus, Lord, hear our prayer: May we rest in Thy care,

Je - sus, Lord, hear our prayer: May we rest in Thy care. A - men.

316

From Felix Mendelssohn-Bartholdy, 1809–1847

Hear Thou in love, O Lord, our cry, In heaven, Thy dwell - ing place on high.

317 Soldiers of Christ, Arise

DIADEMATA. S. M. D.

CHARLES WESLEY, 1707-1788

GEORGE J. ELVEY, 1816-1893

1. Sol - diers of Christ, a - rise, And put your ar - mor on,
2. Stand, then, in His great might, With all His strength en - dued;
3. From strength to strength go on; Wres - tle, and fight, and pray;

Strong in the strength which God sup - plies Through His e - ter - nal Son;
But take, to arm you for the fight, The pan - o - ply of God:
Tread all the powers of dark - ness down, And win the well-fought day:

Strong in the Lord of hosts, And in His might - y power,
That, hav - ing all things done, And all your con - flicts passed,
Still let the Spir - it cry, In all His sol - diers, "Come!"

Who in the strength of Je - sus trusts Is more than con-quer - or.
Ye may o'er-come thro' Christ a - lone, And stand en - tire at last.
Till Christ the Lord who reigns on high, Shall take the con-querors home. A-MEN.

Responsive Readings

Jesus the Light of the World
John 1. 1-9

In the beginning was the Word, and the Word was with God, and the Word was God.

The same was in the beginning with God.

All things were made by Him; and without Him was not any thing made that was made.

In Him was life; and the life was the light of men.

And the light shineth in darkness: and the darkness comprehended it not.

There was a man sent from God, whose name was John.

The same came for a witness, to bear witness of the Light, that all men through Him might believe.

He was not that Light, but was sent to bear witness of that Light. That was the true Light, which lighteth every man that cometh into the world.

I John 1. 5-7

This then is the message which we have heard of Him, and declare unto you, that God is light, and in Him is no darkness at all.

If we say that we have fellowship with Him, and walk in darkness, we lie, and do not the truth:

But if we walk in the light, as He is in the light, we have fellowship one with another, and the blood of Jesus Christ His Son cleanseth us from all sin.

Jesus the Way
John 14. 1-7

Let not your heart be troubled; ye believe in God, believe also in Me.

In My Father's house are many mansions: if it were not so, I would have told you. I go to prepare a place for you.

And if I go and prepare a place for you, I will come again, and receive you unto Myself; that where I am, there ye may be also.

And whither I go ye know, and the way ye know.

Thomas saith unto Him, Lord, we know not whither Thou goest; and how can we know the way?

Jesus saith unto him, I am the way, and the truth, and the life: no man cometh unto the Father, but by Me. If ye had known Me, ye should have known my Father also: and from henceforth ye know Him, and have seen Him.

The Name of Jesus
Philippians 2. 5-11

Let this mind be in you, which was also in Christ Jesus:

Who, being in the form of God, thought it not robbery to be equal with God;

But made Himself of no reputation, and took upon Him the form of a servant, and was made in the likeness of men:

And being found in fashion as a man, He humbled Himself, and became obedient unto death, even the death of the cross.

Wherefore God also hath highly exalted Him, and given Him a name which is above every name:

That at the name of Jesus every knee should bow, of things in heaven, and things in earth, and things under the earth;

And that every tongue should confess that Jesus Christ is Lord, to the glory of God the Father.

JESUS THE SHEPHERD
John 10. 1-5, 7-15

Verily, verily, I say unto you, He that entereth not by the door into the sheepfold, but climbeth up some other way, the same is a thief and a robber.

But he that entereth in by the door is the shepherd of the sheep.

To him the porter openeth; and the sheep hear his voice: and he calleth his own sheep by name, and leadeth them out.

And when he putteth forth his own sheep, he goeth before them, and the sheep follow him: for they know his voice.

And a stranger will they not follow, but will flee from him: for they know not the voice of strangers.

Then said Jesus unto them again, Verily, verily, I say unto you, I am the door of the sheep.

All that ever came before Me are thieves and robbers: but the sheep did not hear them.

I am the door: by Me if any man enter in, he shall be saved, and shall go in and out, and find pasture.

The thief cometh not, but for to steal, and to kill, and to destroy: I am come that they might have life, and that they might have it more abundantly.

I am the good shepherd: the good shepherd giveth his life for the sheep.

But he that is an hireling, and not the shepherd, whose own the sheep are not, seeth the wolf coming, and leaveth the sheep, and fleeth: and the wolf catcheth them, and scattereth the sheep.

The hireling fleeth, because he is an hireling, and careth not for the sheep.

I am the good shepherd, and know my sheep, and am known of Mine.

As the Father knoweth Me, even so know I the Father: and I lay down My life for the sheep.

JESUS THE CHRISTIAN'S SUSTENANCE
John 15. 1-8

I am the true vine, and My Father is the husbandman.

Every branch in Me that beareth not fruit He taketh away; and every branch that beareth fruit He purgeth it, that it may bring forth more fruit.

Now ye are clean through the word which I have spoken unto you.

Abide in Me, and I in you. As the branch cannot bear fruit of itself, except it abide in the vine; no more can ye, except ye abide in me.

I am the vine, ye are the branches: He that abideth in Me, and I in him, the same bringeth forth much fruit: for without Me ye can do nothing.

If a man abide not in Me, he is cast forth as a branch, and is withered; and men gather them, and cast them into the fire, and they are burned.

If ye abide in Me, and My words abide in you, ye shall ask what ye will, and it shall be done unto you.

Herein is My Father glorified, that ye bear much fruit; so shall ye be My disciples.

LOVE

1 Corinthians 13

Though I speak with the tongues of men and of angels, and have not charity, I am become as sounding brass, or a tinkling cymbal.

And though I have the gift of prophecy, and understand all mysteries, and all knowledge; and though I have all faith, so that I could remove mountains, and have not charity, I am nothing.

And though I bestow all my goods to feed the poor, and though I give my body to be burned, and have not charity, it profiteth me nothing.

Charity suffereth long, and is kind; charity envieth not; charity vaunteth not itself, is not puffed up.

Doth not behave itself unseemly, seeketh not her own, is not easily provoked, thinketh no evil:

Rejoiceth not in iniquity, but rejoiceth in the truth;

Beareth all things, believeth all things, hopeth all things, endureth all things.

Charity never faileth: but whether there be prophecies, they shall fail; whether there be tongues, they shall cease; whether there be knowledge, it shall vanish away.

For we know in part, and we prophesy in part.

But when that which is perfect is come, then that which is in part shall be done away.

When I was a child, I spake as a child, I understood as a child, I thought as a child; but when I became a man, I put away childish things.

For now we see through a glass, darkly; but then face to face: now I know in part; but then shall I know even as also I am known.

And now abideth faith, hope, charity, these three; but the greatest of these is charity.

GRACE

Ephesians 2. 1-10

And you hath He quickened, who were dead in trespasses and sins;

Wherein in times past ye walked according to the course of this world, according to the prince of the power of the air, the spirit that now worketh in the children of disobedience;

Among whom also we all had our conversation in times past in the lusts of our flesh, fulfilling the desires of the flesh and the mind; and were by nature the children of wrath, even as others.

But God, who is rich in mercy, for His great love wherewith He loved us,

Even when we were dead in sins, hath quickened us together with Christ, (by grace ye are saved;)

And hath raised us up together, and made us sit together in heavenly places in Christ Jesus:

That in the ages to come He might show the exceeding riches of His grace in his kindness toward us through Christ Jesus.

For by grace are ye saved through faith; and that not of yourselves; it is the gift of God:

Not of works, lest any man should boast.

For we are His workmanship, created in Christ Jesus unto good works, which God before ordained that we should walk in them.

Jesus' Message to the Churches

Revelation 2. 1-7; 3. 14-21.

Unto the angel of the church of Ephesus write; These things saith He that holdeth the seven stars in His right hand, who walketh in the midst of the seven golden candlesticks;

I know thy works, and thy labor, and thy patience, and how thou canst not bear them which are evil; and thou hast tried them which say they are apostles, and are not, and hast found them liars:

And hast borne, and hast patience, and for My name's sake hast labored, and hast not fainted.

Nevertheless I have somewhat against thee, because thou hast left thy first love.

Remember therefore from whence thou art fallen, and repent, and do the first works; or else I will come unto thee quickly, and will remove thy candlestick out of his place, except thou repent.

But this thou hast, that thou hatest the deeds of the Nicolaitanes, which I also hate.

He that hath an ear, let him hear what the Spirit saith unto the churches; To him that overcometh will I give to eat of the tree of life, which is in the midst of the paradise of God.

And unto the angel of the church of the Laodiceans write; These things saith the Amen, the faithful and true witness, the beginning of the creation of God;

I know thy works, that thou art neither cold nor hot; I would thou wert cold or hot.

So then because thou art lukewarm, and neither cold nor hot, I will spue thee out of My mouth.

Because thou sayest, I am rich, and increased with goods, and have need of nothing; and knowest not that thou art wretched, and miserable, and poor, and blind, and naked:

I counsel thee to buy of me gold tried in the fire, that thou mayest be rich; and white raiment, that thou mayest be clothed, and that the shame of thy nakedness do not appear; and anoint thine eyes with eyesalve, that thou mayest see.

As many as I love, I rebuke and chasten: be zealous therefore, and repent.

Behold, I stand at the door and knock: if any man hear My voice, and open the door, I will come in to him, and will sup with him, and he with Me.

To him that overcometh will I grant to sit with Me in My throne, even as I also overcame, and am set down with My Father in His throne. He that hath an ear, let him hear what the Spirit saith unto the churches.

Selections From the Psalms

Psalm 1

Blessed is the man that walketh not in the counsel of the ungodly, nor standeth in the way of sinners, nor sitteth in the seat of the scornful.

But his delight is in the law of the Lord; and in His law doth he meditate day and night.

And he shall be like a tree planted by the rivers of water, that bringeth forth his fruit in his season; his leaf also shall not wither; and whatsoever he doeth shall prosper.

The ungodly are not so; but are like the chaff which the wind driveth away.

Therefore the ungodly shall not stand in the judgment, nor sinners in the congregation of the righteous.

For the Lord knoweth the way of the righteous: but the way of the ungodly shall perish.

Psalm 15

Lord, who shall abide in Thy tabernacle? who shall dwell in Thy holy hill?

He that walketh uprightly, and worketh righteousness, and speaketh the truth in his heart.

He that backbiteth not with his tongue, nor doeth evil to his neighbour, nor taketh up a reproach against his neighbour.

In whose eyes a vile person is contemned; but he honoreth them that fear the Lord. He that sweareth to his own hurt, and changeth not.

He that putteth not out his money to usury, nor taketh reward against the innocent.

He that doeth these things shall never be moved.

Psalm 23

The Lord is my shepherd; I shall not want.

He maketh me to lie down in green pastures: He leadeth me beside the still waters.

He restoreth my soul: He leadeth me in the paths of righteousness for His name's sake.

Yea, though I walk through the valley of the shadow of death, I will fear no evil: for Thou art with me; Thy rod and Thy staff they comfort me.

Thou preparest a table before me in the presence of mine enemies: Thou anointest my head with oil; my cup runneth over.

Surely goodness and mercy shall follow me all the days of my life: and I will dwell in the house of the Lord for ever.

Psalm 24

The earth is the Lord's and the fullness thereof; the world, and they that dwell therein.

For He hath founded it upon the seas, and established it upon the floods.

Who shall ascend into the hill of the Lord? or who shall stand in His holy place?

He that hath clean hands, and a pure heart; who hath not lifted up his soul unto vanity, nor sworn deceitfully.

He shall receive the blessing from the Lord, and righteousness from the God of his salvation.

This is the generation of them that seek Him, that seek Thy face, O Jacob.

Lift up your heads, O ye gates; and be ye lift up, ye everlasting doors; and the King of glory shall come in.

Who is this King of glory? The Lord strong and mighty, the Lord mighty in battle.

Lift up your heads, O ye gates; even lift them up, ye everlasting doors; and the King of glory shall come in.

Who is this King of glory? The Lord of hosts, He is the King of glory.

Psalm 37

Fret not thyself because of evildoers, neither be thou envious against the workers of iniquity.

For they shall soon be cut down like the grass, and wither as the green herb.

Trust in the Lord, and do good; so shalt thou dwell in the land, and verily thou shalt be fed.

Delight thyself also in the Lord; and He shall give thee the desires of thine heart.

Commit thy way unto the Lord; trust also in Him; and He shall bring it to pass. And He shall bring forth thy righteousness as the light, and thy judgment as the noonday.

Rest in the Lord, and wait patiently for Him: fret not thyself because of him who prospereth in his way, because of the man who bringeth wicked devices to pass.

Cease from anger, and forsake wrath: fret not thyself in any wise to do evil.

For evildoers shall be cut off: but those that wait upon the Lord, they shall inherit the earth.

For yet a little while, and the wicked shall not be: yea, thou shalt diligently consider his place, and it shall not be.

But the meek shall inherit the earth; and shall delight themselves in the abundance of peace.

Psalm 40

I waited patiently for the Lord; and He inclined unto me, and heard my cry.

He brought me up also out of an horrible pit, out of the miry clay, and set my feet upon a rock, and established my goings.

And He hath put a new song in my mouth, even praise unto our God:

Many shall see it, and fear, and shall trust in the Lord.

Psalm 46

God is our refuge and strength, a very present help in trouble.

Therefore will not we fear, though the earth be removed, and though the mountains be carried into the midst of the sea;

Though the waters thereof roar and be troubled, though the mountains shake with the swelling thereof.

There is a river the streams whereof shall make glad the city of God, the holy place of the tabernacles of the most High.

God is in the midst of her; she shall not be moved: God shall help her, and that right early.

The heathen raged, the kingdoms were moved: He uttered his voice, the earth melted. The Lord of hosts is with us: the God of Jacob is our refuge.

Come, behold the works of the Lord, what desolations He hath made in the earth.

He maketh wars to cease unto the end of the earth; He breaketh the bow, and cutteth the spear in sunder; He burneth the chariot in the fire.

Be still, and know that I am God: I will be exalted among the heathen, I will be exalted in the earth.

The Lord of hosts is with us; the God of Jacob is our refuge.

Psalm 91

He that dwelleth in the secret place of the most High shall abide under the shadow of the Almighty.

I will say of the Lord, He is my refuge and my fortress: my God; in Him will I trust.

Surely He shall deliver thee from the snare of the fowler, and from the noisome pestilence.

He shall cover thee with His feathers, and under His wings shalt thou trust: His truth shall be thy shield and buckler.

Thou shalt not be afraid for the terror by night; nor for the arrow that flieth by day;

Nor for the pestilence that walketh in darkness; nor for the destruction that wasteth at noonday.

A thousand shall fall at thy side, and ten thousand at thy right hand; but it shall not come nigh thee.

Only with thine eyes shalt thou behold and see the reward of the wicked.

Because thou hast made the Lord, which is my refuge, even the most High, thy habitation;

There shall no evil befall thee, neither shall any plague come nigh thy dwelling.

For He shall give His angels charge over thee, to keep thee in all thy ways.

They shall bear thee up in their hands, lest thou dash thy foot against a stone.

Thou shalt tread upon the lion and adder: the young lion and the dragon shalt thou trample under feet.

Because he hath set his love upon Me, therefore will I deliver him: I will set him on high, because he hath known My name.

He shall call upon Me, and I will answer him: I will be with him in trouble; I will deliver him, and honor him.

With long life will I satisfy him, and shew him My salvation.

Psalm 103

Bless the Lord, O my soul: and all that is within me, bless His holy name.

Bless the Lord, O my soul, and forget not all His benefits:

Who forgiveth all thine iniquities; who healeth all thy diseases;

Who redeemeth thy life from destruction; who crowneth thee with loving-kindness and tender mercies;

Who satisfieth thy mouth with good things; so that thy youth is renewed like the eagle's.

The Lord executeth righteousness and judgments for all that are oppressed.

He made known His ways unto Moses, His acts unto the children of Israel.

The Lord is merciful and gracious, slow to anger, and plenteous in mercy.

He will not always chide: neither will He keep His anger for ever.

He hath not dealt with us after our sins, nor rewarded us according to our iniquities.

For as the heaven is high above the earth, so great is His mercy toward them that fear Him.

As far as the east is from the west, so far hath He removed our transgressions from us.

Like as a father pitieth his children, so the Lord pitieth them that fear Him.

For He knoweth our frame; He remembereth that we are dust.

As for man, his days are as grass: as a flower of the field, so he flourisheth.

For the wind passeth over it, and it is gone; and the place thereof shall know it no more.

But the mercy of the Lord is from everlasting to everlasting upon them that fear Him, and His righteousness unto children's children;

To such as keep His covenant, and to those that remember His commandments to do them.

Selections From Psalm 119

Blessed are the undefiled in the way, who walk in the law of the Lord.

Blessed are they that keep his testimonies, and that seek him with the whole heart.

Wherewithal shall a young man cleanse his way? by taking heed thereto according to Thy word.

With my whole heart have I sought Thee: O let me not wander from Thy commandments.

Thy word have I hid in mine heart, that I might not sin against Thee.

Open Thou mine eyes, that I may behold wondrous things out of Thy law.

Teach me, O Lord, the way of Thy statutes; and I shall keep it unto the end.

Give me understanding, and I shall keep Thy law; yea, I shall observe it with my whole heart.

For ever, O Lord, Thy word is settled in heaven.

Thy faithfulness is unto all generations; Thou hast established the earth, and it abideth.

O how love I Thy law! it is my meditation all the day.

Thy word is a lamp unto my feet, and a light unto my path.

The entrance of Thy words giveth light; it giveth understanding unto the simple.

Righteous art Thou, O Lord, and upright are Thy judgments.

Thy testimonies that thou hast commanded are righteous and very faithful.

Great peace have they which love Thy law: and nothing shall offend them.

Psalm 150

Praise ye the Lord. Praise God in His sanctuary: praise Him in the firmament of His power.

Praise Him for His mighty acts: praise Him according to His excellent greatness.

Praise Him with the sound of the trumpet; praise Him with the psaltery and harp.

Praise Him with the timbrel and dance: praise Him with stringed instruments and organs.

Praise Him upon the loud cymbals: praise Him upon the high-sounding cymbals.

Let every thing that hath breath praise the Lord. Praise ye the Lord.

Services of Worship

BEING FOUND OF GOD

I
GRACE

MUSICAL MEDITATIONS
HYMN: "Spirit of God, Descend Upon My Heart"..................No. 75
SILENT PRAYER. The people seated and bowed
ORAL PRAYER. By the Leader

II
GOD SEEKING MEN

SCRIPTURE: John 3. 14-17
      John 12. 32
HYMN: "In Tenderness He Sought Me".........................No. 96
SCRIPTURE: John 10. 11
      John 10. 14
      John 13. 1
HYMN: "The Mercy of God Is an Ocean Divine"..................No. 97
SOLO: "I Was a Wandering Sheep".............................No. 95

III
SURRENDER

SCRIPTURE: Luke 9. 23-25
      Luke 16. 13
HYMN: Solo—"Live Out Thy Life Within Me"....................No. 139
MOMENTS OF MEDITATION

IV
PRAYER AND GUIDANCE

SPIRITUAL: "All I Want".....................................No. 290
MEDITATION
SPIRITUAL: "Balm in Gilead"................................No. 285

V
WITNESSING

SCRIPTURE: John 13. 17
      James 1. 27
HYMN: "O Master, Let Me Walk with Thee"....................No. 116

VI

CONSECRATION

SPIRITUAL: "Lord, I Want to Be a Christian"......................No. 284

CHORAL BENEDICTION: "Let the Beauty of Jesus Be Seen in Me".....No. 294

THANKSGIVING

MUSICAL PRELUDE. Preferably a glad or patriotic march

PROCESSIONAL HYMN: "God of Our Fathers, Whose Almighty Hand"..No. 226

SCRIPTURE READING: Deuteronomy, Chapter 8

PRAYER

RESPONSE: "Praise God, From Whom All Blessings Flow"............No. 304

SCRIPTURE READING: Psalm 19

HYMN: "This Is My Father's World"............................No. 11

READING FROM: "A Little Te Deum of the Commonplace." *Oxenham*

HYMN: "Peace in Our Time, O Lord"............................No. 232

A MEDITATION on the implications of the day

RECESSIONAL HYMN: "Come, Ye Thankful People, Come"...........No. 27

THE NAME OF JESUS

MUSICAL MEDITATIONS on "Jesus, the Very Thought of Thee".......No. 56

CHORAL SENTENCE: Refrain, "Holy, Holy, Holy," from "Day Is Dying
    in the West"...No. 297

SILENT PRAYER. People seated and bowed

AUDIBLE INVOCATION. By Leader

(The Scripture may be read by the Leader or by various members of the group)

I

SALVATION IN HIS NAME

SCRIPTURE: Matthew 1. 21; Luke 24. 47; Acts 4. 12

HYMN: "Jesus! The Name High Over All" ....No. 60

II

FAITH IN HIS NAME

SOLO: "There Is No Name So Sweet on Earth"....................No. 69

SCRIPTURE: Acts 3. 16; Acts 16. 18

HYMN: "How Sweet the Name of Jesus Sounds"...................No. 58

III

PRAYER IN HIS NAME

SCRIPTURE: John 14. 13-14; John 15. 16

HYMN: "Take the Name of Jesus With You"......................No. 65

IV
LIFE IN HIS NAME
SCRIPTURE: John 20. 30-31
HYMN: "O for a Thousand Tongues to Sing".......................No. 67

V
PRAISE TO HIS NAME
SCRIPTURE: Psalm 113. 1-2; Philippians 2. 9-11
HYMN: "All Hail the Power of Jesus' Name".......................No. 53

VI
BENEDICTION IN HIS NAME
SCRIPTURE: Ephesians 5. 20
CHORAL BENEDICTION: "The Lord Bless Thee and Keep Thee".......No. 299

THE CROSS
MUSICAL PRELUDE, Instrumental
HYMN: "On a Hill Far Away;" ("The Old Rugged Cross") The People
standing...No. 46
SILENT PRAYER. The people seated and bowed
SPOKEN PRAYER. Leader
HYMN: "Beneath the Cross of Jesus"............................No. 39
SOLO: "Above the Hills of Time the Cross Is Gleaming"..........No. 41
SCRIPTURE READING: Isaiah 53
COMMENTS: By leader on the Scripture Reading
HYMN: "When I Survey the Wondrous Cross"....................No. 44
PRAYER AND CHORAL BENEDICTION: First stanza of "In the Cross of
Christ I Glory"..No. 43

CHORAL SERVICE
FOR EARLY EASTER MORNING
MUSICAL PRELUDE, for Organ, Piano, or Small Orchestra
ANY ARRANGEMENT OF "Christ the Lord Is Risen Today"...........No. 48
Leader: "Christ is risen from the dead and is become the first
fruits of them that slept."
HYMN: "Christ the Lord Is Risen Today" ....No. 48
Leader: "For as in Adam all die, even so in Christ shall all be
made alive."
HYMN: "Low in the Grave He Lay" ....No. 47
(The stanza may be sung by a solo voice or selected group, the refrain by
choir and congregation.)

Leader: "Thanks be to God, who hath given us the victory"
Hymn: "The Strife is O'er, the Battle Done" ....No. 52
PRAYER OF REJOICING AND DEDICATION
Hymn: "Welcome, Happy Morning".................................No. 51
Leader and People in Unison:
"Hallelujah, for the Lord
God omnipotent reigneth."
Hymn: "All Hail the Power of Jesus' Name" ....No. 54
(Sing to the tune "Diadem")
BENEDICTION
NOTE—A short message may be added, and further Scripture reading, at discretion of Leader, but let the message of the Easter Hymnody dominate.

PEACE

MUSICAL PRELUDE
CHORAL SENTENCE: "May the grace of Christ our Saviour".........No. 305
INVOCATION
RESPONSE: "Hear Our Prayer, O Lord"..........................No. 306
Hymn: "Not So in Haste, My Heart!"...........................No. 171
SCRIPTURE: Psalm 23. Read in unison
RESPONSE: Hymn, " 'Mid All the Traffic of the Ways"..............No. 165
MEDITATION on peacefulness as productive of peace, and vice versa
Hymn Solo: "Like a River Glorious".............................No. 172
PRAYER HYMN: "Peace in Our Time, O Lord".....................No. 232
BENEDICTION: "The Lord Bless Thee and Keep Thee"..............No. 299

ADORATION

MUSICAL PRELUDE: "Largo"..................................... *Handel*
CHORAL SENTENCE: The Sanctus ....No. 300
PRAYER OF ADORATION
CHORAL AMEN: "Threefold"....................................No. 303
SCRIPTURE: Psalm 95
CHORAL RESPONSE: "Alleluia"...................................No. 307
Hymn: "We Praise Thee, O God, Our Redeemer, Creator"...........No. 5
READING: Credo, from "Bees in Amber"................... *John Oxenham*
Hymn: "Jesus, My Lord, My God, My All".......................No. 4
SHORT TALK on Adoration, based on the ancient Israelitish or the modern Church ideas. Perhaps on an exhibit of prints of well-known masterpieces
SCRIPTURE: Isaiah 6. 3
Revelation 4. 8

HYMN: "Holy, Holy, Holy, Lord God Almighty"..................No. 1
BENEDICTION
CHORAL AMEN: "Dresden".......................................No. 302

JESUS AS SHEPHERD

MUSICAL PRELUDE, Instrumental

LEADER: On the face of the earth from earliest times, there have been spots where, by common consent, men have massed, building themselves cities and finding their unity. So on the great continent of sacred literature there have ever been points of centralization, where human souls instinctively have gathered, forgetting the things that divided them, and remembering only those that made them one. Such a metropolitan seat and center is the Twenty-third Psalm. It has been the meeting point of the ages. Around it men and women of every rank and race have gathered with profound and holy joy, and from it have drawn the courage to attempt, the power to achieve, and the patience to endure.—*Dr. Henry Howard.*

PRAYER: People seated and bowed

UNISON READING OF THE TWENTY-THIRD PSALM

RESPONSE: "Gloria in Excelsis Deo".............................No. 296

READING: God Seeks His Own (Ezekiel 34. 11-16, 30-31)

HE GOETH BEFORE

We stand on the threshold, a new day beginning,
And wonder, perhaps, what the future may be,
The past is illumined by God's love and mercy,
But the day which we enter no mortal can see;
Untried and untrodden it lieth before us,
We pause, as we pass through its wide-open door,
Yet need not be fearful if only we follow
The footsteps of Jesus, who goeth before.

HYMN: "Footprints of Jesus"..........................Refrain of No. 201

LEADER: For our comfort and blessing He makes us lie down in pastures of tender grass; for our refreshment He leads us beside the waters of quietness. But there is something further that He has in view. Not only is *our blessing* an object that He pursues, but the glory of His own Name. Hence we read that He leads us in certain paths for His *name's sake.* Surely this awakens a response in our hearts. We desire that there should be something for the glory of His Name in our walk, and therefore we are glad to be led in paths of righteousness.—*Harold P. Barker.*

CHORAL BENEDICTION: First stanza of "In Heavenly Love Abiding"..No. 167

JESUS AS SAVIOUR

MUSICAL PRELUDE, Instrumental

CHORAL SENTENCE: "This Is My Story, This Is My Song"...........No. 292

PRAYER OF THANKSGIVING FOR SALVATION IN JESUS CHRIST. The people seated and bowed

CHORAL RESPONSE: "Saviour, Hear Us, We Pray"................No. 315

HYMN: "Lord Jesus, I Love Thee"................................No. 179

SCRIPTURE READING: The people standing. In unison, the leader announcing the references

Matthew 1. 21: "And she shall bring forth a Son, and thou shalt call His name JESUS, for He shall save his people from their sins."

Luke 2. 11: "For unto you is born this day, in the city of David, a Saviour, which is Christ the Lord."

Luke 2. 29, 32: "Lord, now lettest Thou Thy servant depart in peace, according to Thy word; For mine eyes have seen Thy salvation. . . . A light to lighten the Gentiles, and the glory of Thy people Israel."

Acts 4. 12: "Neither is there salvation in any other: for there is none other name under heaven given among men, whereby we must be saved."

John 3. 17: "For God sent not His Son into the world to condemn the world; but that the world through Him might be saved."

1 Timothy 1. 15: "This is a faithful saying, and worthy of all acceptation, that Christ Jesus came into the world to save sinners."

Hebrews 7. 25: "Wherefore He is able also to save them to the uttermost that come unto God by Him, seeing He ever liveth to make intercession for them."

MEDITATION ON THE SAVIOURHOOD OF JESUS

SILENT PRAYER: Of short duration concluded by brief audible prayer

HYMN: "I Have a Saviour, He's Pleading in Glory"................No. 83

CHORAL BENEDICTION: "May the Grace of Christ Our Saviour"......No. 305

A SERVICE OF MEDITATION

MUSICAL PRELUDE

CHORAL CALL TO WORSHIP: First stanza of hymn, "Rejoice, Ye Pure in Heart" ....No. 9

INVOCATION: People seated and bowed

A MESSAGE WITH CONGREGATIONAL RESPONSES:

Leader: Here is the message that we learned from Jesus and announce to you: "God is light, and in Him is no darkness, none."

Congregation: If we say, "We have fellowship with Him," when we live and move in darkness, then we are not practicing the truth; but if we live and move within the light, as He is within the light, then we have fellowship with one another, and the blood of Jesus His Son cleanses us from every sin.

Leader: If we say, "We are not guilty," we are deceiving ourselves, and the truth is not in us. If we confess our sins, He is faithful and just, He forgives our sins and cleanses us from all iniquity.

Congregation: If we say, "We have not sinned," we make Him a liar, and His word is not in us.

Leader: This message comes to you that you may not sin.

Congregation: But if one does sin, we have an Advocate with the Father in Jesus Christ the Just: He is himself, the propitiation for our sins, though not for ours only, but also for the whole world.

Leader: This is how we may be sure we know Him, by obeying His commands.

Congregation: He who says, "I know Him," but does not obey His commands, is a liar and the truth is not in him.

Leader: Dear children, the message is sent unto you.

Congregation: Because our sins are forgiven.

Leader: Fathers, the message is sent to you.

Congregation: Because we know Him who is from the beginning.

Leader: Young men, the message is to you.

Congregation: Because we have conquered the evil One.

Leader: Children, the message is to you.

Congregation: Because we know the Father.

Leader: Fathers, the message is for you.

Congregation: Because we know Him who is from the beginning.

Leader: Young men, the message is to you.

Congregation: Because we are strong, and the word of God remains within us, and we have conquered the evil One.

(Adapted from 1 John 1 and 2. Moffatt's translation)

HYMN: "Be Still, My Soul, the Lord Is on Thy Side"...............No. 121
Leader: The Lord be with you.
Congregation: And with thy spirit.
Leader: Praise ye the Lord.
Congregation: The Lord's name be praised.
CHORAL RESPONSE: "Alleluia"....................................No. 307
HYMN: "Lead On, O King Eternal"................................No. 210
READING OF HYMN: "That Cause Can Neither Be Lost Nor Stayed"..No. 125
PRAYER OF THANKSGIVING:
   a. Directed
   b. Invocational
HYMN: "How Firm a Foundation, Ye Saints of the Lord"...........No. 122
PRAYER AND BENEDICTION

Topical Index

(Titles of songs are capitalized)

TOPICAL INDEX

Index of Responsive Readings

Index of Worship Programs

Index of Responses

Alphabetical Index of Songs

(Titles of songs are capitalized)

ALPHABETICAL INDEX OF SONGS

NUMBER

NUMBER

ALPHABETICAL INDEX OF SONGS

ALPHABETICAL INDEX OF SONGS